ADVANCE PRAISE

"The Peloton story is a fascinating tale of entrepreneurship, creative destruction, and innovation. Like Amazon or Netflix, Uber or Sonos before, it almost always takes an outsider to envision an entirely new way of serving customers and disrupt a well-entrenched industry. That is exactly what Georgia Tech alums John Foley, Yony Feng, and their co-founders did, and I can't think of better person to tell this story than David Miller, who's been studying and teaching entrepreneurship for years and who for years tried to sell me on this concept until he finally succeeded!"

—DR. ÁNGEL CABRERA, president, Georgia Institute of Technology

"In *Sweating Together,* David Miller takes a deep dive inside the phenomenon that is Peloton, one of the most fascinating and unexpected startup success stories of our time. He shows how Peloton is a combination of technology startup and wellness brand, whose success is predicated on a community of loyal users. A must-read for entrepreneurs, venture capitalists, fitness gurus, and anyone who wants to understand and navigate the exploding market—and world—of technology, fitness, and wellness."

—RICHARD FLORIDA, author of *The Rise of the Creative Class*

"Peloton has reset the recreation landscape, and David Miller tells us how and why the founders were able to make Peloton something much bigger than an iPad connected to a stationary bike. Miller also tells his own story of his journey from Peloton skeptic to addict so we can understand the brand's hold on the consumer's mindset and why he thinks Peloton could become one of the world's largest companies."

—SETH GOLDMAN, co-founder of Honest Tea, Eat the Change, and PLNT Burger and board chair of Beyond Meat

"David Miller delivers a first-of-its-kind deep dive into one of the world's most fascinating companies, documenting his own journey from skeptical academic to self-described Peloton addict along the way. *Sweating Together* details how a company became a movement and why Peloton has changed everything—from working out in the basement to creating a community-driven megabrand."

—JASON KELLY, author of *Sweat Equity: Inside the New Economy of Mind and Body*

"In *Sweating Together*, Dr. Miller powerfully captures the benefits of social connections in physical exercise. While he highlights the successes of Peloton through the lens of entrepreneurship, it's clear that what emerged from this successful company is a large community of passionate and dedicated Peloton enthusiasts. A powerful lesson from this book is the importance of social support in our physical activities. *Sweating Together* is a brilliant case study of leadership, entrepreneurship, well-being, and innovation."

—NANCE LUCAS, PhD, executive director and chief well-being officer, Center for the Advancement of Well-Being, George Mason University

"David combines his passion for and understanding of entrepreneurship and innovation and his own personal journey to illustrate key features that have driven the remarkable growth of a highly adaptive and entrepreneurial company, Peloton. Peloton's journey, with its relentless focus on the customer, is an excellent case study providing key insights for any innovator looking to make a meaningful difference in the lives of the people and communities they serve."

—SARAH E. NUTTER, PhD, Edward Maletis dean and professor of accounting, University of Oregon, Lundquist College of Business

"David J. Miller has colorfully and carefully captured the spirit of the Peloton brand, its founders, and its impact on how humans across the world consume their workouts. Expect a deep, meticulous dive into the behind-the-scenes moments that will surprise and delight Peloton lovers and skeptics alike, whether they're interested in the sweat or the sweat equity that goes into creating a globally-adored, billion-dollar business."

—LIZ PLOSSER, editor-in-chief, *Women's Health* and author of *Own Your Morning: Reset Your A.M. Routine to Unlock Your Potential*

"David Miller, a leading entrepreneurship professor with a passion for Peloton, was practically built in a lab to write this book. In *Sweating Together,* he combines his love of the brand with his knowledge of branding to create a riveting look at the wild and rapid rise of Peloton. Whether you're part of the Peloton phenomenon or perplexed by it, this book is a must-read."

—CRYSTAL AND TOM O'KEEFE, hosts of *The Clip Out*

SWEATING TOGETHER

SWEATING TOGETHER

HOW PELOTON BUILT A BILLION DOLLAR VENTURE AND CREATED COMMUNITY IN A DIGITAL WORLD

DAVID J. MILLER, PhD
#ChicagoBorn

IDEAPRESS
PUBLISHING

WASHINGTON, D.C.

IDEAPRESS
PUBLISHING

Printed in the United States.

Ideapress Publishing | www.ideapresspublishing.com

Cover Design: Tim Green, Faceout Studios
Interior Design: Jessica Angerstein

Cataloging-in-Publication Data is on file with the Library of Congress.

ISBN: 978-1-94085-897-5

Special Sales
Ideapress Books are available at a special discount for bulk purchases for sales promotions and premiums, or for use in corporate training programs. Special editions, including personalized covers, a custom foreword, corporate imprints, and bonus content are also available.

To Emily, Levi, Sari, and Lincoln for supporting me through this evolving ride

TIMELINE OF SELECT EVENTS IN PELOTON'S HISTORY

2012
- Peloton founded
- $400,000 seed round of funding
- $3.5 million Series A Fund Raise

2013
- First prototype bike designed and created
- Kickstarter Campaign raised a little over $300,000, sells 200 bikes
- First Instructor Hired - Jennifer Schreiber Sherman (JSS)
- First Retail Showroom - Short Hills Mall in New Jersey

2014
- Generation 1 bike released and delivered
- $10.5 million Series B Fund Raise

2015
- Apple iOS App launch
- $30 million Series C Fund Raise
- $75 million Series D Fund Raise

2016
- 35,000 Connected Fitness Subscribers (midyear)
- Commercial/Hotel bikes Announced at Consumer Electronics Show (CES); later discontinued
- Palo Alto Showroom opens
- Author clips in for the first time

2017
- Commercial bike announced at CES (later discontinued)
- Denver showroom opens in Cherry Creek Shopping Center
- 108,000 Connected Fitness Subscriptions (midyear)
- $325 million Series E Fund Raise

2018

- Tread (later known as Tread+) Unveiled at CES, deliveries begin in fall
- Robin Arzón streams classes from the Winter Olympics in Pyeongchang, South Korea
- Tread Studio Opens in NYC (will be used for yoga also)
- Outdoor Runs and Walks - app renamed Peloton Digital
- 245,000 Connected Fitness Subscriptions (midyear)
- Author visits Mothership for the first time
- New Bethesda Showroom Opens (author meets Jess King)
- Peloton Yoga announced with full time yogis
- St Louis Showroom opens
- UK and Canada Launch

2020

- Bike+ launched, tread launched (original tread renamed Tread+)
- Covid-19 global pandemic
- Peloton closes production, pauses opening of Peloton Studios New York (PSNY)
- Instructors across disciplines teach from their homes (including UK instructors)
- Author completes 1,000 cycling class
- ESPN - Peloton All-Star Challenge produced and aired
- 1.09 million Connected Fitness Subscriptions; 316,000 Digital Subscribers (midyear)
- 3.1 million total members on the platform (people with accounts)
- Fit Family classes introduced, including cardio and yoga
- Peloton Pledge introduced; $100 million commitment over 4 years
- Health and Wellness Advisory Council announced and initial members introduced
- Barre classes and Bike Bootcamp classes introduced (September)
- Beyoncé x Peloton partnership announced with HBCUs
- Peloton announces acquisition of Precor, including 2 U.S. manufacturing facilities
- Announcement and opening of Harrod's showrooms
- Global Showroom Count 118 (37 international)

2019

- Live yoga streaming begins
- Peloton is a clue on Jeopardy game show
- Music Publishers sue Peloton; class purges begin
- German Launch (first foreign language)
- Peloton Home Rider Invasion renamed Peloton Homecoming
- 511,000 Connected Fitness Subscriptions (midyear)
- 102,00 Digital Subscribers (midyear)
- Initial Public Offering (September); PTON opens at $27 and closes at $25.76
- Peloton introduces Artists Series classes
- Amazon Fire App launched
- Peloton acquires Tonic, a Taiwanese maker of its hardware
- Open showroom in O'Hare Airport in Chicago (later closed)
- "Peloton Wife" television commercial controversy

2021

- U.S. and Canada tread deliveries begin
- Peloton completes $1 billion convertible bond offering
- Consumer Product Safety Commission issues Tread+ advisory
- Peloton issues recall of 125,000 Tread+ and treads and suspends sales of both
- Introduction of Mood Series classes
- Collaboration with Adidas | Adidas x Peloton
- Peloton announces; later breaks ground on manufacturing facility in Ohio
- Expansion to Australia with bike and Bike+
- Peloton announces corporate wellness with United Health Group
- 2.33 million Connected Fitness Subscriptions; 866,000 Digital Subscribers (midyear)
- 5.9 million total members (accounts on the platform)
- Peloton tread sales resume; unclear when Tread+ will be sold again
- Peloton announces its own, private label apparel line
- Peloton Studios London open, UK tread instructors introduced
- Author passes 5,000 total classes taken on the Peloton platform
- *Sex and the City* uses Peloton bike to end the Mr. Big character
- Sweating Together sent to printers

CONTENTS

I DO NOT WANT
THOSE SHOES

The day started as it begins in millions of American homes, with a discussion about money. It was November 2016 and we were heading into the holiday season.

"You spent how much on an exercise bike?" I growled at my wife, Emily.

"Two thousand dollars," she replied with confidence. My wife is a beautiful, successful physician; a partner in a top medical group at a top hospital in suburban Washington, D.C.; and has always been serious about fitness. It was not surprising for her to make this kind of purchase without consulting me. It was silly of me to protest.

In my defense, I had not yet prepared a simple cup of coffee, and our three kids (all under 10 years old at the time) were awake and in search of toys, iPads, milk, and food. Our two dogs, Moose and Scout, with a combined weight of 230 pounds, were unaware that their main caregiver had spent so much on an exercise bike, and they barked loudly in the background.

The problem for me was that we already owned a treadmill and a stationary bike, and Emily was a member at a high-end gym (an Equinox), less than a mile from our home. Moreover, our neighborhood was exercise friendly, with plenty of green space amid quiet streets and pathways from Rock Creek Park and the Potomac River to the National Mall.

When Emily told me she had bought the $2,000-plus Peloton indoor cycling bike, I was a jogger. I would plod slowly around our neighborhood or high school tracks or run on our 10-plus-year-old Precor treadmill in the basement. The treadmill and a string of desirable neighborhood choices had saved me from health club memberships for more than a decade. Throw in some push-ups and other random exercises, and I was a decently healthy 44-year-old father of three when the Peloton appeared in our home in 2016.

If I had to run on the Precor *dreadmill* in the basement, I would. In reality, this meant I often evaded exercise when the weather was foul or the daylight was fleeting (October through February). I commuted in D.C. traffic, often getting home well after dark and rarely wanting to run in the basement, no matter what was on TV or how good a music playlist I believed I had created.

Besides not joining a health club, I did not participate in "trendy" fitness classes, whether yoga, cycling, or bootcamps. As I soon would find out, the bike my wife had purchased came from the boutique segment of the fitness industry. I had always felt that sweating and suffering were a private affair unless one was on a team. However, sports teams ended for me in college, and those intramural experiences were mostly social.

That initial Peloton discussion did not last long. I'd known Emily for more than 20 years, and we'd been married for more than 10 years: the Peloton bike was coming to our house.

When I found out that it carried a subscription fee of $39 a month, I nearly revived our talk about the purchase, but also immediately realized that the company founders were super sharp. Clearly this fitness equipment had a different business model from any other we had owned, a recurring payment. It was interesting as well as irksome.

Little did I imagine that the Peloton bike and platform would change our lives forever. When the bike arrived I was still annoyed with Emily, and I ignored the Peloton in our basement. The sleek, black carbon frame of the new bike made the treadmill look archaic, and we shoved our old Tectrix stationary bike against the basement wall where it would eventually find a purpose holding water and towels for the Peloton rider.

While the bike certainly looked attractive, and Peloton commercials featuring a supermodel-type mother and her family enjoying a beautiful modern life with it made the lifestyle appear intriguing, I did not even consider riding during its first two months in our home. Emily insisted on purchasing cycling shoes for me as most users choose to clip in to the Peloton bike's pedals, something I had never done. Also, I wear a size-15 shoe, so locating a pair was not an easy task for her.

When the Giro brand cycling shoes arrived, I refused to look at them, much less use them or the bike, and the shoes sat on the top step of the basement staircase. I remember thinking to myself: "I am not touching those clip-in shoes." Emily refused to return the shoes and ignored my childish behavior and the size-15 cycling shoes sat in limbo at the top of our basement stairs for weeks.

I walked past the cycling shoes on the stairs and the Peloton bike itself a few times in the fall of 2016 as I jogged on our Precor treadmill, communicating my disapproval of the Peloton through my cardio choices. Fate, of course, had other plans, and by late December 2016, I would be brought to the Peloton by an embarrassing performance in a low-level adult hockey game, which included me vomiting a burrito on the bench. That incident jarred me into questioning what kind of shape I was really in.

On December 30, 2016, I took my first ride on the Peloton. It was also the first time I took an indoor cycling class and clipped in to a bicycle. As a kid in the 1980s, I rode BMX and freestyle bikes, and in the 1990s I rode mountain bikes. The Tectrix bike we owned was the proverbial coat hanger so it had been nearly 20 years since I had any real two-wheel action of any type.

My first Peloton ride was a 20-minute "Beginner Ride" with an instructor named Jennifer Jacobs. It was an on-demand class. It was no different from streaming a TV show or movie except the content was coming to an exercise bike and the data from my effort was feeding back to the Peloton service in real time, which was reflected in my placement on the class leaderboard, a list that ranked everyone that had ever taken the class. My plan was to find out what indoor cycling was about with an engaging, motivating instructor. I was a rookie, and my last group fitness class was a Krav Maga self-defense class with a bunch of cops and FBI agent types in Rockville, Maryland, outside of D.C. I had no idea what might happen in an indoor cycling class.

I would quickly learn that Peloton had an ensemble of about a dozen instructors, some with larger-than-life personalities. The vibrant social media presence of the instructors' and the riders' passion for them were among the first clues that told me Peloton was different from any fitness program and possibly any company I had ever seen before, as a consumer or an entrepreneurship researcher.

In early 2017, just weeks after my first ride, I took notice of Peloton members' fanaticism when Emily introduced me to the Official Peloton Member Page on Facebook (it was called the Official Peloton Riders Page at that time). People were posting fantastic tales of health benefits and more from riding their Peloton bikes. The page was like a 24-hour-a-day digital revival service on Facebook, members recounted miracles of diseases overcome and control over life regained.

Peloton riders were posting pictures of themselves riding with disco lights flashing in their homes, sharing their rides, even crying while riding, planning group rides, and referring to their leggings as "magic pants." Peloton members were constantly referring to themselves by their Peloton usernames, or leaderboard names, employing hashtags as they identified themselves (#ChicagoBorn is the leaderboard name I would eventually settle on). It was odd and I was shaking my head in confusion as I read all those posts, but I could not turn away.

I began discussing what I was witnessing with my entrepreneurship students at George Mason University, even opening my Facebook account in class to show them this consumer behavior, and then asking whether my business students had ever seen anything like this and what entrepreneurial and business principles were at play.

I slowly started to ride the Peloton more frequently in early 2017, using our treadmill less than in past winters. First, I began to appreciate the challenge of indoor cycling and the quality of the instructors and their fun, demanding approach. Then I would begin learning about the diversity of class types and different approaches to fitness. I truly enjoyed the convenience of choosing from thousands of challenging workouts in my home and loved seeing the "Pelo-puddles" (a term I learned on the Facebook page) of sweat forming under the bike. They were proof that I was getting something done. I wanted to ride more.

As I began to ride more and share more with my students into 2017, I realized that my growing desire to ride was part of a phenomenon envisioned by CEO John Foley and the other four founders of Peloton. The team began to build the venture in 2012, and by 2017 I was a convert and growing fascinated by their business model. Since I was 16, I had gone into gyms—ranging from local owner-operated neighborhood facilities to franchises of international chains and national leaders in the high-end segment, including the East Bank Club in Chicago, where Oprah also sweat it out. I had never been gripped by any gym or exercise program the way that Peloton took hold of me.

I grew addicted to riding, and I found fellow fanatics, tried different instructors, and visited Peloton-related accounts on Instagram and Facebook. My fitness levels improved dramatically. I agreed with *Men's Health and Fitness* in its 2015 write-up that Peloton was "the best cardio machine on the planet."

By spring of 2018, I was waking up at 5:15 am on Tuesdays to ride grueling *tabata* style classes in the "pain cave" at 6:00 am with "Pelo-friends" from across the country and Peloton instructor Robin Arzón. I was spending an hour a day with Peloton working on my fitness and overall well-being, and I was going beyond that searching for new workouts, places to explore, and options for food and fuel. I was a daily active user of Peloton's platform, and I was loving it. I began streaming Peloton's stretch, yoga, and strength workouts. I wanted more and more, and the company would provide it, offering new products, services, and features to feed my demands.

I was not alone. The Official Peloton Member Page on Facebook was getting bigger each month as I watched the company. When I joined that Facebook group in February 2017, it had just over 25,000 members. By early 2018, membership topped 75,000; by late January 2019, the number was 146,000; and by September 2019, it approached 200,000. In September 2020, over 335,000 people were members of the Facebook page and when the four year "Peloversary" of my first ride arrived on December 30, 2020, there were nearly 380,000 on the page. By February 2021, four years after I started watching the Facebook page, it went over 400,000 members. Thousands of other Peloton groups emerged on Facebook, Reddit, and Instagram with millions of members and followers. We will explore the major role of social media throughout this book as it has been leveraged by many segments of the Peloton community.

The growth of Peloton-related social media represents the growth of product sales and membership. While our bike was one of the first 100,000, according to the company, by mid-2019, more than 1.4 million users were registered on the Peloton platform, which by then was streaming indoor cycling, running classes, boot- camps, strength training, yoga, and more. By March 2020, there were 2.6 million registered members representing more than 1 million connected fitness devices (Peloton bikes and

Treads, which are the company's treadmills). This number would grow even greater through the Covid-19 pandemic and Peloton would boast more than 3 million registered members working out on more than 1.4 million connected Peloton machines by fall 2020. By mid 2021, the company counted over 5 million registered members and 2 million connected devices (bikes and treadmills).

The book that follows will tell three stories: one of a fitness, innovation, and business revolution that arrived via a New York startup's "bike that goes nowhere"; another of a consumer (me) who became addicted to that venture's products and services, altering their approach to fitness, health, well-being, and life; and lastly, the story of the rise of the business of well-being across the global economy.

This is a book I never planned to write. In fact, I was working on a manuscript based on my research into high-growth student entrepreneurs such as Bill Gates of Microsoft, Mark Zuckerberg of Facebook, Wendy Kopp of Teach for America, Phil Knight of Nike, Larry Page and Sergey Brin of Google, and more. But my wife bought a Peloton bike and some clip-in shoes for me and somehow here we are discussing the future of our society, community, and economy through the lens of that bike and the world that has emerged around it.

LIVING IN AN ENTREPRENEURIAL WORLD

Madonna sang about a material world in the 1980s. Today we live in an entrepreneurial world. For some time we called it the post–Cold War era, the information age, and the knowledge age, but it is clear at this point that innovation and entrepreneurship are the driving forces behind societal and economic change.

You can see it everywhere: on TV shows such as *Shark Tank*, *The Profit*, and *Bar Rescue* and in the public's fascination with empire builders such as Jeff Bezos of Amazon, Elon Musk of Tesla, Oprah Winfrey of media fame, and Sarah Blakely of Spanx. It seems as if every athlete, musician, and celebrity dreams of crossing over to entrepreneurship. MBA achievers want to be founders now, not bankers or consultants.

Moreover, America's lionization of founders has gone international with the global innovation economy expanding to Latin America, India, Russia, and China. The billionaire population grows each year, proving that this entrepreneurial economy is the real deal, and people of all cultures and geographies want to participate.

Entrepreneurship and innovation have not always been a global aspiration. Consider the Cold War, General Motors, and IBM. For most of human history, few individuals had the notion, let alone opportunity, to create a new organization. Today people from Moscow to Michigan and Madagascar know that an inspired individual can build a venture that changes the world and creates billions of dollars in wealth along the way.

The entrepreneurial economy that we are living in (and by most accounts enjoying) has been brewing for decades, but we are just beginning to understand what is going on. The *Economist Magazine* produced a special issue focusing on the "Entrepreneurial Revolution" in 1976, and management guru Peter Drucker published the book *Innovation and Entrepreneurship* in 1985. Only now are we comprehending the art and practice of entrepreneurship.

A LOSER'S BUSINESS

"Entrepreneurship is a loser's business." I make this statement to my students during the second session of my entrepreneurship classes each semester. I get the students hyped during the first session, introducing myself and my research into student startups such as Facebook, Boosted, Grubhub, Google, Nike, and Teach for America. I remind them that undergraduates started most of these ventures and that young leaders changing the world is becoming a regular occurrence. I ask my students to share their favorite company, founder, or new product with the class. Responses in recent years range from Musk and Bezos to Berkshire Hathaway CEO Warren Buffett and Oprah, with Apple, Airbnb, Spotify, and other consumer brands regularly mentioned. The students recognize the innovators and their wares, and love them.

When the students arrive for the second class, I tell them the truth: "Entrepreneurship is a loser's business." I repeat this throughout the semester at extracurricular events and clubs and in small meetings and office hours with students, alumni, and community members.

"Entrepreneurship is a loser's business." I say it often because we need people to understand how difficult it is to create any business, especially anything that employs more than a handful of people.

The data are there to prove that entrepreneurship is a loser's business. Most new ventures fail. It does not matter whether we are talking about a bunch of Ritalin-fueled engineers in California's Silicon Valley attempting to be disruptive and innovative or a team trying to run a seemingly simple business, such as a cupcake bakery or a suburban landscaping service.

In most cases new ventures die young. A majority of new businesses in the United States will not make it to five years. If you don't believe me, check the Small Business Administration website, call your local banker or chamber of commerce, or score the portfolio win rate of the most successful investors in Silicon Valley, Boston, or New York.

All that failure aside, some ventures will survive, and a few will prosper, hire many people, and change communities. A smaller group will become high-growth ventures and change industries, cities, regions, and lives. Peloton falls into that last category.

These high-growth, disruptive companies catch the public's eye because of their ability to radically change how we live, work, and play as well as to create massive wealth for their leaders, investors, and others. They are about the future and many find this part of the economy intoxicating.

Learning about world-changing new ventures and figuring out how they grow and thrive is a big part of my job as a professor at a major public research university with a range of stakeholders. Students and community members want to learn about entrepreneurship and build their tool kits for the day when they launch their own business. In fact, surveys show that most Millennials hope to own a business, so there is strong demand for our courses and extracurricular programs. Generation Z, growing up with eBay and Etsy and the gig economy, see the world in much the same way.

I was among the business school students in the 1990s who first began taking entrepreneurship classes and choosing startups over banking and consulting careers. Today entrepreneurship is the hottest field in business education.

In my first experience with entrepreneurship, I decided to leave the University of Chicago's business school midway through my MBA studies to join RollingStone.com and eventually another venture-backed dot-com. It was the late 1990s and I didn't want to miss the internet rush (bubble). Because of those experiences,

I became fascinated by student founders and the entrepreneurial ecosystems of universities and colleges in the United States. I chose to research these topics in earning my PhD.

The database of student-founders and their ventures that I created and manage includes some of the most innovative and impactful companies in the world, such as Boosted, Dell, Equity Residential Properties, Facebook, FedEx, Google, Groupon, Grubhub, Intuit, Microsoft, Nantucket Nectars, Netscape, Teach for America, TerraCycle, Under Armour, and many more.

In addition to tracking student ventures, I always looked for amazing new ventures that could provide clues into what is to come and how to best understand and effectively convert on the great opportunities across the economy and society.

Though I fought the Peloton bike when it arrived, by early 2017, it became obvious to the entrepreneurship researcher in me that this venture was something very special and different, and it was the customers who were providing the clues.

In February 2017, four instructors (Jenn Schreiber Sherman, Steven Little, and Hannah Corbin were the next three I tried) and about fifteen rides into my Peloton career, I noticed something on the Official Peloton Member Page on Facebook that shocked me. A single post screamed to me that there was a real power to the bike and the service that the company was building.

A Peloton member in Minneapolis posted that she was about to turn 40 years old, and for her birthday she was going to New York City to take a live class in the Peloton Studio, where the streaming cycling classes are filmed and produced. Wow, I thought, kind of like watching a taping of Oprah. This member also stated that she had never visited New York before. That was what stopped me cold. Something about the fact that she had never been to NYC made the trip to Peloton more meaningful.

My mind raced through some of New York City's great attractions: Broadway, Central Park, Ellis Island, the Empire State Building, the Guggenheim and other art museums, Madison Square Garden, the Statue of Liberty, *Saturday Night Live,* and the *Today* show.

None of those world-famous sights or experiences had motivated this woman to come to New York City, but a stationary bike that she rides at home, with instructors and people she had never met—that was a reason to visit?

For some reason that I did not understand then, this woman wanted to be inside of the box, to use TV lingo. In this case, she was going to a fitness studio in the Big Apple to be with a Peloton instructor and other members, face to face, in real life, sweating together. I assumed she did not know the instructors or the other people that would be in the classes with her. I would soon learn that Peloton members referred to the studio in New York City as the "Mothership" and the Minnesotan member's desire to visit was common.

It did not compute for me. I thought the whole point of the bike was to avoid the inconvenience of going to the gym. Now people were going to New York to take classes? I understood the workouts were great and convenient, but Peloton members (customers) were behaving in ways that did not make sense to me. This unexpected consumer behavior fascinated me. They were also really happy and posting about it. I wanted to know: What the hell was going on with this bike and who were the people behind it?

THE INTERNET, SCHUMPETER, AND THE CRAZY ONES

After I graduated from the University of Michigan in 1995, I was lucky to head straight to London for a year to complete a master's degree in Asian Studies at the University of London. I lived in a small studio apartment and had no television— shocking this American as I had lived on a diet of cable TV for the previous decade.

However, I had a laptop and a basic dial-up modem, which put me ahead of 99 percent of the world at the time. As slow as that modem was, it was revolutionary for a young American graduate student in Europe. It provided basic text and some pictures— no games, videos, or streaming sports in the mid-1990s—but it was mind blowing. Since the first popular browser, Mosaic, had recently been released, I was on the digital frontier reading articles and news from around the globe in my tiny London flat.

As much as I enjoyed the pubs of London and pints of Guinness, I wanted to be in my little apartment on Bloomsbury Square browsing the emerging World Wide Web. I spent countless hours a day pulling down articles from the first basic sites of magazines such as the now-defunct *Far East Economic Review*, academic websites, and other outlets that covered the People's Republic of China, the country I was studying in London. I wrote a dissertation about the impact of the internet on state actors that rely on the control of information as part of their political system. Although I didn't fully realize it at the time, this early experience with the web was the beginning of my research into the role of innovation and entrepreneurship in social and economic change.

More than a decade later, when I began my doctoral studies, I quickly learned that it was Joseph Schumpeter, an Austrian economist known for his theory of "creative destruction," who brought the concept of the entrepreneur into economic theories around growth, change, and innovation. Schumpeter was the first to point out the central role that innovators and entrepreneurs, as individuals and in small groups, could play in an economy. Before Schumpeter, economists would try to measure the size and potential of an economy using concepts such as total labor, total capital, and stores of knowledge that the economy had at its disposal. There was no role for individuals and their ventures.

In addition to pointing out the importance of what he called changemakers, Schumpeter highlighted creative destruction as an important part of a capitalist economy. The value-producing innovations that the changemakers bring to society also would cause problems and, potentially, the demise of existing providers.

For example, the rise of Craigslist in the early 2000s hastened the decline of the newspaper industry as the classified advertising business disappeared almost overnight. Another traditional example of creative destruction is the case of Henry Ford and other affordable automobile producers and the destruction of the horse-drawn buggy, saddle, and whip industries it supported. Creative destruction hurts many no matter how great the innovation. My wife, Emily, dropping her Equinox membership when she bought the Peloton is a perfect example of the creative destruction that connected fitness has brought to the health club and fitness equipment industries.

Disruptive innovators bring social, technical, political, and cultural change and often invite resistance. In the 1990s, Apple Computer ran an advertising campaign with the slogan "Think Different," featuring historical innovators and changemakers including Jane Goodall, Jim Henson, John Lennon and

Yoko Ono, Louis Armstrong, Cesar Chavez, Amelia Earhart, Mahatma Gandhi, Pablo Picasso, Jimi Hendrix, and others. This campaign, one of many successful emotive ads Apple has pulled off over the years, included the following copy as part of the iMac release in 1997:

> Here's to the crazy ones. The misfits. The rebels. The troublemakers. The round pegs in the square holes. The ones who see things differently. They're not fond of rules, and they have no respect for the status quo. You can quote them, disagree with them, glorify, or vilify them. But the only thing you can't do is ignore them. Because they change things. They push the human race forward. And while some may see them as the crazy ones, we see genius. Because the people who are crazy enough to think they can change the world, are the ones who do.

The crazy ones that Apple was celebrating were the types of people that Schumpeter was writing about and that I was looking for as an entrepreneurship researcher. For most people, the crazy ones themselves—whether Steve Jobs, Walt Disney, or Peloton founder John Foley—are interesting, but not as important as the products, services, worlds, and experiences they create.

When my wife brought the Peloton into our home, she saw it as an awesome workout. She had no real care or concern about the people building the company, the business model they were developing, or the future growth path of Peloton Interactive, Inc.

(the official corporate name). As I spent more time riding the bike and observing the Peloton community—mostly through scanning third-party platforms such as Facebook and Instagram, but also by watching my wife and her friends—it became clear that many great elements of creativity, innovation, and entrepreneurship were present in the company's products and services. Moreover, Peloton member actions and behaviors were taking place online and off, unlike anything I had witnessed since joining the internet rush 20 years earlier when I left business school to join RollingStone.com.

As I took more Peloton classes, met riders and instructors (through social media and classes), and experimented with my own health and fitness, I began to see Peloton as some strange, sweaty mix of Apple, Lululemon, and Tesla with a social media community breathing a cult-like positivity one might find around Oprah Winfrey, Joel Osteen, or Tony Robbins.

In the pages that follow, I will share my journey into the phenomenon of Peloton and my exploration of the revolutionary business that John Foley, his team, and his customers are building.

Exploring this high-growth startup and how it sucked in a middle-aged, moderately healthy professor from the Midwest and millions of others provides incredible insights into our economy and society and where we are heading. It did not matter that I hadn't taken a cycling class before, or that I drove a Ford F-150, or that I was an avid watcher of UFC (cage fighting). Somehow the culture of an indoor cycling studio in New York captured me and millions of others.

According to the company's S-1 filing in August 2019, the Peloton platform had more than 1.4 million registered users, with more than 500,000 paying subscription fees of $39 a month for a connected piece of equipment and another 102,000 paying for an app-based digital subscription (allowing those digital subscribers to take classes on non-Peloton hardware by streaming to the members device). Just about a year later, by September 2020, Peloton revealed more than 1.1 million connected devices, over 3.0 million registered members, and nearly 500,000 digital-only subscribers. With revenue of almost 2 billion dollars in fiscal year 2020, just eight years after its founding, Peloton was truly unlike anything else in fitness or across the economy. This was before the pandemic struck in spring 2020. By mid-2021, a year into the pandemic, Peloton counted 2 million connected devices and more than 5 million total members.

Growing any kind of venture to Peloton's scale is nearly impossible, and doing it in a way that is making customers happier and healthier is almost a miracle. This is among the core reasons that the Peloton journey is worth researching, discussing, and trying to understand. The ability to make people happier, healthier, stronger, more resilient, and more connected is not to be taken lightly. The business of creating and delivering well-being is growing and where the economy is headed.

Throughout these pages we will dig into the company that Foley and his colleagues have built as well as the community that is Peloton, with stories of members (customers) and the celebrity instructors. From the rise of well-being, social media, and gamification to the role of physical space in a digital world, talent retention, and community building, there is no better venture for understanding where our economy is heading than Peloton and its community of people sweating together.

I must warn you that this book is based on my experiences owning and using Peloton products and services. This is a *consumer memoir* of sorts; I just happen to be an entrepreneurship researcher and spend much time trying to understand new venture creation and its impact and meaning for society. This is neither an exhaustive account of Peloton's founding nor a financial analysis for investing in its stock. My experiences with Peloton may have similarities and vast differences from other members. As many of the instructors state, and the members often repeat, "Your ride is your ride."

CHAPTER 1

JOHN FOLEY, PELOTON, AND ITS SWEAT-DRIVEN BUSINESS MODEL

John Foley, co-founder and CEO of Peloton, is known as John on digital leaderboards across the Peloton platform and as KeyLargoFoley on Twitter. As his Twitter handle suggests, John grew up in Florida, was the son of a Delta Air Lines pilot, and attended Georgia Tech for college.

In order to help pay for his education, Foley spent his college summers working midnight factory shifts, wearing a hairnet, hard hat, and steel-toe boots for Mars, the giant confectionary and food business. Foley went on to begin his career with Mars after graduating from Georgia Tech.

These years with Mars gave Foley an early view of what his life would be like working in consumer packaged goods within traditional corporate America. On the job in the mid-1990s, Foley would create spreadsheets of the future value of his retirement accounts: stable and predictable, but not necessarily enjoyable or exciting. He would call his father and explain that he was not happy with his work. His dad, a veteran, would reply, "If it was fun, they'd call it play." Foley expected to adopt this stoic approach for himself.

During my interview with Foley, he pointed out that for young, capable workers, career expectations were reaching an inflection point in the mid-'90s; the balance of power was swinging away from employers and to talent. Mars was the old corporate model that generations of workers had experienced. Like many Generation X members, Foley knew that he wanted something different from his career, it just was not clear to Foley early on what that different could be.

Foley eventually transferred to Kal Kan, a Mars pet food division. This moved him to East Los Angeles, a gritty industrial part of the City of Angels. Fortune smiled on Foley, and his brother-in-law introduced him to some people at an internet startup, CitySearch. Foley was given a shot to join the venture.

Like many young people who joined the internet boom of the mid-1990s (including me), Foley was forever changed by the experience. Gen Xers and subsequent generations (Millennials, Z's, and beyond) were moved to demand more from work than just a paycheck.

When we discussed this part of his career Foley described how working with so many young, educated, and optimistic people was intoxicating and impactful. The idea that "the sky was the limit" was totally different from his years of experience in consumer packaged goods manufacturing.

Foley wouldn't look back after joining the internet rush in Los Angeles and working for several more startups. Eventually, he headed to Boston for Harvard Business School, then on to New York for more media startups, including Barry Diller's gigantic IAC and Evite. He joined BarnesandNoble.com, where he experienced digital content and hardware creation via the Nook eReader and experienced first-hand the power of Amazon and others developing and controlling platforms and networks.

In our discussion about the dramatic changes taking place in the workplace during the internet boom era and how Foley interpreted and navigated that era, it became crystal clear to me what a deep, analytic, and macro thinker Foley is. Foley would apply that strength when he began to develop the Peloton idea.

FOUNDERS MATTER BECAUSE THEY IDENTIFY PROBLEMS

Like Foley, I became intoxicated by the internet rush of the late 1990s. Because of what I witnessed and experienced during the boom and bust, I spent almost a decade researching student founders such as Mark Zuckerberg, Bill Gates, Michael Dell, Kevin Plank, and Elizabeth Holmes, and I know that these brilliant people could never have created Peloton.

A 19-year-old in a dorm room never would have identified and understood the problem that Peloton set about to solve.

Alternatively, John Foley has exactly the LinkedIn profile one might expect for a venture of Peloton's complexity. (It is far more than a bike with a iPad, no matter what the critics contend.)

Foley's life before launching Peloton gave him a great blend of education, work, and life experience that enabled him to understand how an interactive, hardware-producing streaming fitness company might work and why people would want to join. Foley's engineering degree from Georgia Tech, MBA from Harvard, and years in a variety of consumer, technology, and content companies prepared him to launch a high-growth company of some sort.

However, Foley's personal life experiences uniquely positioned him to identify a problem and develop a vision for a connected fitness company with offerings on par with the best boutique fitness studios in New York or Los Angeles.

Around 2010 Foley's life was going well. He had young children, a high-powered job in the tech world, and a happily working wife, Jill. Foley, a competitive triathlete and indoor cycling enthusiast, realized that his and Jill's successes and responsibilities in life would override their indoor cycling habit. Getting to classes was a challenge and reserving a spot in top boutique studio classes was a logistical nightmare on par with getting hot concert tickets.

As an experienced technology executive, Foley had a good understanding of supply chains, hardware, consumers, and digital content. His opportunity and goal became obvious: boutique group fitness in the comfort of your own home, live and on demand.

When one meets Foley, or watches an interview with him, it becomes clear he is a serious, competitive guy and this intensity and passion is one of the reasons co-founder Tom Cortese and so many others have joined him for what Foley told me was a "once in a lifetime opportunity to build one of the special companies of all time."

Cortese, a colleague of Foley's from IAC, said that one of his reasons for joining Peloton after months of discussing the concept and taking indoor cycling classes with Foley was that "there is no one more aggressive and passionate all at the same time than John." In my full interview and over the course of several other interactions and talks with Foley, I found determination in his gaze and authenticity and warmth in his person every time. I was actually surprised by how engaging Foley was in person, but once I met him and experienced his energy, I completely understood how he was able to win team members over in the early years.

Foley ultimately launched Peloton in 2012, lining up the initial funding from his personal wealth and a small group of friends and family investors. In the next two years the founders would develop the Peloton bike, software, and some early classes. They also ran a Kickstarter campaign, moving the first 200 bikes via online crowdfunding, learning that many potential consumers wanted to see and test the bike before purchasing. Some members of the core founding team went along part-time in the first year or two. However, they were committed to Foley and the enormous opportunity in the health and fitness space he had uncovered. By the beginning of 2014, Peloton started to deliver its black-framed, connected, indoor bikes.

SHARING VISIONS OF THE FUTURE

One of the great challenges for entrepreneurs with innovative ventures is convincing people that the founding team's vision of the future is correct and that the team can actually execute on the opportunity. Founders of disruptive ventures (the crazy ones) must communicate a totally new future that is not easy to see. They need energy and answers to convince potential investors, partners, customers, and employees.

For Tom Cortese, Yony Feng, John Foley, Hisao Kushi, and Graham Stanton (the five people listed as Peloton's co-founders), it was challenging to communicate the idea that people could have fun sweating together digitally, but doing it while all alone at home. Many investors, including top venture capitalists in Silicon Valley and leading players in the health club and fitness industries, were not interested in working with Foley and the team.

The Peloton concept was something that many people just could not get their heads around. Academic observers from Joseph Schumpeter to Clayton Christensen, author of *The Innovator's Dilemma*, have pointed out that true disruptors are hard to spot (even when they are out there openly asking for money) and, more often than not, are understood after the fact.

The digital economy, which is clearly part of the Peloton model, has scaled with low-cost computers, high-speed connections, and lots of software. This amazingly vast frontier with low barriers to entry has attracted the smartest in our economy, such as Bill Gates, Jeff Bezos, Jack Ma, and many more.

The ease, speed, and low capital requirements of entrance to the digital space are likely among the reasons why Foley and his founding team at Peloton had trouble getting support from venture capitalists early on. The Peloton business model, with expensive hardware purchase via the initial Peloton bike and constant content creation from a studio in New York, did not match what investors were looking for. Social networks, apps, enterprise software, and e-commerce were the sweet spots for most venture investors as Foley and the team began to build Peloton. Fitness hardware and content, even if connected, did not match the models and patterns investors at the time expected.

For many fitness operators, the concept of people working out in live group classes from home, away from the physical studio space did not make sense. The personal interaction with the instructor and the small class community were what boutique members sought. Foley and his team understood, but believed they could replicate the experience with the right hardware, software, instructors, and social engagement tools.

Even the best investors and corporate leaders can face domain limitations, blind spots, and arrogance. The Silicon Valley investors that Foley and Peloton met with early on were not familiar with indoor cycling or boutique fitness companies such as SoulCycle, Flywheel, and Barry's Bootcamp, brands that were growing dramatically at the time. During our conversation, Foley lightheartedly relayed the story of a Silicon Valley Sand Hill Road investor stating dismissively, "Out here there are two types of biking: mountain biking and road biking." Hundreds of investors would turn Foley and the team down in the first few years. In my interviews with Foley and Cortese in 2019, after they had raised hundreds of millions and were on the path to an IPO, it was obvious they were still smarting from the early rejections.

Pride, ignorance, and limited models are the reasons that most investors turned down early iterations of Airbnb, Amazon, and countless other innovative and impactful firms. The new disruptors did not match the investors' models of successful past investments and ventures. Instead of being curious enough to explore the new model, most backed away, sticking with well-known investing patterns.

For the early Peloton team, a world full of mobile apps, streaming content, and high-demand boutique fitness inspired a connected at-home bike providing high-quality, convenient workouts. In this scenario—with high capital needs and a product concept new to the world, the founding team had to stay resilient, and the initial product had to be compelling to users in order to power through the biases of industry leaders and capital holders. Fortunately for Peloton, customers saw the value in the team's concept and Foley's vision well before the investing and fitness community did.

THE INITIAL PELOTON BUSINESS MODEL

At its simplest, a business model is how a venture or organization creates products and services and sells those products and services. To quote innovation expert and Stanford University Professor Steve Blank, a business model is how an "organization creates value, delivers value, and captures value."[1]

For Peloton, the venture initially created and delivered value through a high-end, at-home, indoor bike that streams high-quality cycling classes live and on demand. Peloton captures value by selling the bike and charging a monthly subscription fee. The core value of the first Peloton bike and the company's later offerings is convenient access to world-class workouts at home. As it states on the side of Peloton delivery vehicles, "Live studio fitness from the comfort of your home." Convenience is highly valued and Foley understood that.

In many ways Peloton has merged two traditional models in the fitness space: buy a piece of home equipment or pay a monthly membership at a gym. Peloton has pulled them both off with some critical adjustments. There is no central gym or physical location, but there are updates and improvements to the home equipment through continual software and feature upgrades and content creation. With the physical space being the Peloton member's location and the content streaming to the members, in the Peloton model there are no limits on the number of seats available in a class, thus Peloton makes world-class fitness content accessible to members no matter where they live or travel. Additionally, while there are live classes scheduled, the opportunity to take on-demand classes at the time of their choice is a value offered to Peloton members. The traditional gym model has the manager or studio owner determining which classes are available and when.

That straightforward offering of convenience, accessibility, and choice was Foley scratching his own itch and those of his co-founders. Foley and his peers were busy professionals who took their fitness seriously. For many market segments in our modern world, convenience is one of the attributes that users are willing to pay for. From a car ride with Uber, to self-serve kiosks at a Wawa convenience store, to check deposits via smartphones, the market wants convenience, and that is one of the basic building blocks of the Peloton business model.

CONVENIENCE AND CHOICE

Having regular live classes each day and a massive library of on-demand classes gives Peloton members a convenience that traditional gym and studio-based fitness offerings cannot match. With class lengths of five to 90 minutes and cycling class styles including low-impact, music theme, interval rides, and climb rides, Peloton quickly built its library into a veritable tapas bar of fitness.

Members not only can control when they workout, but also choose what types of workouts they do. They need not worry about the logistics of signing up, getting a spot in the class, driving, and parking. There are no sold-out classes, waiting lists, or rushing to the shower afterward.

When members log into their Peloton account, from the equipment or a digital device, they have a range of options to put on their plate for that workout. Users can sample small dishes or gorge on one big favorite (like a 60-minute climb ride!) or do anything in between. Peloton has expanded far beyond cycling to provide ever greater choice. The Peloton Timeline in this book highlights the introduction of new fitness and well-being disciplines as well as hardware offerings between 2014 and 2021.

For an example of the choices available, a member with only a 30-minute window to work out can choose from: a) a 30-minute bike class; b) a 15-minute bike class, a 10-minute core strength class, and a 5-minute stretch class; c) a 10-minute flow yoga, a 10-minute ride, and a 10-minute walking class; or d) any other combination they make up from the thousands of classes available.

A Peloton member's ability to mix and match workout types, lengths, and intensities is a value that no one else in the fitness space had offered before Peloton. Yes, a fitness consumer could go to a massive gym and use a range of machines, spaces, and weights, but it would be impossible to find a 10-minute arms class, 20 minutes of yoga, or a 20-minute cycling class, all with world-class instruction and at the time that the member wanted the classes. Peloton has evolved to provide this unique value very quickly. The ability to "stack" workouts is a feature that Peloton members love and mention repeatedly in describing how they use their membership. Eventually Peloton created a stack feature in its software to allow members to program and schedule their personal stacks ahead of time.

As time on the Peloton platform passes, the instruction from a consistent group of coaches allows members to learn more and gain confidence in creating personal stacked workouts. This has happened for me and is one of the extra values I have received—confidence in my fitness knowledge and approach.

In one of my favorite Peloton groups on Facebook, members share planned stack workouts with others and meet on the Peloton leaderboard to complete the workouts together at specific times. While completing the stacks together from across the country, they provide virtual high fives and chat with one another.

AMAZING TALENT AND CONTENT CREATION

Beyond introducing an attractive and incredibly smooth bike for home riders (and later a treadmill and other digital fitness offerings), the Peloton founders set a goal of delivering the best content in the world to their members.

The team wanted their classes to be as good as any available at the best studios. Foley and his crew were competitive and had experience in consumer markets and media, and they knew their content had to be spectacular for the company to thrive. They had lived and worked out in New York and Los Angeles, so they were familiar with leading fitness offerings. For owners of at-home exercise equipment, this was a radical change: interactive, live instruction from some of the best instructors in the world. No one had tried this before.

While amazing fitness instructors are scattered around the country and the world, the challenge for most in the health club industry is that those great instructors can only teach a limited number of times to a limited number of students. By finding elite instructors and streaming their classes live and on demand, co-founder Tom Cortese believes that Peloton has begun solving an issue that had plagued the gym industry since inception.

The Peloton founders believed that their location in New York would enable them to find some of the most talented instructors around. Even as the venture has grown and scaled, Peloton's talent needs are smaller than those of the largest players in the health club industry. Most of the increased demand for talent has been driven by Peloton adding content well beyond the original cycling classes. When I joined Peloton in 2016, there were 12 core cycling instructors, by the end of 2021 there were more than 50 instructors across cycling, strength, yoga, and running. The instructors were teaching out of NYC and London and were delivering content in English, German, and Spanish.

With a digital fitness streaming model, there would be no limit to how many people could enjoy an incredible session with an amazing, motivating instructor or how many times they could enjoy it. Peloton is a rare institution that has shown how to scale education. Yes, fitness instruction is education.

WORLD-CLASS HARDWARE
FOR THE HOME

For companies to become industry changers, first and foremost, the product or service must be great. It must deliver something so new and different that people are blown away. Examples are Amazon offering a book selection even larger than the mega stores or Tesla offering an electric performance car rather than a golf cart–like electric car as previous auto makers had done.

The choice of an indoor bike as Peloton's entry to the streaming fitness market was made for a variety of reasons. Foley and his peers loved indoor cycling and understood the importance of having of a base of users familiar with the concept.

Also, a real-time group connection, formed through good instruction and music, was a regular feature in top cycling studios and gyms. Another consideration for the Peloton team was the lower cost of an indoor bike versus a treadmill. Also, as Cortese pointed out during our interview, with an indoor cycling class, both the bike and the instructor were stationary, which would make video and audio production easier for the new venture as it started.

In my opinion, with nearly 35 years of general consumer experience using exercise equipment, the original Peloton bike is an amazing product. Most early Peloton owners and reviewers felt the same way. Although I had never taken an indoor cycling class before my wife brought the Peloton into our home, I later tried other bikes and classes. To most who try it, the Peloton looks better, uses digital controls, and provides a quieter, smoother ride than other indoor bikes. If you search for reviews of the bike, they have been largely positive. Most writers from 2014 through the present have been taken aback with elements such as the bike's belt drive and HD touch-screen tablet. One early reviewer described seeing the instructors' sweat glisten.[2]

The team pulled off the hardware side of the offering by hiring Eric Villency of New York–based Villency Design Group, a high-end industrial design firm. Villency had a long list of successful fitness and wellness clients, and he was called the "wizard of wellness design" by *Well+Good*, a leading media outlet in the well-being space.[3] *Bloomberg Businessweek* referred to Villency as a "kind of Jony Ive of stationary bikes." Ive was the Apple design chief behind iconic offerings such as the iPhone and earbuds. As fate would have it, Peloton and Villency would later have a legal fallout.

As co-founder Cortese said in a 2016 speech, the Peloton team wanted to create a superior bike that was beautiful enough to fit in one's living room. The sleek, black finish has a very New York look to me; the Peloton offering looks nothing like the standard silver Schwinn bikes that populate most health clubs and small indoor cycling studios.

When it comes to design, the bar for most in-home exercise equipment has been low. Foley has pointed this out repeatedly when explaining how big the opportunity is for Peloton. Peloton's sophisticated style and approach to at-home fitness equipment helped it stand out immediately. More important, the team assembled the back-end software engineering talent to connect the bike, members, and unique and engaging instructors.

COMMUNITY

One of the elements of boutique fitness that customers, including Foley and his co-founders, love is the boutique aspect of the offerings. The spaces and the classes are small, whether they're for cycling, yoga, Pilates, or bootcamps. Individuals in the class can receive personal attention and the class is an intimate shared experience. This high-touch experience often means customers are willing to pay up to $50 per class or extra fees on top of their regular health club membership.

According to many, including Foley, the right class with the right instructor and classmates is well worth paying for, like a special dining experience. The community aspect of indoor cycling is one of the reasons top cycling studio brands such as SoulCycle and Flywheel grew quickly in New York and beyond, and attracted riders like Foley and my wife, Emily.

Most, including many industry leaders and investors, did not think the Peloton team could recreate the community aspect of a group fitness class online. It is why none of the top players, no matter how credible Foley's background and pitch, wanted to partner with him when he started Peloton. However, the Peloton founders, with decades of combined experience in the online world, knew that community was something that the internet and technology could do well.

From early message boards and sites like Craigslist and Facebook to basic group chats, technology, when deployed properly, can strengthen communities and extend them over time and space. The choice of the name Peloton comes from the word for the pack of riders who ride together in a road race, both cooperating and competing. It signaled the company founders' intention to create a community that would sweat together while completing fitness classes.

Software and user-interface design followed this intention with the creation of a leaderboard of participants allowing members to see who was on the ride and what that member's output was. The riders (and later runners) are dynamically ranked on the leaderboard as the class progresses. The in-class community energy coming through the leaderboard was part of the social experience Foley and the team planned and hoped for. The leaderboard is not only for competing, but it also works as a simple social tool for members to communicate through names and hashtags to the community, reinforcing the social experience of a class on the Peloton platform. Video chat was another element the team put into place using hardware (cameras and microphones) and software to create a social element to classes on Peloton's connected platform.

Early in Peloton's existence, the community element of the business model morphed as members and instructors behaved in a range of ways to push the community in directions the company founders never imagined. When I interviewed Foley in early 2019 he acknowledged that the "intensity" of the Peloton community "surprised" him and that he was "studying it" just as I was. Much of the Peloton community experience migrated from the actual fitness offerings (classes) to social media spaces as members wanted to share information about the bikes, the rides, the instructors, and one another. As early adopter John Bernstein (#YukonJack),[4] a Minneapolis father who bought the bike in 2015, explained to me, the community formed naturally online as riders wanted to share what they were learning—how to clip in and out, for example—and what great rides they were taking. The only way to learn these things in the early days was from other riders.

Peloton members, before the Covid disruption, as we noted earlier, also had the ability to visit the New York studio where the classes are filmed and meet the instructors and other members. As we will explore, the community grew dramatically in the digital space and expanded into the physical world. Physical interaction and space is an important part of the Peloton story.

When Foley and I discussed the emergence of the community, he referred to it as an X factor in Peloton's success that "might be the most powerful thing we have created." I believe Foley is correct. The community around the Peloton platform is unlike anything I have witnessed studying startups or experienced in my 40 years as a serious American consumer. It is one of the most powerful forces behind the company's rise; members have turned the mix of social media, engaging talent, hardware, software, and sweat into a community that is an immense asset creating and delivering value for other members and the company.

DATA AND GAMIFICATION

Because I was born in the Chicago suburbs in the early 1970s and raised mostly in the mainstream of American consumer culture, I've come of age with video games. Pong, Mattel Handheld Football, Pac-Man, Ms. Pac-Man, Donkey Kong, Mario Bros., Madden, Angry Birds, Wii, Xbox, and others have gained my time and attention since the 1970s.

While massive improvements in technology is a core reason for the amazing expansion of gaming, the addictive nature of smart game design has been a not-so-secret sauce for the industry.

Good performance in games leads to positive reinforcement in a range of forms: victories, improved rankings, peer respect, awards, pride, self-confidence, funny noises, coins, flashes of light, and on and on.

These concepts were not invented with video games. Leafy crowns were awarded to victors at the original Olympics. However, video games have allowed game creators to intensify and focus these efforts. Digitization and data allow for an unlimited amount of goodies to be created and awarded to users. The positive reinforcement generated through good gaming design keeps players coming back for more.

Eventually the value of *gamification,* applying game design elements and principles to achieve goals and increase engagement, became a well-known and used strategy across many industries and sectors, from education and training to policy making and health.

One recent gamified trend in health, fitness, and technology has been the idea of the quantifiable self, the concept that the more we can measure and track ourselves, the better we can do, and perhaps the more motivated we will be to do more. CrossFit, Orangetheory Fitness, and many other popular workouts use statistics and gamification elements to strengthen their offerings and bring more value to their customers. Basic data and gamification go hand in hand with fitness and health, as Fitbit, Strava, Garmin, and Apple have shown.

Metrics were not traditionally part of the indoor cycling offering; a talented instructor, encouraging music, and a strong community were what most people wanted. Then in 2010 New York–based indoor cycling studio, Flywheel, entered the marketplace with a leaderboard in the studio, a few years after SoulCycle began to make its mark as a boutique indoor cycling studio.

While SoulCycle, founded in 2006, was known as rhythmic and meditative, Flywheel went a different route. A Flywheel class had a leaderboard on the wall based on the bike output of the riders in the room. The output of a rider is determined by their bike's resistance (how hard it is to pedal) and cadence (how fast the rider is pedaling). Riders loved the gamification option for indoor cycling, as evidenced by Flywheel's growth from one location in 2010 to more than 40 locations across the U.S. by 2017. It is worth noting that New York indoor cycling legend Ruth Zukerman was a co-founder of both SoulCyle and Flywheel.

For Peloton, recording members' data and presenting it to them simply and clearly in real time has been an important part of the business model. While exercising on the Peloton bike and later the tread, output becomes a key measure for many members as they track their progress or earn personal bests on different class types and lengths. It's worth noting that on the Peloton platform the output is always calculating on the bikes and treads and translating to a place or ranking on the leaderboard. The leaderboard can be sorted a range of ways on the user's screen (e.g., age, gender, friends, hashtags) or can be completely hidden by the member.

Digital badges like a gold star are awarded for personal best outputs and for participating in special-event classes such as the Thanksgiving Turkey Burn workouts and All for One workouts over the Fourth of July holiday, where ensembles of instructors teach classes together and other celebratory sessions are offered. Artist Series classes (featuring entire class playlists of a single musical act or artist) and their badges have become a fun, pop-culture gamification element of Peloton that members love.

The Century Club milestone and badge, awarded for a member's 100th class in any discipline (usually riding) is typically the gamified element that can become a gateway badge and event for many members. It's worth noting that members also earn a Century Club T-shirt with the milestone and can go online after their milestone class to order their shirt.

Howard Stern, the media superstar and a Peloton member, discussed his surprise at learning about his 100th ride (via a congratulatory email from Peloton) and earning a Century Club T-shirt. At first Stern mocked the notion with his co-host Robin Quivers and stated that he deleted the email initially out of cynicism. Moments later, Stern went on to recount that a few days later he realized that he was proud of his achievement and that he wanted his shirt. Stern instructed his assistant to retrieve the email and order his shirt.[5]

As Peloton's offerings have expanded, the opportunity to celebrate milestones and earn digital badges for milestone workouts (100 rides, 500 yoga classes, 300 bootcamps, etc.) has grown. Although the Peloton badges appear in digital formats on the members' accounts, the real value is the pride the members feel in their progress and commitment to self and the respect and support they receive from the community of instructors and other riders. Various badges can be earned for working out "with" a certain number of Peloton friends. For example, working out with one friend earns you a Dynamic Duo badge while working out with 20 or more friends earns a Swarm Badge.

For me, the simple gamification of earning a blue dot on my Peloton calendar for each day I take a Peloton class is the one that has really made me obsessed and changed my life. When a member views the calendar on their Peloton account, each day has a gray dot. As soon as a class is taken that day, the dot becomes blue. About a year and a half into my membership, I became obsessed with keeping my daily blue dot streak going.

Earning a month of blue dots is a pretty common goal for Peloton members. My streak started when I added that goal as one of my monthly goals in the summer of 2018. What ended up happening was that between July 16, 2018, and January 26, 2021, I logged into the Peloton platform and took at least one class every single day. That is a streak of 924 days! Most days I took multiple classes, perhaps a morning yoga, then later in the day a bike class and a cool down and a stretch. Then Peloton added strength and running and bootcamps and more, and it became easier and easier to earn a blue dot.

Missing my blue dot on January 26, 2021 is something I won't forget because I had a lot going on that day. I returned to the physical classroom at George Mason University for the first time in almost a year when campus closed due to the pandemic. That was exciting and nerve-wracking and new (masks, half the class at home online, social distancing in the room, etc.)

Later that day, after teaching those first two classes back on campus (masked and socially distanced), as dusk arrived, it was time for me to head to a local suburban Maryland clinic to receive my first Covid vaccine shot. Because I am an educator, I was eligible for vaccination in late January of 2021 in Montgomery County, Maryland.

By the time I got home from my 5:50 pm vaccine appointment, it was almost 8:00 pm and I was hyped up from classes and the nervous excitement of the shot. Not long later, after eating a bit and playing with my kids, I crashed on the couch and then woke groggy, and headed off to bed. I forgot, for the first time in 924 days, to do a simple five-minute mediation or stretch or yoga before calling it a day.

Yes, some days (maybe 20 of the 924) I did a simple mediation or yoga or stretch for five minutes. Some people would find this cheating and weak, but I settled on a completely different feeling for those short classes: pride. When I did those little five-minute mediations or standing yoga classes or stretches to get my blue dot, sometimes as I was preparing to go to bed at night, I would smile with pride. Those short classes that I remembered to get in proved to me that my well-being and fitness had become a true lifestyle and the gamified blue dots helped me make it a daily habit.

Members and groups have developed other, deeper sets of gamification elements through challenges, groups on social media, websites and apps, and participation in non-Peloton events and celebrations. The gamification and metrics associated with Peloton interact with other elements of the model (community, social media, talented instructors, physical spaces) to deepen the pull of Peloton business model and create more value for members.

PHYSICAL SPACE

While the initial core value of Peloton is talent-driven content conveniently delivered to members' homes, a digital proposition, physical spaces play an important role in the venture's growth and ability to provide value to its members.

The range of physical spaces and uses runs from the studios where Peloton produces its content, its network of global retail showrooms, and data facilities, manufacturing and fulfillment centers across the world, vehicles to deliver and service Peloton bikes and treads, and accommodations to host special member events and meetups. Physical space is a central element in Peloton's digital business model.

The importance of space and its role in revenue generation and community building must be mentioned up front so it is not overlooked as technology, social media, content, and talent garner a lion's share of attention from the media and other Peloton watchers. As more members sweat together in their homes, outside, in Peloton spaces, or institutional settings, it has become clear that the business is a digital-physical hybrid, blending the best elements of being together and being apart while sharing physical experiences.

GOING FORWARD, GOING DEEPER

There is more depth to the Peloton model than the elements listed above, and we will explore the nuances and interactions of the business model's building blocks throughout the rest of this book. In many cases, the community of members actually pushed the model and its elements forward.

It is important to note that Foley and his team chose to enter growing markets in fitness, digital content, and well-being. Spending on health and well-being has been growing for decades and is likely to increase as economies and societies move to a new era of well-being with new values and expectations. Well-being and health trends of all sorts have accelerated with the pandemic as new challenges and existing problems have been exposed.

As a Peloton member, I discovered an inertia to health and well-being consumption. On Friday December 7, 2018, less than two years after my first ride, I completed my 500th during a live 45-minute rock class at 8 am. As I wrote on the Facebook page of one my favorite Peloton groups (the Peloton Monthly Challenge Team or #PMCT) after the ride, "Truly happy day as I hit 500 rides with so many from #PMCT that have helped me so much over that past 11 months . . . I've come to realize that the best way to celebrate health and well-being is with more health and well-being (especially with others)."

It was in fact true. Two years and 500 rides in, I was happy and wanted to do more, and I was not alone. As Peloton members used the platform and experienced it, they wanted to consume more health and well-being goods and services. It was evident in the social media posts, Peloton's growing sales, and the milestones and workout counts of members.

The desire to become stronger, healthier, happier, and more engaged is one of the most fascinating and central elements of the Peloton story and why it is so important to try to understand. From ever-rising obesity rates and political divisiveness to social challenges and media madness, the world needs organizations that create positive change, hope, and connectivity now more than ever. For Peloton and others focused on providing well-being and improved health, the future is theirs to write.

CHAPTER 2

FITNESS IN THE MIDDLE OF THE AMERICAN BELL CURVE

I completed a marathon. Yay me! It was 2004, the race was the California International Marathon, and the point-to-point course started in cow country outside Sacramento and ended near California's Capitol downtown. My experience was slow, painful, lonely, cold, and a bunch of other negative adjectives. But I completed a marathon. As it turns out, lots of people have.

In fact, about 500,000 people a year complete a marathon in the United States, so by my rough calculations, there must be at least 10 to 15 million people who have run 26.2 miles as part of an organized race. It has become some kind of bucket list item for many, but a pedestrian fitness experience, nearly 50 years after the running boom took off in the United States in the 1970s. Marathon events have grown for the past four decades, and a broader range of people with a broader range of fitness levels have participated.

Years before my marathon experience, my wife ran the Marine Corps Marathon when she was in her twenties and finishing medical school. Decades later I talked my childhood buddy Taz into visiting and running the Marine Corps Marathon in Washington, D.C., when we were in our forties. That race was slower and colder than the one I ran in my thirties in California and I bailed on him when I lost my glove somewhere near Georgetown. It was easy to quit because I had already crossed the marathon off my bucket list.

In 1980, 90 percent of marathon finishers in the U.S. were male, but by 2014, that number dropped to 57 percent.[6] The famed New York City Marathon, which hits all five boroughs, had an average finish time of 3:31 in the 1970s, its first decade; by the 1980s, the average finish time crept to over 4 hours, and by the 2010s, the average finish time was more than 4:30.[7] By 2017, more than 50,000 people a year were completing the marathon, versus the 127 who started the race in 1970 (only 55 finished). This democratization of the mighty marathon, once the purview of elite athletes, is representative of how deeply entrenched and broad-based fitness has become in American culture.

I have witnessed and participated in many parts of the growth of the fitness industry for most of my life. As a typical suburban kid on the outskirts of Chicago (think of films *Risky Business* or *Ferris Bueller's Day Off* for era and geography), I played a variety of sports, including ice hockey, tennis, baseball, basketball, and even water polo. I rode Schwinn bikes, then BMX and mountain bikes, and I owned Rollerblade inline skates and Vision and Powell & Peralta skateboards.

By high school in the late 1980s, I was listening to Van Halen and Run DMC, wearing Air Jordans, and drinking gallons of Gatorade. However, I was not an athlete "like Mike." As I got older and team sports faded away, I began "working out," a catchall term for doing something physical to improve overall health and appearance. This meant I tried a range of gyms, exercises, and fitness approaches.

In most ways, my fitness journey before Peloton was plain vanilla, including that California marathon. During the past 30 years, I've worked out at Bally's, Crunch, Powerhouse Gym, Gold's Gym, a few Young Men's Christian Association (YMCA) sites, and Jewish Community Centers from London to San Francisco. I've also used regional fitness chains, martial arts gyms, local and high school tracks, hotel fitness centers, university gyms, and independent gyms in the various cities and towns I've lived in and visited across the United States, Europe, Japan, and other places. Before kids arrived, I had a number of years as a member of elite urban clubs such as the Sports Club LA's San Francisco location and the East Bank Club in downtown Chicago.

Additionally, I've owned a variety of home cardio equipment, including the Precor treadmill and the Tectrix stationary bike, as well as free weights, a heavy bag, mats, blocks, and other random fitness items. My parents, in-laws, and other friends and family members have owned equipment I have used over the years, everything from steppers and treadmills to Bosu balls and weight benches. Some get my attention for weeks of use, some for months, and others, like the Precor treadmill, limp along for years.

Regardless of my inconsistency with jogging and countless fitness trends, booms, busts, and false prophets, the growth of the industry has been steady, and various strong segments and niches have emerged in the fitness and well-being markets. Just as microchip makers have gone from producing for mainframes to personal computers to mobile devices, gaming systems and the Internet of Things, fitness industry entrepreneurs and businesses have found growth in many directions.

As recently as 2019, more than 64 million Americans were health club members, generating over $35 billion in membership fees.[8] The sale of fitness products for home use reached more than $5 billion in 2017 and was estimated to be worth over $24 billion total (home, gym, office, hotel, etc.) globally by 2019 according to researchers.[9,10] After the United States, Germany and the United Kingdom boast strong health club industries, with Germany at 11.7 million members and $6.3 billion (USD) and the UK with 9.9 million members and $6.2 billion (USD) annually.[11]

Of course, apparel, shoes, travel, events, supplements, and electronics (Fitbit, headphones, and more) account for billions of dollars more spent each year. The Global Wellness Institute's 2019 Physical Activity Economy Report, in looking at the size of the sports and active recreation industry holistically, sees equipment and supplies, apparel and footwear and technology as accounting for over $466 billion in 2019.[12] Peloton sits at the intersection of all of these markets. According to the Global Wellness Institute, the global wellness market, including spas, personal care, beauty, fitness equipment, supplements, and more, was $4.5 trillion in 2018 with physical activity accounting for nearly $850 billion globally.[13]

No matter which data one chooses, the health and fitness industries in the U.S. and globally have continued to reshape and grow with new innovators, technologies, and models attempting to meet consumer and public demands for exciting and effective solutions. This leads some to argue that Peloton is just another hot product that will be copied as others try to reap profits. Eventually the whole connected fitness segment will slow and settle at a steady state.

The historical range of evidence might support this view, from the Thigh Master and the Stairmaster to Tough Mudder races and plogging (jogging and picking up trash), trends are ever present. Today's must-take class or activity almost always becomes a flavor of the month that ends just as our parents and grandparents get comfortable with it. Like kips and downward-facing dog, everything that goes up must come down.

While I believed Peloton was just another piece of equipment when it came into my world, and I argued against its purchase, that old-school view changed as I began to experience Peloton. I began to believe that Peloton might be on the verge of completely reshaping how we experience health and well-being (and major parts of the economy, too). A quick review of the emergence of the health and fitness industry and some previous trends in its growth can put the Peloton experience in context.

HIGHLIGHTS FROM THE HISTORY
OF HEALTH AND FITNESS

Americans, like most people around the world, did not always spend vast amounts of time and money on fitness and well-being. In fact, for most of human history, strength, mobility, and endurance were determined by the day-to-day life of each individual, from hunters and gatherers to blacksmiths, farm workers, and soldiers.

The Greeks and Romans often looked beyond the military and practical uses of the body and celebrated the beauty and strength of the human form. Those ancient European cultures embraced the notion that physical training, not just mental sharpening, was part and parcel of a well-rounded person. They stressed having a sound mind in a sound body, and their governments implemented policies for a fit populace, including building public gyms and creating the original Olympic Games.

Of course, this connection between the mind and the body could be found in other parts of the ancient world. Yoga, which means unite, bind, or attach, highlights the connection of the mind, body, and universe. It originated in India more than 5,000 years ago. Various forms of martial arts throughout Asia developed the body in tandem with the spirit, mind, and soul.

While physical and mental fitness and the culture of the body emerged in many societies, it took thousands of years for a mass culture of fitness and body to gain prominence across major segments of humanity. Eventually, capitalism and the rise of the industrial economy brought fitness opportunities to large swaths of the world.

The Industrial Revolution and sedentary lifestyles, combined with the nation-state fervor of Europe in the 1800s, led to the development of organized fitness methods, routines, and businesses for the masses. As new states emerged in Europe, fitness movements matched the muscular, nationalistic mood of many nations in the eighteenth and nineteenth centuries.

The Germans led the charge with movements built around gymnastics, fencing, and riding in the late 1700s. The first gymnastics textbook was published in 1800 in Germany, and the first open-air gymnasium, or *turnplatz*, was opened in 1811 in Berlin, with parallel bars, rings, and high bars to develop a strong, young population. The large, wood-framed structures of the *turnplatz* show a remarkable resemblance to many obstacles we see on challenge courses and children's playground structures. The movement would spawn a countrywide drive for athleticism as Germany began to ramp up its strength.

By the 1870s, fitness facilities, often sponsored by militaries, and various national games and competitions would spread across Europe.[14] In London, the first YMCA was created in 1844 because a dozen young London dwellers were concerned over the lack of healthy activities for men coming to work in the city. The Highland Games in Scotland began during this era of nationalism and industrialism. The games included traditional Scottish physical challenges including caber (giant log) tossing, hammer throwing, and stone shot put, along with running races, wrestling matches, and jumping competitions.[15] Do a quick search on YouTube, and you can find countless videos of large-muscled competitors in kilts performing all kinds of feats of strength and athleticism as part of modern Scottish games played today around the world.

In the United States as well, industrialization led to a rise in physical fitness and a focus on activities that engage the body.

Perhaps there is no better embodiment of the physical reaction to the industrial era in the United States than President Theodore Roosevelt. His intense efforts famously took his weak, asthmatic, aristocratic body and transformed it into that of a warrior, hunter, boxer, outdoorsman, and politician willing to take on any challenge, physical, mental, or social.

That said, Roosevelt's personal approach to fitness and America's growing appreciation for the natural world, as evidenced by the creation of the Boy Scouts in 1910 and the National Park Service in 1916, did not mean the country as a whole was in fine form. In fact, when World War I rolled around, the government found that one-third of all draftees were unfit for combat.[16]

Although many Americans got into shape to fight the war, when it ended, the Roaring Twenties arrived with good times and booze to wash away the horrors in Europe. Fitness for the masses was not quite what the market wanted.

Through the middle of the twentieth century, there were some pushing for physical health such as bodybuilder Charles Atlas, who campaigned for exercise; physical educator Dudley Sargent, who invented fitness tests such as the vertical jump; and fitness and nutrition pioneer Jack LaLanne, who opened his first health club in Oakland in 1936. However, there was little focus on or interest in fitness for the masses until after World War II and the Baby Boomers' dominance of daily life in the United States.[17]

Following World War II, U.S. government agencies issued reports and recommended programs for physical fitness education for young Americans. While this represented a renewed call for fitness for the masses, it was an effort inspired by national security in the wake of the war, not health and wellness for individuals or communities.[18] This Cold War, government-led awakening was supported by policy makers and political leaders.

BABY BOOMERS AND THE EVOLUTION OF HEALTH AND FITNESS IN THE US

Just as a pig distorts the body of the python digesting it, the Baby Boomers have impacted fitness, health, wellness, and body image since the end of World War II. The mass organization and promotion of fitness started as the huge post-war baby boom generation entered school. President Dwight Eisenhower established the President's Council on Health and Fitness, and in 1957 the council released a seminal report calling for specific annual tests for students in American schools. Many pushed for increased health and fitness for young Americans, developing leagues, clubs, competitions, and more to create a vigorous youth. President John F. Kennedy, himself the image of health and virility, published a piece titled "The Soft American" in *Sports Illustrated* in December 1960, just before he took office. He referenced the poor results that Eisenhower's Council had uncovered:

For physical fitness is not only one of the most important keys to a healthy body; it is the basis of dynamic and creative intellectual activity. The relationship between the soundness of the body and the activities of the mind is subtle and complex. Much is not yet understood. But we do know what the Greeks knew: that intelligence and skill can only function at the peak of their capacity when the body is healthy and strong; that hardy spirits and tough minds usually inhabit sound bodies.

In this sense, physical fitness is the basis of all the activities of our society. And if our bodies grow soft and inactive, if we fail to encourage physical development and prowess, we will undermine our capacity for thought, for work, and for the use of those skills vital to an expanding and complex America.

Thus the physical fitness of our citizens is a vital prerequisite to America's realization of its full potential as a nation, and to the opportunity of each individual citizen to make full and fruitful use of his capacities.[19]

Kennedy asked his citizens to take care of themselves and thus help take care of their nation. A month later, during his inaugural address, Kennedy continued this altruistic theme stating, "Ask not what your country can do for you—ask what you can do for your country."

While Kennedy's idealism about fitness supported more fitness testing and teaching on behalf of the nation, in reality, the rise of fitness among Baby Boomers was sparked by a concept that Kennedy was all too familiar with: body image and lust.

Eventually Baby Boomers would care greatly about the health side of fitness, but in the 1960s and 1970s, rock music, the sexual revolution, and feminism would mingle and help speed the growth of the health and fitness industry. From Muscle Beach in Venice, California, which gave rise to Gold's Gym, to the creation of aerobics, the coming of age of Baby Boomers created an insatiable demand for various types of health and fitness spaces, products, systems, and services.

Working women with independent minds and their own money to spend demanded that the fitness market move beyond the boxing gyms, YMCAs, and dirty weightlifting rooms that dominated public spaces. Barriers to fitness fell and options emerged. Events such as the introduction of Jazzercise in 1969 and the release of *The Joy of Running* in 1976 helped make it easier and more acceptable for anyone and everyone to focus on their health, fitness, and looks.

By the 1980s, the health and fitness industry was on fire, the country was coming out of a major recession, and many Baby Boomers had kids of their own. Sports and fitness marketing was revolutionized by the likes of Nike and Jane Fonda's fitness videos. It seemed as if all of America wanted to be a perfect "10" like Bo Derek in the 1979 movie. Fifty percent of Americans claimed to do some kind of exercise in 1981 versus 24 percent in 1960, and nearly 13 million Americans were members at one of the 5,000 gyms that had grown across the United States.[20]

No matter how fat or greedy the population became during the 1980s (remember TV series *Dallas, Dynasty, Magnum PI,* and *Silver Spoons*?), Americans were obsessed with fitness and open to new approaches. Nautilus machines and Lifecycle bikes (with circuit boards from the emerging computer industry) became must-haves for top gyms and wealthy individuals.

Many giant tennis clubs built during the 1970s tennis boom morphed into full health clubs during the 1980s, converting court space to pools, cardio areas, and aerobic rooms. The 1985 movie *Perfect*, a romantic drama featuring Jamie Lee Curtis as an L.A. aerobics instructor and John Travolta as a *Rolling Stone* writer covering health clubs as singles bars, introduced many Americans to the concept of group fitness. It also highlighted health club culture as a scene full of flirtation and sexual energy. Step aerobics were introduced in 1989, and group fitness continued to spread.

Most health clubs in the 1980s were independent, locally owned ventures—much like movie rental businesses at the time. Consolidation would come with mega gyms and national fitness brands taking over the marketplace, just as Blockbuster, Hollywood, and a few others rolled up the video rental industry.

Bally's began buying gyms and became the first of the major health club operators during the 1980s.[21] By the 1990s, the industry hit high growth, and 24 Hour Fitness, Bally's, LA Fitness, and other large brands appeared across the United States.[22] These large gyms offered massive numbers of cardio machines, resistance equipment, and free weights; aerobic, group fitness, and locker rooms; basketball courts, stretching areas, and swimming pools; spas and salons; and cafes. The bigger the space and the more options available the better was the general strategy of the era.

This era of the rise of the mega gym is when indoor cycling (aka Spinning or studio cycling) would emerge and grow, setting our path toward the Peloton bike and platform. Indoor cycling was one of many new fitness concepts that helped to fill the health club chains, independents, nonprofits and franchise systems that sprouted across the country through the 1990s.

Treadmills, rowing machines, resistance machines, stair steppers, and ellipticals also went into high production and became affordable as low-cost electronics and international supply chains allowed growth and experimentation in the fragmented fitness machine industry. Mega gyms, their local competitors, nonprofit fitness centers, hotels, apartments, offices, and home users soaked up the products from the fitness producers and suppliers that emerged.

Eventually buyers could find home fitness equipment almost anywhere. Discounters such as Sears offered treadmills, stationary bikes, and more. Sports retailers such as Dick's Sporting Goods made it possible to grab free weights and a tennis racquet in one visit. Meanwhile, local specialty fitness stores spread across the U.S., offering a wide range of choices from many manufacturers. There were also many direct-from-producer sellers such as Nordic Track and Total Gym (think Chuck Norris). The fragmented equipment industry grew as large gyms and home users appeared to have a never-ending demand for fitness hardware.

JOHNNY G AND THE CREATION OF INDOOR CYCLING

As large health club operators and equipment makers were building fitness empires through the 1980s and into the 1990s, their members, personal trainers, suppliers, instructors and managers were experimenting with offerings. The blossoming market was creating opportunities in every direction, from video tapes and televised classes to home gyms and apparel.

Amid this landscape of fitness industry growth appeared Johnny Goldberg, a South African immigrant settled in Los Angeles. He was an avid road cyclist and completed many multi-stage races throughout the world. In the mid-1980s, while training for the 500-mile Race Across America, Goldberg was nearly killed on a training ride one night. According to Johnny G, as he became known:

It happened in 1987 for me, where I nearly got killed on the road one night, and I decided not to do my nighttime training on the bicycle, and bring it indoors into the house. My wife was pregnant, and it was safer and also allowed an opportunity for me to be around her, so she wouldn't have to worry. It was at this point that I realized I could simulate everything I needed to do as an athlete outdoors. I could train heart rate, time, distance by monitoring intensity, and I could also work the most important part of the endeavor, and that was myself. This was when I started to think of constructing a commercial training program that anybody could do at any age . . . So I formulated some principles and named the program Spinning.[23]

As a serious road cyclist, Goldberg had two burning problems: first, time away from his young family, and second, safety while training. Johnny set to work with his friends, building bikes by hand and experimenting. Soon Johnny G built a road cycle for indoor training with a training approach and an instructor certification program, and by 1990 he had a small studio. Not long after that, he was offering classes and bikes at a couple of small gyms and in 1994 Johnny G opened the Spinning World Headquarters in Culver City, California, with a fleet of 40 prototype bikes built by Schwinn.[24]

From there, Johnny G's company, Mad Dogg Athletics, would certify hundreds of thousands of instructors and sell millions of bikes over the ensuing decades as large gyms and fitness centers became huge consumers of his bikes and training programs. At some point the venture switched to a licensing venture, and others used his intellectual property: designs, brands, trademarks, teaching materials, and more. (Mr. Wonderful from TV's *Shark Tank* would have loved Johnny G's method.) In just a handful of years, the Spin bike became a worldwide phenomenon with a countless gyms and health clubs offering indoor cycling sessions. The growing health and fitness industry fell in love with Johnny G's concept as an effective means to fill gyms with machines, people, and energy and drive more revenue.

BOUTIQUE FITNESS, URBAN TRENDS, AND MILLENNIAL DEMANDS

With the mega gyms aggregating large market share from local independent gyms, franchises, and nonprofit facilities in the 1990s, many were looking for new entry points to the industry. Just as Johnny G was reimagining a road bike for use inside and within a group setting, Greg Glassman, in Santa Cruz, California, was exploring functional fitness concepts.

Glassman grew up a gymnast and experimented with weights and body weight exercises in search of exercises that allowed him to perform his best. Although he was impressed with all of the action on Muscle Beach (where Arnold Schwarzenegger pumped up his fame), Glassman observed that bodybuilders' impressive-looking physiques were not really functional for many activities.

Later in life, as a professional trainer, Glassman's search for intense, functional fitness options continued in reaction to the development of static strength machines and station-based systems such as Nautilus. Most exercise machines in gyms and homes controlled the movement of the body and the flow and intensity of the workout and they allowed work on only one or two muscle groups at a time. Few machines offered anything like the movements Glassman made in gymnastics on the rings or the pommel horse, or what his clients, many in law enforcement and firefighting, experienced in their daily jobs. Eventually Glassman created his own high-intensity functional fitness approach that pushed clients to the limits.

For Glassman and his clients, the health and fitness industry of the 1990s, with large gyms and rows of machines, was unable to meet their needs. In fact, their high-intensity training was often unpopular in traditional gyms. Not only were Glassman's sessions loud and expressive, but they did not use the rows of fitness machines that the managers and owners had invested in.[25] Glassman had created CrossFit.

Glassman and his followers were kicked out of countless gyms, and in 2000 he opened his own space in Santa Cruz, subletting 400 square feet from a jiu-jitsu gym. Glassman was backed by the new credit card of one of his clients, a local school principal. Word of his intense workouts and his results spread. Soon Glassman leased his own space, and by 2002 Glassman was giving seminars on his CrossFit methods and posting his workouts to the internet. By 2005 Glassman's CrossFit had five affiliate gyms, and that number grew quickly, supported by the effectiveness of the workouts and the low cost business model.

The limited gym size and standard daily routine of CrossFit (known as the WOD, or workout of the day) went a long way toward creating a community mentality among the athletes and the owners of the independent affiliates (they are not known as franchises) that sprouted across the United States after 2001.[26] The daily routine connected CrossFit enthusiasts no matter where they were or what level they achieved. Functional activities such as Tough Mudder, Spartan Race, Parkour, and even American Ninja Warrior made workouts such as CrossFit useful in the worlds of entertainment and competition. By 2018, CrossFit reached more than 15,000 affiliates globally, making it the largest fitness system in the world.[27]

Glassman and CrossFit, like Goldberg and indoor cycling, discovered, drove, and represented a massive shift across the health and fitness landscape. Customers no longer wanted mega gyms with huge choices and anonymity. Fitness enthusiasts, often led by urbanites and followed by suburbanites, craved a more personal and measurable experience on a human scale.

CrossFit, spinning, and yoga were a few of the fitness and well-being disciplines that seemed made for this new trend emerging in the 2000s: boutique fitness. Boutique fitness meant small, focused facilities that provided a more intimate and exclusive experience with a limited menu of options.

The creativity and innovation, with higher revenues, that boutique fitness offered was a savior for the fitness industry as older Baby Boomers and Gen Xers alike were ready for something new and different. Boutique fitness also attracted the emerging Millennial generation. Millennials were said to seek new experiences rather than things, making boutique classes preferable to warehouse-style gyms. New, smaller fitness opportunities were emerging to meet the desires of a range of experienced and new fitness customers.

As boutique fitness emerged, large gyms would adopt new boutique concepts such as kickboxing or Spinning to stay fresh. Johnny G and his Mad Dogg Athletics relied heavily on sales to large gym operators to grow the base of Spinning customers, instructors, and providers across the country and the world.

Whether yoga, boxing, indoor cycling, or high-intensity interval training (HIIT) like Barry's Bootcamp, F45, and Orangetheory Fitness, the decades after 2000 witnessed the rise of boutique fitness. In many cases, these offerings have been tested and refined in urban centers, and users spend as much as $40 for a one-hour session.

While their spaces might average between 800 and 1,200 square feet, and they offer only one type of activity with multiple variations, many boutique providers have been able to extract a much higher fee per use than traditional gyms because of the intimacy of the time there and direct engagement with a fitness professional. If you ask a regular user, from barre classes based on ballet training to indoor cycling, why they keep returning, their answers generally center around the personal experience, community, and results. In most cases (save CrossFit and a few others), the spaces are more attractive and upscale than traditional large gyms.

For members the boutique experience of being pushed to your limits by a well-trained, motivating instructor with a small group of like-minded people in a sensory-pleasing environment is well worth the cost.[28] In a world of 24-hour work communications, factory-farmed food, McMansions, and urban congestion, boutiques provide a special break from modern life. The intimate, intense, and inspiring experience of boutique offerings was what the fitness industry needed in a world of large, impersonal facilities.

Athletic teams, clubs, and the military have known for ages that group exercise can be effective. There is science to show the same. Danielle Wadsworth, an academic who leads an exercise and obesity lab at Auburn University, interprets the boutique fitness movements success: "Being with a group of people who have the same goal, even if it's just a short-term goal like trying to complete the workout, helps motivate you. At a boutique, you aren't just working out with the group that wandered in for a 2:30 class. You're working out with people who have bought into a particular philosophy, who went out of their way to reserve a coveted spot, and who are accordingly enthusiastic about being there."[29] Exclusivity and intimacy and shared goals, in contrast to solitary workouts in a large gym, have been central to growing the boutique approach to fitness.

Ruth Zukerman, dancer turned housewife turned entrepreneur, launched two successful indoor cycling brands, SoulCycle and Flywheel, based on exclusivity, intimacy, and dedicated communities of instructors and members. Zukerman initially built these boutique cycling offerings out of the cloistered worlds of New York City and the Hamptons between 2006 and 2010. Her experiences taking boutique fitness concepts national and dealing with investors, employees, partners, and members during this boom era is described in full detail in her book *Riding High* (2018). Zukerman's serial success speaks not only to her personal dynamism as an instructor and leader, but also to the desire of so many for intimate, sweat filled sessions that meet their emotional and social needs as well as burning calories and building muscle.

It is worth remembering that the community also involves the instructors and staff at boutique facilities. More personal instruction and attention are paid to customers as the gym is smaller, there is little room to roam, and the fees are generally much higher. From reservation systems and a welcoming front desk to abundant towels and follow-up emails, strong boutique offerings engage customers before, during, and after the class.

According to the International Health, Racquet and Sportsclub Association, from 2012 to 2015, membership surged by more than 70 percent at boutique fitness studios across the United States while membership at traditional clubs grew by 5 percent, and nonprofits such as YMCAs saw a drop of more than 10 percent. Boutique offerings that have grown in recent years include Flywheel, Orangetheory Fitness, and Barry's Bootcamp. Boca Raton, Florida–based Orangetheory Fitness, founded in 2010, has used the franchise model to grow its membership to over one million, store count over 1,200 and system wide revenues to more than a one billion dollars by 2018.[30]

Another sign of the incredible demand for boutique fitness offerings is fitness app startup ClassPass. Founded in 2013, ClassPass is a website and mobile offering created by Payal Kadakia, a 28-year-old MIT graduate working at Warner Music in Manhattan.[31] Kadakia was sick of searching for open spots in boutique ballet classes and came up with the idea for a service to act as a market-clearing mechanism for excess space in boutique fitness classes. Basically, ClassPass serves as a Priceline or Expedia for the boutique fitness world. The service allows users to buy various boutique classes at gyms at discounted prices. Since its founding in 2013, the venture has raised more than $200 million in venture capital, operates in more than 28 countries, has partnered with more than 30,000 fitness and wellness providers, and as of 2020 had a private market valuation of more than $1 billion.[32, 33]

While Peloton is firmly rooted in the boutique studio segment of the health and fitness market, Foley and team fused elements of technology, content creation, and physical space to create a new kind of well-being company driven by its membership and community. Peloton's model has turned out to be unlike any fitness movement the world has ever seen. Who are the members that responded to Peloton's offerings and vision? That is what we will race to next.

CHAPTER 3

MEMBERS, MEMBERS, MEMBERS: CUSTOMERS

It was the inexplicable behavior of Peloton riders that I observed in early 2017 that pulled at my curiosity. I needed to know what kind of people went to social media and proclaimed that this exercise bike was a special experience, often a life-changing experience. The Peloton riders had their own language with terms such as "magic pants" (leggings worn while riding) and "Pelo-pups" (a rider's dog). Like the woman from Minneapolis, many wrote of going to the Mothership in New York. The celebration of members' Century Rides seemed to be on par with a high school graduation, replete with #100 mylar balloons next to their bikes, signs and cakes and countless congratulations from "Pelo-family" friends on social media.

I couldn't quite understand how these people were so motivated by a cotton T-shirt after spending thousands of dollars on a bike and subscription fees? Were they all like my wife? Were they outdoor cyclists trying to train safely? Were they techno hermits? I was not sure.

No matter where they were located or how fit or not they seemed, based on my view of social media and the leaderboard results in 2017, growing thousands of them loved their bikes and their workouts to a degree I had not witnessed before in any product category. I was racking my brain and consumer history and was having a hard time coming up with another product or service or brand that customers seemed to love so much.

CUSTOMERS ARE REALLY WHAT MATTER

In the past 10 years or so, a theory called *customer development* has taken hold in the field of innovation and entrepreneurship. It was developed by serial entrepreneur turned Stanford professor Stephen Blank, whose definition for a business model we used earlier—how an organization creates, delivers, and captures value.

The key concept of customer development is that customers and their problems or needs are in the center of the business model. The model focuses on the customer, not the product. While this may seem obvious to focus on the customer's needs, in an age of technological advances, it is easy to get sucked into product development and technical specifications and abandon the customer. The business world is littered with products and services built because it's possible and funding and talent are available, not because customers need or really want them. Products must solve a real problem, not be a solution looking for a problem.

The ultimate validation of any product or service is whether people will pay for it, regardless of what investors or industry insiders believe. This is why the first question on the popular television show *Shark Tank* is almost always, "What are your sales?"

For many, the simple concept of sales as validation is often confusing because so many products in the digital economy, from web browsers and apps to cloud storage, appear to be free because customers don't have to pay directly with cash out-of-pocket. Massive amounts of venture capital investments also muddle the issue by allowing companies to provide free or deeply subsidized products and services as they search for a business model.

In Peloton's case, the customers drew my attention with their eccentric behavior, but I knew from those early arguments—er *conversations*—with my wife about Peloton that the customers paid up front for the bike and on a monthly basis for the subscription. This was 100 percent customer validation. Now who were these Peloton members?

UNDERSTANDING PELOTON CUSTOMERS

The first thing I did was try to understand who these Peloton customers were and what value they were paying for. I explored the basic demographics of age, gender, location, and income as well as the more important psychographics of motivations, fears, and hopes. Foley learned about his customers from the ground up when he worked retail in the first store that Peloton opened in late 2013 in suburban New Jersey.[34]

As I explored the riders via the leaderboard in classes and their posts on social media sites, the wide range of Peloton members became clear very quickly. While the advertisements, including the many television spots I saw in 2017, made the product aspirational with gorgeous homes, views, and people, the membership never matched that early imagery in my experience. The following sections will cover the customer segments I identified and some of the individuals I've come across through thousands of hours participating in the Peloton community and also conducting research with questionnaires and interviews of members.

There are a range of members for a range of reasons, but I learned they function as a community on the leaderboard and just as often outside of the class in the real world and social media. As bike instructor Jess King said during our interview in 2019, "you can feel the pulse" of the community on the leaderboard during rides. When you look at the names, ages, locations, and exercise output, it's clear that a diverse group of people is sweating together across the Peloton platform.

PELOTON MEMBERS YOU WILL FIND ON THE LEADERBOARD

As it all started with my wife, I tried to make sense of what customer segment she was part of. I quickly realized that Emily is part of what I call the **Healthy Wealthy Buyers**. These Peloton members were among the initial entrants to the fold. They are generally middle- and upper-income Americans who have a history of spending money on their health and well-being. Eventually Peloton started offering financing options to make the product more affordable so that by the year 2019, 50 percent of sales of bikes and treadmills were financed, often at zero percent interest. Initially however, a core segment were buyers with a history of fitness spending.

Healthy Wealthy Buyers have been fueling the well-being market for decades, were some of the first to sport athleisure outside the gym, and are often the pioneers when new fitness and health trends emerge. This is a core market that Nike, Lululemon, and others have targeted for years to buy their higher end, innovative products. From professional settings and my years in metro areas, I know many people who belong to this segment, spending for their health and wellness, including on food, apparel, travel, fitness, and many areas of self-care.

Prior to Peloton, my wife had a long history of spending on healthy food, self-care, fitness apparel and footwear, club memberships, and other products and services intended to improve her health and overall well-being. The range runs from new water bottles and a decades long search for the perfect running shoe to skin and hair doc visits and e-commerce purchases. This market continues to grow. In 2017, spending on personal care alone was more than $1 trillion, with healthy eating at $700 billion and fitness and mind body at nearly $600 billion. Given the size and scope of the well-being marketplace, it is no surprise many of Peloton's members come from this pre-existing market.

Like my wife, Peloton CEO Foley and his wife Jill fit into the Healthy Wealthy Buyer category, but Foley also fit in the **Spinning**

and Boutique Enthusiasts segment. Many indoor cycling and boutique fitness enthusiasts moved to Peloton quickly when they learned about the offering.

Like so much of society, many Spinning and Boutique Enthusiasts are short on time, but not on money or passion. While they would love to book as many indoor cycling, yoga, or bootcamp classes as possible, life gets in the way as it did for Foley. Few want to battle for seats in a class as if they are tickets to a Super Bowl.

For other Spinning and Boutique Enthusiasts, a move or a job change made getting to their studio challenging or impossible. In my survey of Peloton riders, there were cases of losing a favorite instructor and the entire boutique studio experience changing for them. In my survey, Jen (#Dawnbreaker), a Northern Virginia Peloton member since 2017, described her path to Peloton, "My favorite Spin instructor left my local studio. I didn't love the new instructor, and a friend recommended Peloton." Randi (#ThereIsNoTry), a Maryland-based member I met at a public Peloton meetup explained she, "purchased the Peloton because I loved Spinning classes but couldn't get to workout consistently after I had a baby."

Peloton gives many a second shot at amazing instructors and the convenience of accessing them in a way that is not possible with traditional boutique studio, large or independent gym business models. Tiss (#Tiss_is_It), a member since 2017, wrote, "I moved to a new (small) town. Was an avid Spinner in CA, but the bikes here and the classes were lame."

Many of the longtime indoor cyclists that I talked to understood from the beginning what value Peloton could bring and what a game changer it would be for access. In sharing their stories, many described wanting the bike the minute they saw an ad for it.

Jenn Sherman, the first instructor hired by Foley and Peloton, was an indoor cycling addict before becoming a certified instructor. As she prepared to open her own spinning studio in New Jersey in 2013, she read about Peloton in a *Well+Good* article titled "How Peloton Plans to Revolutionize Spinning—at Home."[35] According to Sherman, she knew right away it was "fucking brilliant" (how Jenn described it to me during our interview). This belief in the idea inspired Jenn to write a cold email to Peloton to inquire about teaching for the early-phase venture.

More than a few of the Peloton members I met in this customer segment were, like Sherman, certified instructors and many were still actively teaching in their hometowns at a range of independent studios, nonprofits, and other fitness facilities. Spinning and Boutique Enthusiasts understood Peloton and why its value proposition was so different, even if investors and industry participants did not see it.

A third core Peloton segment I discovered were the **Health Buyers;** members facing some type of health challenge that needs a fitness component to solve or manage it. The range of health challenges that members have told me or posted about runs the gamut from depression and bad knees (often from a lifetime of running) to cancer diagnoses, diabetes, strokes, heart disease, and hip replacements. New Jersey–based member Stephanie (#GoldnGrl) responded to the question of why she initially bought the bike by writing, "Was unable to run after surgery. Needed to find my new stress outlet and bought the bike." In many cases, these members chose Peloton as the fitness option for their recovery, because of the convenience and in-home aspect of the offerings.

Samantha (#thePugMother), one of the creators of a Facebook-based Peloton challenge group (#PMCT) that I joined about a year into my membership, received the bike as a gift from her husband after a scary visit with her doctor. At the time, Samantha was a successful litigator at a large law firm and a mother of two. Her work cycle of being really busy for months at a time while on a trial took its toll on her health, and she gained 40 pounds over 10 years while building her career. Samantha's doctor warned her of a dangerous future after a sky-high cholesterol reading and even said that she would have to change her diet, giving up her beloved cheese, if she didn't do something. Sam was only 36 and of Italian descent and told me she could not imagine her future without pasta and pizza and cheese. Sam's husband, David, a stay-at-home dad, super chef, and CrossFit addict, was also concerned about the challenges her career presented for her health.

In early 2017, David had the bike delivered to their apartment in New Jersey. Samantha had no clue it was coming and was furious with David when the bike arrived. It took Sam some time to accept the bike, but knowing that she had to get her health in order and refusing to give up cheese, she tried it. Initially Sam rode under David's account, but she knew she was missing something as she read through all of the vivid, excited posts on Facebook. Sam decided to reach out on the main Facebook page in July 2017, looking for others that wanted to ride every day for 30 days straight. This led to the creation of a Facebook group called the Peloton Monthly Challenge Team and over time to Sam becoming healthier and stronger than ever before. Sam has been active with the group for over four years and by age 40 was stronger and healthier than ever before in her life. David and Sam eventually bought a second Peloton bike and a Peloton tread, as Sam has also become a runner.

The Health Buyers, when asked, "How or why did you originally start using Peloton?," offered a multitude of answers, from the generic "for health benefits" and "weight loss" and "to lose baby #3 weight" to the more dramatic like Samantha's story or the survey respondent that explained, "I had a double mastectomy and was extremely weak after and was too embarrassed to go to the gym so I bought it, even though I hated cardio."[36]

What is really interesting to me as I look at the diversity of Health Buyers on the Peloton platform is that it appears to be a real solution for many of them. The combination of exercise, community, data tracking, and the "safety" of use at home appears to fit the bill for many people.

During Peloton's annual member celebration, known as Homecoming, in May 2019, I was asked to sit on a panel at the Bethesda, Maryland, showroom to share how Peloton membership had changed my life. My member co-panelists were a teenage cancer survivor who rode for strength and a personal trainer named Sarah John who uses Peloton to work with parents of kids battling cancer.

Peloton's observable results: physical, mental, and social, have helped create a strong connection among the members. There are countless moments on social media where members claim life-saving benefits from Peloton that getting misty-eyed becomes normal. If it were not the customers making all of the fantastic claims, you might think Peloton was some kind of digital snake oil.

As was explored earlier, endurance athlete Johnny G was concerned about safety in training and time away from his family when he invented the concept of Spinning, or indoor cycling, so it is not surprising that road cyclists, triathletes, and mountain bike riders can be found all over the Peloton platform. These **Endurance Athletes,** like Johnny G and Peloton founders Tom Cortese and John Foley, often see Peloton and its offerings as a perfect complement to their training and an antidote to weather and safety problems.

Peloton co-founder Cortese was a triathlete before joining Foley to create Peloton, but he quickly saw the value of boutique fitness after Foley began taking him to classes in New York. Cortese also noticed that indoor cycling was far more fun than traditional training for endurance events. The amount of fun Cortese was having with indoor cycling, something he was not used to as an endurance athlete, became one of the reasons that he was confident in the idea.

Peloton member Mike (#MikeRidesMtTam), a father and outdoor rider from the Bay Area, was not sold on indoor cycling when he tried it out for his first ride in early 2018. Mike's explanation of his experience, "My wife saw it in a mall and wanted one. I'm already an avid outdoor bike rider and pooh-poohed the thought of Peloton and it being a substitute for real biking. Now I love it, ride the Peloton nearly daily, and will often Peloton over an outdoor ride because it's so convenient (not having to worry about clothing layers, food), and the instructors are much more interesting and motivating than I would have thought."

As Cortese stated when we talked at Peloton headquarters in early 2019, "We were able to make working out something you want to do." For many people and especially endurance athletes, having fun while working out was something they had never experienced before. As someone who now works out with Peloton daily, I agree with Cortese.

I would like to note that I have witnessed Peloton members become endurance sports athletes because of their experience with Peloton and indoor cycling. Jerry (#EvryBdyLvsJery), a Peloton member I randomly met at a New York Peloton event and then bumped into a year later in the original Peloton tread studio, explained that he became a runner with Peloton, after buying the original Peloton Tread. Through Peloton, Jerry met a group of runners and joined them to run a half-marathon in 2019. This would have never occurred before he became part of the Peloton community.

For those interested in traditional endurance training, Peloton has programmed specific content ranging from heart rate zone classes and power zone training to cycling classes taught by professional cyclists such as Tour De France veteran Christian Vande Velde. With the introduction of outdoor running and the treadmill products (in 2018), Peloton has pushed into marathon training as part of its portfolio of content and there will likely be more endurance-related offerings as the company grows.

As I tried to understand and segment Peloton members (customers), another group that emerged quickly were the **Technology Buyers**. These Peloton members are people that love buying new products and being early adopters, whether it is hardware such as the Peloton bike or a smart scale or the latest electric vehicle. There are gadget lovers of all types in our entrepreneurial economy and many of them have joined Peloton.

These members are excited about the technology behind the bike and the service, technical specifications of further offerings, upgrades to the software and the app, and different metrics available to members. I met Chris (#SunshineKnight), a "Pelo-friend," through the Peloton Facebook world. Chris lives near Green Bay Wisconsin, is a Tesla driver, drone pilot, nudist, professional racquetball player, technology entrepreneur, beyond-talented photographer, and fitness enthusiast. Chris tries to improve his performance through measuring data such as his output per minute during different ride lengths. Chris also tracked the impact of warm-up rides and fans on his performance, and he does ride in the nude at home. His love of data generated by the technology behind Peloton and how these numbers connect to his performance is common in this world.

Chris and others also love that Peloton is a technology firm with software upgrades, extensions to other platforms (such as Apple TV, Roku), new product introductions and opportunities for members to engage with the technology. Connecticut-based Peloton member John Mills (#RunLiftLive) originally bought the bike for his wife to make her love of indoor cycling more accessible. When John, an IT architect, learned he could stream classes to the large screen in his entertainment room, he was hooked and excited to bring Peloton into his workout world, which mostly consisted of lifting and running at the time. These members wait for new software upgrades, hang out on the Feature Friday open thread on the main Facebook page and are constantly looking for opportunities to upgrade and extend Peloton's technical capabilities.

As Foley noted in our interview, most early buyers had some early-adopter mentality as it was clear that Peloton was a new technology venture with offerings unlike anyone else. In the first few years (2014–2017), Peloton members faced a risk that the company might go under, and the bike and their investment could be worthless. #RunLiftLive acknowledged that he considered that Peloton might fail when he made the initial bike purchase.

I have come to know a handful of the Technology Buyers in person and through online groups, and they love to take their stats from workouts and extend and analyze them. Often technical members create spreadsheets to track their progress and to lead and support discussions online around hardware, software, and streaming challenges that come with being new to the world.

A group of Peloton riders created an app called mPaceline that connects to Peloton and allows members to see their power output and other statistics related to their performance in classes. It also creates new graphs to track performance over time for those who want to use the data that the Peloton platform generates from its users.

Another group of members created a community, website and service called the Power Zone Pack that allows members to analyze their rides through the well-known power zone frameworks, participate in challenges (with prizes), and pay for upgraded data analysis features. The Power Zone Pack, led by Angie VerBeck (#AngieVerb) has a massive presence on Facebook and across social media with tens of thousands of active participants. This growth has led to additional data, more challenges and optional premium upgrades on the Power Zone Pack website, which host riding challenges that hundreds of thousands of Peloton members participate in. Data organization and presentation will likely grow in intensity as more users join and disciplines are added to the Peloton platform. The mix of classes generating data and innovative hardware and software connecting people, places, and hardware make Peloton membership a great option for many interested in technology, innovation, and well-being.

Celebrity Members are also a key group of customers you will come across if you spend time with the Peloton community. In this case we are talking about mainstream society celebrities, not Peloton based. While celebrities always have been tied to fitness crazes because of the demands of their careers and their residences in NY and LA, countless celebrities have made it clear that they absolutely adore their Pelotons.

Thanks to Peloton's roots in boutique fitness in New York City (a media, entertainment, and sports mecca), many celebrities began riding the bike early on. The first celebrities I remember hearing about were actors Rob Lowe and Hugh Jackman, both NYC residents. The excitement felt by riders at the possibility of being on the leaderboard with heartthrob Rob Lowe or Wolverine was almost too much for them, especially for women in their forties and fifties. Less sexy but still popular riders include the likes of TV weather forecaster Al Roker, actress Reese Witherspoon, rapper Diddy (Sean Combs), and actress and media personality Kelly Ripa.

Then at some point came talk that Michael Phelps was on the bike, which led to speculation about what kind of numbers (output, miles, Power Zones) he produced while riding and whether anyone had any chance against him on the Peloton leaderboard (versus the Olympic swimming pool). The fact that the most decorated Olympian of all time was doing the same workout as I was made me, like many Peloton members, feel like a badass. Ironically, but not surprising, by 2021 as the connected fitness market was exploding, Phelps would become a paid spokesperson for NordicTrack iFit brand fitness equipment, a Peloton competitor.

In August 2019 Heisman Trophy winner and NFL MVP Cam Newton came to ride live in NYC with instructor Alex Touissant. The quarterback allowed the experience to be filmed and in the special video posted online about his ride, Cam appeared as excited by the chance to ride in the studio as any suburban parent from Dallas or Ironman competitor from Northern California. In December 2019, not long after Newton, I rode in the studio with Alex Touissant, my wife, and my 13-year-old son, and it was an experience we will never forget.

Googling celebrities and Peloton or scrolling social media will yield a broad and deep list, including power couple Steph and Ayesha Curry, former First Lady Michelle Obama (apparently her bike's camera and microphone were disabled), comedian Kevin Hart, and entrepreneurial icon Sir Richard Branson. Radio host Howard Stern, ESPN personalities Mike Golic Jr. and Booger McFarland, and media powerhouse Reese Witherspoon are all Peloton members, as are U.S. President Joe Biden, Jamaican sprinter Usain Bolt, and NBA icon LeBron James.

In the age of social media and countless media outlets tracking celebrities, politicians, athletes, and societal scoundrels, the Peloton in the living room or Instagram post is what people are looking for. The bike, and later the tread, confirmed that a celebrity was fit, cool, and technically savvy.

Beyond the celebrities who are using the Peloton platform and often discussing and posting about it, Peloton has become part of the cultural landscape through its rise, often appearing in the background or as a prop in TV shows or point of conversation on talk shows across media platforms. The bike was featured as a *Jeopardy* clue in February 2019. This TV milestone made the bike community smile collectively and highlighted the cultural phenomenon that Peloton had become just five years after the introduction of its first product.

Another important segment of members that I discovered is the **Partners, Spouses, and Family Members** of all of the other groups. As you know, I fit into this big market segment. We are the people who did not make the purchase and in many cases didn't understand the value when the Peloton was brought into our lives. Members of this customer segment may even be hostile toward the idea of Peloton, as I was.

Intelligently, like some premium Netflix accounts, but unlike most traditional health clubs and subscription-based services, when customers buy a Peloton bike (or other Peloton hardware) and set up their Peloton account; multiple member IDs (leaderboard names) can be set up on that subscription. This is one of the reasons there are more members than subscribers. When I inquired about the limit in the retail showrooms I visited, I was repeatedly told there is no limit. I have yet to hear of an account holder being told that too many members have joined via their Peloton account.

I became an active Peloton member riding three days a week on average that first year. As the second year began, I used our Peloton membership more than my wife, completing four or five workouts a week.

Two of our three children have become members on the Peloton platform. Our oldest is a travel lacrosse and hockey player, has a profile, and uses various types of classes from cycling and running to strength and stretching. Our daughter, a dancer, loves the stretching and yoga and meditation and occasionally tries a cardio class. Our youngest (just four years old at the drafting of this chapter) does not have a profile. However, he has joined me and his siblings for countless yoga, stretching, and bodyweight strength classes, and he can quickly pull up his little leg for a yoga tree pose. I find it truly disruptive that my children know what HIIT, tree pose, and recovery days are and understand that these activities are part of daily life. Peloton introduced family programming in early 2020, and there is no doubt this will grow.

The goal of being fit for family members, especially children, is a common theme across the platform, but the deep engagement with family members is something that few expected, including those who purchased the bike. The experience of kids getting involved through parents and caretakers is one of the less marketed and less known impacts of the Peloton platform and community. Social media postings and interviews make it clear that improved fitness and engagement with family members extends to vacation hikes, neighborhood 5K runs, and countless other active family outings. This family engagement is building Peloton's brand and will translate to more members and revenues for sure, but the deeper concept of spreading happiness and well-being intergenerationally through sweat and fitness cannot be discounted.

By 2019, Emily and I were talking about Peloton more than anything else except our kids, and there are countless stories of adult siblings and adult parent-and-children sets who ride together across the country to keep in touch. Many of the Peloton groups that I participate in have siblings, cousins, in-laws and other family relationships represented, and it is hard to think of a better way for adult family members and friends to stay connected. I know of at least one case of feuding sistersin-law who were able to build a relationship around the bike after years of discord. It is heartening, but also a bit disturbing.

There's one final customer segment that we cannot forget: the **Peloton Addicts**. I clearly fit into this group, as does my wife and my friend Sam, and many thousands of others. The Peloton Addicts are composed of members from all of the aforementioned segments. These are the bike riders, tread users, and app members who became addicted to the workouts, instructors, and community. Once newbies, now they're always talking about the latest classes or rides or special badges, buying the newest apparel from the Peloton boutique, and going for personal bests and milestones. These addicted members create and lead Peloton-based groups on social media, meet Pelo friends for meals, and even travel to stay with them to run races, vacation, and attend weddings.

When I first began researching the company in February 2017, it was the addicts on the Official Peloton Member Page and on other Peloton-related social media platforms that were calling out to me to keep exploring.

As I researched the Peloton community online, via local meet-ups and in New York at the studios, it became clear that many, many people had caught the Peloton addiction. Some caught it immediately, while others like me and Sam took some time to find our place in the Peloton world.

PATH TO ADDICTION

In my first full year on Peloton (2017), I was a regular, riding the bike 101 times and running a bunch. For me, 150 or so cardio workouts in a year was a record, and if I had to guess, it probably would be a great year for a vast majority of Americans. Woot, woot! I was winning, no doubt. Thank you, Peloton, for a great 2017, likely my most active since college. The convenience and sweat Peloton offered were real and better than any solution I'd experienced in decades. However, in 2018 I truly became a Peloton addict, taking more than 450 cycling classes and more than 800 non-bike workouts (stretching, strength, yoga).

I knew I was working out a lot as 2018 opened, but it was not until that summer when I realized I was fully addicted to sweating with the Peloton community. The realization sneaked up on me slowly, but finally hit me one evening. It was about 6 p.m. and both my son and I were in the basement. We could have and should have been outside on that beautiful summer evening with plenty of light remaining, but we were in the basement of our old colonial style home.

We were in adjoining basement rooms, separated by a set of Home Depot French doors; I could see him, but he was not paying attention to me. I was 30 minutes into a cycling class and really struggling, sweating profusely, and gasping for air. I had chosen this pain, was with friends on the leaderboard, and I loved it and hated it at the same time.

Through my blurry vision, I could see my son, sprawled on the floor, his upper body on a beanbag chair and his legs spread across the rug. He was wearing large headphones with a microphone and was holding wild-sounding conversations, punctuated by laughs, with people who were not in our basement. As I rode on my Peloton bike, my son was playing Epic Games' Fortnite on his Microsoft Xbox One. We were both competing via technology with other users. I was racing up the Peloton leaderboard, trying to earn a personal best and beat my mileage goal, and riding with some people I met via online Peloton groups. My son was counting kills, wins, skins, and an assortment of things I somewhat understood. He was playing with kids he knew from school and his hockey team. It dawned on me at that moment that I was as addicted to my Peloton and the community as he was to Fortnite and friends.

The hard-core Peloton users, like me, are very important customers for a variety of reasons. First, they continue to take classes and populate leaderboards, making classes and experiences more dynamic for those who want to compete or interact with other users (high fives, video chat, social media) whether live or on demand. Importantly, addicted users promote the company, the community, the brand, the instructors, and often the gospel of health and well-being. They spend time on Facebook, Instagram, Reddit, and other platforms sharing information, answering questions, and celebrating and supporting other riders and the instructors.

As Joel Berkowitz (#JoeyB), a local New York City rider I met while riding in Peloton's New York bike studio during a visit, told me, "I enjoy not only being a customer, but I also think of myself as an ambassador of the brand." Whether Joel wears his Peloton gear, posts on Facebook, or tells people about Peloton, he and other addicts are the lowest cost and most effective form of advertising and sales that the company has. This is not a new concept, and Peloton understands this and provides a $100 apparel credit to members who refer new customers. I have seen Joel in person a number of times since our first meeting and very often on the leaderboards and social media.

Joel, who rode frequently in the studio before the pandemic because his office was located nearby, told me he has sold more than twelve bikes. He is not alone. In 2019, #EvryBdyLvsJery shared "I have encouraged six others this year to purchase the bike." Judging from Jerry and Joel's continually climbing workout counts, they are likely still referring customers.

As of late 2020, my wife and I had referred more than 28 Peloton purchases (mostly bikes, but a few treads) in recent years that we have received credit for from Peloton, and we have thousands of dollars worth of Peloton merchandise from these referrals. We also have purchased thousands worth of merchandise on our own! Moreover, Emily placed a deposit on the Peloton tread when it was announced in 2018 and she upgraded us to the Peloton Bike+ in 2020 on the day Peloton announced orders could be placed for their upgraded, premium bike.

Doing the math shows that my wife and I have helped drive at least $70,000 (24 bikes and 4 treads) in additional hardware purchases, plus monthly revenue of $39 on those machines. That could add up to more than $13,000 a year in monthly fees ($39 × 28 × 12 = $13,104 a year).

Additionally, I know I have influenced others to buy but did not receive the referral because they did not know about it or forgot or I was part of a chorus of Peloton advocates that tipped their behavior. For example, the administrative assistant at my entrepreneurship center purchased a bike during the pandemic and did not tell our team until the day before it arrived in the fall of 2020. The point is not that I missed the credits; it is that many addicted Peloton members cannot stop "selling" Peloton. Every business is searching for heavy users who bring in other customers. Peloton has found many of its new members because addicted users can't stop talking about it. This includes some of the celebrity riders mentioned above. The addicted members come from all of the aforementioned groups.

Addicted Peloton members play an important role in revenue generation and community building, one of the key elements in the Peloton business model. This group is one of the reasons that Peloton has grown so quickly, and it's likely one of the strengths that will protect the company as more competitors enter the connected fitness and well-being space.

THE CORONA COHORT

In January 2020, not long after Peloton was publicly lambasted for its Christmas 2019 commercial featuring a sheepish wife showing a video review of her year with the Peloton her husband bought her, reports of a fast-spreading flu began coming out of China.

The novel coronavirus Covid-19 became an immediate topic of conversation in the spring semester of 2020 as my classes discussed world and business news at the start of each session. By March, the virus had made it to the United States, and the country began to shelter, work, and attend school in place as much as possible.

What did this mean for Peloton? Potentially millions of new members for their connected fitness devices (bikes and treads) and Peloton's digital offering. Gyms were closing down across the country, and 65 million U.S. gym members were shut out of their fitness facilities.

During the early phases of the coronavirus in the U.S. in 2020, Peloton extended its free digital trial offer to 90 days versus the standard 30 days. Because of social distancing requirements,

Peloton had to focus on bike sales only as one delivery person could leave that product at the door versus the three delivery people needed to bring a Peloton tread into the buyer's home. The company also had to limit use of its network of showrooms and adjust the ways it could create new content during Covid. Eventually a handful of Peloton instructors began streaming classes live from their homes while studio production policies were being worked out during the spring and summer of 2020.

As the severity and length of the pandemic became clear, new customers came flooding to Peloton from all of its existing customer groups, but also included younger buyers and boutique fitness members that had previously rebuffed Peloton's in-home offerings. When Covid-19 arrived and in-home became their only option, many customers finally joined Peloton after years of resistance. Many of the **Corona Cohort** came from SoulCycle, Barry's Bootcamp, Equinox, Orangetheory Fitness, and countless local studios and health clubs across the country.[37]

The Peloton earnings calls in May and September and November 2020 were shocking, with Peloton crushing sales and membership expectations. Because of the massive increases in demand and global supply chain challenges, Peloton was a must-have product of the pandemic in 2020 and into 2021. Wait times for delivery were "elongated" and customers and the company were stressed but there were few alternatives as the pandemic ground on through 2020. On the Q3 and Q4 2020 earnings calls, Peloton President William Lynch explained that the company's hardware-building subsidiary, Tonic, (located in Taiwan and acquired by Peloton in 2019) would be opening a new facility and would be ready for Christmas 2020, but demand and sales continued to grow beyond expectations through 2020 and into 2021.

The pandemic accelerated mainstream acceptance of the bike and Peloton's model of in-home, streaming fitness. The company was already building the connected fitness market pre-Covid; that is why I began researching Peloton in 2017 in the first place. As Foley reminded everyone in the first post-Covid earnings call in May 2020, Peloton had doubled its sales every year since launching in 2014. Covid accelerated what was already a rocketship phenomenon. The Corona Cohort was huge, but aligned with Peloton's history.

CONNECTING THROUGH SWEAT

This chapter explored the range of buyers that found incredible value in Peloton's offerings. It was obvious as I sorted through what and who I was witnessing on the platform that Peloton's appeal was about more than indoor cycling. Many of the customers had never done indoor cycling and were not road bike enthusiasts. My wife had taken some classes, but she was not a regular at any cycling studio. I had never done it in my life, but within two years I had taken more than 550 indoor cycling classes on the Peloton bike.

The core value proposition, a world-class workout in your home at the time of your choosing, was something that really interested a lot of people, whether they purchased the bike or tread, rode a shared bike in an apartment or office, or used the digital app with another piece of hardware.

Countless members communicated that convenience mattered greatly, but that Peloton is about so much more. A

51-year-old Maryland mother and endurance athlete that I met in the Bethesda Peloton showroom said she received the bike as a "fiftieth birthday present and to enhance her training." She went on to say, "I met one of my now-closest friends through the Peloton. She lives in Michigan, and I'm outside of D.C.! We have met in New York City three times and once locally."

When I started riding the Peloton bike, I found this kind of testimonial almost hard to believe. Since I have gone deep into the community, I understand it. Like the woman from Minneapolis marking her 40th birthday with a trip to Peloton, I have traveled to NYC to ride live and meet other members, including multiple rides with Samantha the litigator. This unexpected value beyond the classes that Peloton delivers often turns regular users into addicted users and ambassadors and salespeople for the brand.

As we proceed, we will explore the parts of the Peloton model that make it so meaningful to such a diverse group of members. How does a company built on sweating and streaming fitness content across great distances build meaningful relationships when society and the marketplace are becoming more fractured and disparate? What about Peloton is bringing so many diverse people together to achieve healthy and positive outcomes? And what role do the instructors play in all of this?

CHAPTER 4

THE INSTRUCTORS: TALENT AND SUCCESS IN TODAY'S ECONOMY

SLIDE INTO MY DM

It was a slow Sunday in early March 2018. My oldest son's travel hockey season was winding down, and I had to do carpooling for his early-season lacrosse and my nine-year-old daughter's religious school. My wife was at work, and our nanny was at the house helping out with our two-and-a-half-year-old son. I squeezed a quick three-mile run around the neighborhood between religious school drop-off and lacrosse drop-off and planned on taking an on-demand cycling ride later in the day, just before the family headed to an end-of-year hockey party. I was addicted to Peloton at that point and it was a tight day, but I was going to fulfill all my family responsibilities and have a couple good sweats. I was deep into my Peloton challenge group and was squeezing workouts into any nook or cranny I could find on the weekend or before and after work.

While waiting in the carpool pick-up lane, I considered what ride to take by scrolling through the Peloton app on my iPhone. Then an Instagram notification popped up. It was a message from Denis Morton, a Peloton cycling and yoga instructor. Earlier, while waiting during the other carpool trip, I had commented on one of his Instagram stories, letting him know I had a great time on his live ride the day before—members often compliment and thank instructors for their efforts via social media.

When I realized that Denis actually replied to me, I could feel my heartbeat pick up as if I were on the actual bike completing a spin-up or sprint. I read his message quickly. "Thanks—me too! Responding to your LB name, my dad was born in Oak Park, and I've still never been to Chicago . . . " Oak Park is a suburb of Chicago and it appeared that my leaderboard name, #ChicagoBorn, was our conversation starter. His message went on from there, and for several hours we exchanged a variety of short thoughts via Instagram direct messages. I was floored, and so was my wife. A handful of our friends with bikes were amused and surprised. Denis was spending part of his afternoon off the Peloton bike, chatting with me about Chicago, family life, and more. I walked around all day with a smile, hardly believing that an elite instructor living the glamorous life working for Peloton in New York was communicating with a middle-aged dad in the

D.C. suburbs! I was so happy! It was brief and via social media, and I accept it might have been an intern on Morton's account, but no matter, it made me super happy. That personal attention made me smile, and it was part of what made the Peloton experience so different and meaningful.

Later that day I reflected on how exciting I found the Instagram conversation. I had three happy and healthy kids, a supportive spouse, and a stimulating and rewarding job at a great university. Yet here I was, gushing with pride and excitement as I shared a few little messages, jokes, and thoughts with Denis Morton. I was barely participating in indoor cycling a year earlier and yet here I was obsessing about workouts and freaking out over messages from a fitness instructor. What was happening to me?

The good news, I rationalized, was that I was not alone. I knew from Peloton class leaderboards that hundreds were with me on live rides in 2017 and 2018 and that thousands would take popular rides on demand in a few days. I knew from the Official Peloton Member Page on Facebook that the counts of riders and members were growing. Media reports highlighted increasing revenues and store openings.

As the Peloton phenomenon grew, instructors became celebrities via the classes, but also via company advertisements, social media, and an unending supply of stories on the venture and the beautifully fit and inspiring talent in front of the camera.

From small podcasts such as *Mothers I'd Like to Know* and digital outlets PopSugar and TechCrunch to major media properties such as the *New York Times*, the *Wall Street Journal*, and *Good Morning America*, Peloton instructors were in demand. Everyone seemed eager to know them and sweat with them, from

Peloton members in Texas and Iowa to celebrities such as Al Roker, Robin Roberts, and Carson Daly.

This chapter begins to explore the important role of instructors in the Peloton community and the company's business model. Although there are limited numbers of instructors (even with the addition of the tread and other disciplines and international markets), there are great lessons to be learned about the economy and talent by following Peloton instructors through the company's incredible success.

First, the Peloton instructors are responsible for engaging with customers and creating world-class fitness content that impacts the members and keeps them coming back. In a customer-centric world, memorable contact with customers can be a crucial differentiator for any venture or organization that wants to succeed and grow. The importance of customer engagement means that the ability to create value might be spread across an organization and can make a range of frontline employees central to both immediate and long-term success.

Additionally, in an economy awash in information, the production of differentiated content that keeps customers returning becomes a strength few can replicate. Instructors and their ability to create engaging content helps makes Peloton as much a media company as a fitness hardware producer.

Beyond their crucial role engaging the customers and creating the content, instructors are a diverse ensemble of fitness and well-being talent. Their diversity can be measured across a range of metrics and lenses, from their coaching and music styles to fitness theories and non-Peloton activities.

The diversity of the instructors matters for at least two reasons. First, customers in today's world demand choice, no matter what the product or service is. Our economy has evolved to the point where customers expect options when making decisions, even at the lower end of many markets. How many kinds of coffee drinks can one buy at a McDonald's in the United States? Different customers want different things. Choice is important.

The diversity of the talent is also crucial to explore because it highlights the varied paths that instructors have taken to Peloton. In a modern economy defined by innovation and change, few careers are linear, even for the superstars. In a digital and globalized economy this lesson is even more true, and Peloton instructors highlight the theme of amazing talent being in a range of places and on a range of career paths.

Another reason that the instructors are worth exploring is that in today's world of highly competitive markets and talented people striving to lead their best lives, a company's culture is crucial to attracting and keeping the best and brightest employees. Foley told me that Peloton leadership is well aware of this and is working hard to create "the best place in the world to work."

While we will focus on the talent in front of the screen, the instructors, Peloton is battling for engineering, design, manufacturing, media, retail, merchandising, and marketing talent with countless firms across New York and the globe. The importance of a talent-supporting culture came up as a repeated theme when I spent time working out with Peloton, talking with its people, and researching the company.

Finally, Peloton's instructors give us great insights into what I call the LinkedIn world. I began to think about this idea when I was researching superstar scientists at leading universities and trying to make sense of the patent policies of major schools. In my analysis, universities were focused on their own priorities rather than those of their scientists, and this did not make sense in an economy based on individual talent.

In my analysis, a LinkedIn world is one where an individual's personal brand and authentic self are more important to them than the brand and goals of the organization they work for. It acknowledges that great performers can move, thus their LinkedIn identity or personal identity (no matter where it resides) is more important than their organizational one.

In earlier economic eras, labor was usually bound to an employer or organization they worked for. That's not so true in today's world. From NBA star LeBron James and top lawyers to marketing executives and software engineers, talented individuals are continually curating their skills and brands, knowing that their organizational affiliation is likely to have a limited lifespan, and new opportunities will appear.

From active Instagram accounts, apparel sponsorships, and hosting live events, Peloton instructors provide a great view of talent and opportunities available to top performers in today's fluid economy. For organizations of all stripes, understanding that team members are also CEOs of their own identities, careers, and side hustles is important, and the Peloton story offers insights into that reality. Peloton instructors make you sweat, cry, and smile, and represent many themes about talent and success while doing it.

CUSTOMER CONTACT AND CONTENT CREATION

The people who interface with customers are critical in every business, and these contacts should bring something of value that is tangible to the customers. It could be as simple as efficient directions (e.g., a help desk employee at a mall or a museum). It could be reliable 24-hour on-call technical support at a company selling real-time stock market information to trading firms globally. The point is that the best ventures make sure that those making regular contact with customers are spot on and always trying to please the customer. Amazon has taken over and created market after market with its relentless focus on customers.

When you start riding or taking classes on the Peloton platform, you quickly realize that the instructors are a key differentiator versus other at-home equipment. The classes the instructors program, the playlists they create, and the way they engage with community members in class, in person, and on social media all play a crucial role in Peloton effectively executing its core business model and keeping users coming back and consuming more content.

While Peloton has retail and logistics teams that make important contact with customers, the face of the company and the main method of engaging with current and potential members is through the instructors and the classes they put together. Initially this contact was exclusively indoor cycling instructors on the bike and in some floor exercises. Over time, as Peloton has introduced new offerings (strength workouts, the tread, yoga, outdoor runs, and more) and entered new markets (Canada, the UK, Germany, and Australia), the number and diversity of instructors has grown.

The instructors understand their need to engage and often inspire members, and they take their roles seriously to work with the production team and others to develop great classes, series, and special events. Music drives many classes, and the playlists planned by the instructors are based on genres such as country, pop, rock, or hip-hop or themes of decades, artists, or holidays.

For example, my wife is a fan of cycling instructor Alex Touissant's Club Bangers series of rides, while I like the 1980s rides that Jenn Sherman offers as well as the New Wave series that Christine D'Ercole puts together. The instructors must be part MTV veejay and part motivational speaker to get members through their often grueling workouts.

Cycling and tread instructor Jess King, whose background in dance and love of movement drive her classes, explained to me that she spends her Friday nights listening to music and devising playlists for the coming week. She told me that it is a date with herself, and she takes it seriously. In fact, King, who joined Peloton in 2014 after being told about a place called 'Pedalton,' said the more the company has grown, the more she has felt compelled to up her game and grow. The artist and athlete in Jess has grown with Peloton as her classes have taken on greater production value (costume, choreography, lights, and more) and she also willed herself into being a tread instructor, spending almost a year training to teach on that platform. It's obvious from Jess's following (aka King's Collective) on Peloton and social media that many appreciate her efforts and love to spend time with her in classes and on social media.

During my interview with co-founder Tom Cortese, he described to me that the power of the instructors' personalities turns classes into must-watch content. Peloton members want to know what Jenn Sherman will talk about during her Sunday NFL Pregame rides or what songs she might play during her Yacht Rock rides. (Yacht rock is soft rock from the 1970s and 1980s;

think *Rosana* by Toto or *I Keep Forgettin' (Every Time You're Near)* by Michael McDonald).

Peloton's reliance on an ensemble of talented and engaging instructors, available live and on demand, gives it a competitive advantage in content creation and customer relationship building that traditional fitness providers and clubs were not prepared to match. The on-demand offerings and social media activities provide opportunities to make the instructors' content and connections an experience not limited by the physical size or location of the boutique or club or time of the class.

For most members, the Peloton class takes place at home, which creates a comfortable and intimate experience. Sweating, breathing heavily, lungs burning in your throat, legs bogging down and heavy, and wondering if you can make it through a class while trying to listen to the instructor's commands and inspiring words can be a truly raw experience. Being at home allows members to let themselves get lost in the classes.

The Peloton class is also a shared experience, with the instructor, unlike other media consumption; this holds true on demand as well. The physical and emotional nature of Peloton classes develops a bond between instructors and members, one of the original attractions of boutique fitness. Peloton instructors have been able to develop bonds at scale and have deepened them within the intimacy and safety of the member's homes.

During my interview with Robin Arzón, Peloton's VP of Fitness programming and a tread and cycling instructor, she explained, "there is something about being in someone's home and having the privilege of being in someone's living room, or in their home gym or on their balcony or in their kitchen, and that isn't lost on me." Robin went on to say, "Even as a rider myself, when you are having that interaction with someone across the screen there is a familiarity there . . . It's a level of intimacy." As odd as it may sound, millions have experienced and crave this intimacy with the Peloton instructors.

When it comes to traditional content creation and consumption, a concept called the fourth wall is worth introducing. It's the idea that the audience is separated from actors in a play, television show, movie, or traditional fitness program (like Richard Simmons or Billy Blanks) by an invisible wall. While the viewers can see through the wall, the players or actors cannot see the audience.

Peloton breaches the fourth wall because the instructors can and do interact with the members whether they are in the studio in New York or riding at home. During live classes, instructors shout out members, reference holidays and popular culture, and acknowledge the reality of the class and the members participating. Moreover, the heavy use of social media allows continual engagement before and after the class is offered.

If members are physically present in the studio for classes, a seven day a week occurrence pre-Covid, they are likely to interact with the instructors before the class while preparing their water bottles and logging into the bikes and treads in the studio. After class, there is often a photo/chat line to meet the instructors and take selfies with them. These physical visits to the studios are and have been an important part of the Peloton story. I grew up in Chicago and lived near Oprah's TV studio for more than a year, I doubt that many visitors to the show were able to meet Oprah, take a picture with her, and share it with their friends far and wide. In contrast, the post-class images of Peloton members and instructors end up all over social media. These images and accompanying stories of the interactions build up the instructors' fame and deepen the relationships among the members, the instructors, the company, and the broader Peloton community.

Member engagement is a central part of the instructors' job, and their successful relations and communications with members, even as Peloton has scaled, is one reason Peloton has built such a loyal customer base so quickly. The idea of extending engagement with members and customers beyond the core product or offering is occurring in many industries and has implications as loyalty is tested, and low pricing is dangled as a selling point in many markets. Memorable customer engagement is a key to satisfied and returning customers.

Over my first two and a half years on the Peloton platform, I took about a third of my cycling classes with instructor Jennifer Jacobs. My main Peloton training group, the monthly challenge team Sam (#thePugMother) created, loved JJ and programmed her classes for countless group rides. Jacobs is tough and demanding as an instructor, and her '80s playlists were amazing.

I loved Jacobs' grueling style so much that I signed up and took a 6 am climb ride with her live in the NYC studio on a January morning in 2019. The 5:30 am walk to the studio from the Hampton Inn two blocks away was bitterly cold and dark. As I changed into my cycling gear in the locker room, my stomach began to feel nauseous. I went and took a seat in the lobby; the pre-ride vibes were that of a funeral. While we all had voluntarily signed up and paid our money to climb live with JJ, everyone nervously sat there knowing the sweaty hell that awaited us and no one could even muster a smile.

Less than six months later, in June 2019, with Peloton having about 500,000 bikes sold by that point, it was announced that

Jacobs would be leaving Peloton to pursue other opportunities. It sent shockwaves through the "Peloverse," especially to my small challenge group and the tens of thousands that loved her '80s rides, vicious climbs, and teaching style. The deep, emotional bonds and relationships that Jacobs, as a Peloton instructor, had built with members (customers) were real.

On Friday June 21, 2019, more than 4,300 riders clipped into their Peloton bikes at 8 am EST to take instructor Jennifer Jacobs' final live class on the Peloton platform. The ride streamed live that first day of summer and was taken more than 22,500 times (a majority on demand) in just over five days.

Jacobs was an instructor with Peloton for over three years and had quite a ridership for her '80s themed rides each Friday. Jacobs' stunning beauty was matched by the intensity of her workouts and the care she put into planning them. Her super challenging climb rides, like the one I took in NYC, were a favorite of many —including me.

When JJ officially announced she was leaving Peloton a few weeks before that final ride, an amazing range of riders across geography, age, fitness levels, genders, lifestyles, careers, pet preferences, and a host of other attributes openly shared their sadness, memories, fears, and gratitude for the incredible impact that Jacobs had on their lives. JJ fans discussed favorite rides, challenges overcome with JJ, and pictures with JJ at the studio in NYC.

My friend Sam, the litigator in NYC, lost more than 40 pounds riding (almost) exclusively with JJ and gained endless confidence and friendships through Peloton over the years with JJ. Because Sam lived in NJ at the time and worked in NY, she rode in the studio with Jacobs for many of her milestone rides (e.g., ride #200, #300,etc.).

For Sam and many of Peloton members, the instructors become as influential in their lives as a special school teacher might be. Peloton instructors become central players in the fitness and well-being of Peloton members.

As the outpouring of emotion enveloped JJ's impending departure it became crystal clear that Peloton, through its hardware and talent led content, had helped facilitate hundreds of thousands of relationships between members and instructors and millions of relationships between members and other members.

While a vast majority of these relationships between instructors and members are new and digitally based, relationships become meaningful to members quickly. I'll admit it, when I learned Jacobs was leaving Peloton I was shocked and experienced a few moments of panic, wondering who I would ride with on Wednesday and Friday mornings and whether JJ's brand of intensity was lost to me forever.

I had not realized how attached I was to Jacobs and a few of the other instructors. In fact, I began to think I was taking them for granted, never considering that they might leave. And while some compared the departure to an athlete leaving a team, I don't see it that way. I was connected to Jacobs more than any athlete as I sweat it out with her and she programmed her classes for me and the other Peloton members. Athletes play for championships, teammates, and money. Fans (customers), in most cases, are just observers and cheerleaders that support the players as they do their thing.

At the time of Jacobs' exit I was kind of surprised by the sadness and concern washing over me, fully aware it was caused by a mostly digital, one-sided fitness relationship that I paid for. This was a new kind of relationship for me and I was experiencing a new kind of loss. I have no name for the end of a digital consumer fitness relationship, but I did feel it. Don't forget, my first Peloton ride ever was with Jennifer Jacobs.

Further, I took my first ever live ride (from home) with JJ and the Peloton Monthly Challenge Team (PMCT) in early December 2017, and my proudest moment on the bike was completing a 90-minute climb ride with JJ in October 2018. That ride had me covering more than 33 miles in one session and grinning from ear to ear for at least a week. Jennifer Jacobs had really impacted my life, I could not deny that.

For Peloton, its members, and other Peloton instructors, the outpouring of emotion around JJ's departure and the massive number of riders (relative to the size of the company at the time) taking her final ride was evidence of the impact Peloton and its instructors were having on members. Was my relationship with Jacobs a friendship? No. But it was some kind of relationship that made my life better. It was a relationship deepened by the fact we had shared some good healthy fun in the studio and via streaming classes. Most importantly, it was a relationship that was also shared and strengthened with tens of thousands of others in classes, in person, and on social media.

The depth of the emotional connections formed between Peloton, its frontline workers, and its members is truly unique. The importance of team members that engage with customers cannot be overstated.

FROM WATER TO FITNESS,
CUSTOMERS EXPECT CHOICE

The first time I looked at a group picture of the 12 core Peloton instructors teaching in late 2016, it reminded me of the Benetton ads I grew up with in the 1980s. The United Colors of Benetton campaign gave rise to the trend of ads with a diverse, curated group of faces. It is now the standard in catalogues, websites, and campaigns for all kinds of products, services, and institutions.

When I clipped into our Peloton in 2016, the ensemble of 12 cycling instructors was diverse across a host of elements. From their physical styles—understated (bike instructor and Martha's Vineyard native Emma Lovewell) to tatted up badass (Robin Arzón)—to their teaching styles—technical and metrics oriented (Matt Wilpers) to entertainment and musically driven (Alex Touissant and Jenn Sherman), the instructors offer a diversity of choice well beyond their physical images.

For Peloton members and potential customers, the motley crew of instructors is crucial because it creates choice and more opportunities to connect with the content and to continue to work out. As Cortese pointed out, with Peloton, fitness becomes fun; something people want to do. The instructor's ability to make people want to want to work out with authentic, engaging, and constantly updated content is truly disruptive.

With so many instructors, with varied classes and teaching styles, there are multiple points of entry for members and a vast menu if and when they decide to spend more time with Peloton; something that happens with many customers. The abundance allows for experimentation and refreshment. For example, a metrics-driven, mileage-obsessed Peloton friend is usually focused on choosing classes to improve her numbers; once or twice a month, she will take a DJ ride with instructor Jess King and DJ John Michael because she finds Jess fun, quirky, and unpredictable, the opposite of her regular training.

My friend and thousands of other Peloton riders also find the banter and antics between DJ John Michael and Jess King incredibly entertaining while sweating. DJ classes feature Peloton's house DJ, John Michael, spinning the tracks as members workout. It's not for everyone, and the first time I tried a DJ ride, I didn't like it. Eventually some online friends got me to try another for a milestone ride of theirs and I became a fan.

The range of choices of instructors and content matters because as members spend more time with Peloton, thinking about fitness and well-being, their needs and demands evolve. From deciding that you like high-intensity rides, or you want climb rides to balance out music-based rides, to joining different gamified challenges or trying bootcamps, the diversity of instructors and approaches helps to ensure that customer needs are met, even as they evolve.

In my fourth full calendar year with Peloton (2020) my number one discipline by hours spent was yoga (81 hours) and number two was running (79.7 hours), while cycling came in third with 73.4 hours for the year. BTW, Peloton delivered this data to me at the beginning of 2021, making my progress and activities for 2020 easier to view and celebrate; my experience was gamified, quantified, and delivered to me.

The expansion of Peloton's offerings, including floor workouts, yoga, treadmill workouts (with running, walking, hiking, and bootcamps), and whatever else is in store will demand new talent and increased production from existing talent. Continuing to offer a range of choices for customers will matter to Peloton just as Baskin-Robbins (31 flavors) and Starbucks need to keep it fresh with new flavors, and WWE (World Wrestling Entertainment) needs to bring in new personalities and rotate out the old and stale.

Eventually most members end up with several favorite instructors and class types, though some train exclusively with one instructor, which poses a real problem if that instructor leaves. There have been departures from Peloton besides Jacobs, and they can be traumatic for members of the Peloton community, like a dramatic breakup. Spend some time on Peloton social media and you may still find hearts aching for past instructors Steven Little, Nicole Meline, Jennifer Jacobs, Oliver Lee, and others.

TALENT CAN COME FROM ANYWHERE

Another reason the diversity of Peloton instructors is important to understand is because it reiterates a truth about markets driven by innovation and creative output: talent can come from anywhere, and the path to the top is almost never straight. It is a mistake to assume that the best performers in any field or occupation should have followed a specific route to achieve excellence, especially in an economy more often defined by change than anything else.

The reaction of members and increasing sales and engagement are evidence that Peloton instructors are world class. But as we dig a bit deeper, we see that their differing paths played a role in forming their specific styles and approaches to teaching classes and connecting with members. The diverse educational and career backgrounds of Peloton instructors highlight the nature of an economy where lateral and forward moves are common, and career changes are accepted and even expected. It's also important to note that like great achievers in any field, none of the instructors ended up where they are by mistake, and for many, Peloton will not be their last career stop.

ARTISTS AND SUITS

I was lucky enough to interview four Peloton instructors as part of this research: Matt Wilpers, Jenn Sherman, Jess King, and Robin Arzón. These interviews were in addition to spending thousands of hours with Peloton instructors in streaming classes, training live in the studio, chatting at special events and at the studio, and tracking and engaging instructors on social media. In reality, I've spent as much time with the Peloton instructors since early 2017 as I have with any people other than my immediate family.

Of the four instructors I interviewed (Matt, Jenn, Jess K., and Robin) not one planned a career in fitness when they were in school and beginning their working lives.

Cycling and tread instructor Matt Wilpers was a track and crew athlete in college in his home state of Georgia, and he earned two degrees in accounting before becoming an auditor in New York City. When he realized finance was not for him, Matt became a trainer and went on to take pre-med coursework at New York University with plans to be a doctor. Though focusing on traditional careers such as finance and medicine, Wilpers knew that his favorite thing to do was coach people and help them improve, even in the pre-dawn hours before reporting to his full-time gig. Matt worked at Equinox as well as with multiple fitness ventures and online training groups before meeting Foley through a former Equinox client. Matt, who had worked on a fitness app while building his training career, told me that after meeting Foley he knew, "If this company doesn't make it, none of them will." Matt's quant background can be seen in his approach to planning and training, including his development of the Power Zone classes on the Peloton platform.

When instructor Jess King was growing up, her mother owned a gym and was a bodybuilder, and while Jess shared her mother's love of movement, Jess viewed herself as a dancer and artist, appearing on *So You Think You Can Dance* and performing in Las Vegas and Los Angeles as she launched her career. Eventually Jess made her way to the East Coast, living and working in New York City. King's initial conversation with Foley had her seeing a career in fitness as an outlet for her passion for movement. Jess has done just that and has not looked back.

For the instructors, their unique backgrounds influence how they approach fitness, their communication styles, and what they talk about in class and across media platforms. Some instructors, such as Robin Arzón (who also holds the title of VP of Fitness Programming) continually provide motivational quotes, challenges, and cues to their classes, something that many people want. Not all instructors are as direct and brash as Arzón; some are more reserved, cerebral, and metrics based while others base much of their approach on their own career paths and personal journeys with fitness and health and music and life. Some share a lot, others not so much.

SWEAT WITH SWAGGER

Peloton instructor Robin Arzón, perhaps the most broadly recognizable Peloton instructor, is a Philadelphia native and former NYC litigator who recreated herself as an ultramarathoner, blogger, and style maker. Arzón offers members opportunities to join her to "sweat with swagger," and throughout her classes she reminds them that they are doing the right thing, taking care of themselves and earning their confidence. "Self-care is not selfish," is something I remember from my time with Robin.

For about six months in 2018 and 2019, I regularly took Arzón's 45-minute *tabata* classes at 6 am on Tuesdays. These sessions were known online in the Peloton Monthly Challenge Team as the "pain cave," and that was a fair name. These were not really fun as *tabata* is a high-intensity training method based on a two-to-one work-to-rest ratio. This means, for example, that for every 30-second hard push, you get 15 seconds to recover, before pushing hard for another 30 seconds. The pushes might be anywhere from 20 seconds to a minute. This might go on for 25 pushes and 25 rests over the 45-minute class. Each time, if you were doing it right, your legs would burn, your lungs would scream, and vomit would threaten.

As we suffered and smiled through these classes, Robin, full of swagger, tattoos, and strength would remind us that, "We don't do basic" and "Yes, you can." Her brand of aggressive, inclusive coaching speaks to a range of riders, and it's no wonder that Robin, who never ran a 5K race before attending law school, could represent the New York brand. During our conversation, Robin told me she was "allergic to exercise" as a child and would even steal her mother's medical notepad (her mother is a physician) and forge notes to get out of gym class. "I was petrified to be the sports kid," Arzón explained to me, "I was made fun of when I was growing up for the way I ran." It is hard to believe when you watch Robin lead a class, whether bike, strength, or running.

As a Type 1 diabetic, Robin has a strength and personal story (including being held hostage at gunpoint in a bar when she was an undergraduate at New York University) that are compelling to young Millennials and middle-age Generation X members like me. Completing those *tabata* rides before the sun came up gave me confidence and strength heading into the day, no matter what I was doing. The positive endorphin rush, fueled by music and Arzón's motivation and my "Pelo-friends," is something I appreciate and value and never found with any other workout.

Arzón, like Matt Wilpers breaking away from finance, had to recreate herself as a side hustle as she was building a successful corporate career. Robin, who began running a bit in law school and then marathon training, knew she had a different view on fashion, fitness, and urban life and began blogging about it in 2010 as a way to "scrapbook and memorialize her marathon training."

Arzón's *Shut Up and Run* blog was a visual conversation with countless pictures to accompany her words and experiences; this was years before Instagram. Arzón told me, "I realized it was resonating with folks; that it was sparking conversations for maybe perhaps unconventional athletes or folks who didn't really consider themselves athletes in a former life like I did." Arzón had slowly changed the narrative of her life and others loved it and were inspired by it. In 2016, Arzón would take her blog approach and publish a best-selling book: *Shut Up and Run: How to Get Up, Lace Up, and Sweat with Swagger.*

After spending seven years in law and moonlighting as a fitness and style blogger and journalist, she went to fitness and media full time in 2012. Robin became a certified coach and indoor cycling instructor. Arzón ran ultramarathons, was the subject of a documentary as she ran five marathons in five days to raise money for multiple sclerosis research, and she worked with Nike Women. As an archived Tumblr social media page of her early blog's "about me" page said, "SHUTUPANDRUN is for athletes who think medals are the highest form of Bling. We sweat with swagger on the streets of our cities. And we never sacrifice style for function. Fueled by the ethos that there is no finish line, I channel the collective energy of the world's running crews, a family forged in sweat."[38] The blog Arzón created and shared with the world was a long way from legal briefs and Arzón's childhood image of herself as an "arts and crafts, straight-A, honor-roll student," that avoided movement at all costs. She had recreated herself as a full-time fitness professional; she had rewritten her narrative publicly with images, sweat, and swagger, and by 2014 was part of Peloton, well off the corporate law path, and about to help ignite a well-being revolution.

JENN FROM NEW JERSEY

It was 2013 and a stay-at-home mom turned New Jersey cycling instructor was about to achieve her dream of opening her own indoor cycling studio. She had financing, a lease, a business partner, and a loyal following of indoor cyclists who loved her. Jennifer Schreiber Sherman was ready to launch, then she learned about Peloton and her plans were disrupted.

I took some fun rock rides with Sherman, known as JSS by her adoring fans, early in my Peloton riding career and began to ride frequently with her during my second year, when I began looking for 60- and 90-minute rides. JSS was offering 60-minute NFL pregame rides on Sundays, and I tried one on Super Bowl Sunday in 2018. I loved the ride and her humorous analysis of the game and the players. It was clear she was a real NFL fan, in addition to being a huge music fan.

Sherman, I would learn, is a bit older than me and did not become a fitness instructor until later in life. After attending Syracuse University and having an early career in the live events side of the music business, family life came calling. She spent years as a stay-at-home mom with her two kids and found indoor cycling after some personal challenges left her taxed and stressed out.

Jenn had always been a gym rat and went through lots of phases, including step aerobics, but she had never been an athlete or a cheerleader. When she discovered indoor cycling, she fell in love with it. Music, which had always been a passion and had influenced her pre-motherhood career, was the main attraction for her. As Jenn began riding at a local studio she was blown away by the power of a great class with a great soundtrack and a great instructor.

Not long after falling in love with indoor cycling, Jenn got certified to teach and began instructing at the studio where she had been a rider; Jenn quickly developed a sizable following in Bergen County, New Jersey. She told me that she made it a point to make everyone feel comfortable in her classes. The riders loved Jenn and her music and kept coming back. Sherman was killing it, even serving as a Lululemon ambassador when the brand was beginning to grow the athleisure apparel segment. She was happy with her new second career. Her kids were in school during the day and she was able to teach and make people feel amazing.

Sherman was kicking so much ass that a family member of a successful studio owner in Connecticut approached her to see if she was interested in partnering to open studios in New Jersey. This opportunity appeared to be Sherman's dream, and she went to work writing a business plan, finding space, and preparing to take on financing with her new partners.

It was then, in 2013, as she was about to start her own studio that Sherman learned about Foley and his idea for Peloton. When I interviewed JSS, she relayed the story of reading a *Well+Good* article where Foley described how he was going to revolutionize indoor cycling and she knew it was "fucking brilliant" immediately (Sherman drops many F bombs, for those who have not taken a class with her). JSS wrote a cold email explaining why Peloton should hire her. They did and JSS joined the team, changing her dream on the fly. Boutique fitness was truly peaking at that time and Sherman, a mother of two in suburban New Jersey, was ascending that peak with the launch of her own studio when she decided to leave it to join Peloton and a vision, not yet real.

When I describe Sherman to those who don't know Peloton, I often explain that her personality is large and "New York," like Elaine from *Seinfeld,* but Sherman has incredible rhythm. JSS has a huge following, known as the JSSTribe, online and many members who regularly rode with her in the studio pre-Covid. Because Sherman was the first instructor hired, many of her most ardent supporters are among the oldest Peloton members, often referred to as OGs.

I have met many JSSTribe members while riding in the studio in NYC, online, and at my local showroom, and they are spirited before, during, and after classes—reflecting the fun #JFDI personality of Sherman. Jenn told me that she has always tried to know her riders, dating back to her earliest days teaching in New Jersey and she loves Peloton members to come in and ride so she can match the leaderboard names with faces, no matter how big the classes become. This open accessible attitude that Sherman brought as the first instructor has become part of the Peloton brand and matched the accessibility that the founders were going for when creating the venture.

Wilpers, Arzón, King, and Sherman highlight some of varied paths that instructors have taken and support the concept that talent can come from differing backgrounds. Other Peloton instructor backgrounds include primary education (tread and cycling instructor Jess Sims), years as a professional makeup artist (cycling instructor Tunde Oyeneyin), and many in the performing arts; cycling instructor Christine D'Ercole was an extra in *Dead Poets Society* as an aspiring actor, and instructors Cody Rigsby, Hannah Corbin, and Rebecca Kennedy were all professional dancers before becoming fitness professionals. Some are technical and fit the traditional coaching mold, while others make you think (Denis Morton), and many bring the party to class—most members know to take a Cody Rigsby class when you need to smile. The variety and choice that Peloton's ensemble of instructors offer with their skill sets, personalities, attitudes, and soundtracks keep members engaged and satisfied and has been crucial to the venture's success. As this book went to print in fall 2021, Peloton was nearing 50 full-time instructors—from yoga and bike to tread and strength. This is four times more than when I first road in late 2016.

TALENT AND THE CREATIVE ECONOMY

I started working on my PhD at George Mason University in 2006 and I became a good friend and then colleague of a brilliant academic named Richard Florida. In 2000, well before I met him, Florida wrote an award-winning and fascinating book, *The Rise of the Creative Class,* exploring the significant role that creative thinkers play in innovative sectors of the economy. Florida used data to highlight why some places, such as New York or Miami, could attract talent and others could not retain talented people.

Organizations, especially high-growth ventures, have waged a battle to attract and retain talent for decades. Leaders of great organizations understand this. James Goodnight, founder and CEO of software maker SAS Institute, once wrote, "Ninety-five percent of my assets drive out the gate every evening. It's my job to maintain a work environment that keeps those people coming back every morning."[39] Goodnight is correct. Keeping talent happy and engaged is central to the long-term survival of any organization.

Making sure talent is happy, supported, and engaged, with opportunities to flourish, is a must for organizations that want to lead. That means a measure of independence and the ability to improve and grow. In many ways, just as Peloton is a platform for its paying members to improve their health and well-being, it is a platform for talented individuals to grow their skills, careers, and in the case of many instructors, their brands. As the company scales, it is providing learning experiences and opportunities for its employees. Jess King pointed out how much she has learned about corporate management and approaches as part of such a talented organization with structures and strategies supporting her growth.

Foley truly believes that the team can build one of the greatest companies of the century, but that talent across the spectrum is crucial, especially software and in front of the camera. In our interview at Peloton headquarters Foley spent as much time discussing the development of what he called "the best company in the world to work for" as he did talking about developing fitness products.

Foley described in detail a cultural off-site session that the company runs annually to identify and resolve problems that can affect the ability of Peloton's team to execute on this "once-in-a-lifetime opportunity," to build the best workplace culture in the world. The off-site on culture brings people from across the organization to discuss these challenges and create a plan of action. The goal is to find internal problems and solve them so that the company can become the best in the world to work for and attract and grow the best, most diverse workforce in the world.

Foley also stressed the importance of continually bringing in more talented people. He acknowledged that as the scale gets larger and Peloton heads into the unknown, there are fewer people with appropriate experience, so they must bring in more talent to support the growth. An example Foley noted was bringing William Lynch, his boss and colleague at IAC and Barnes&Noble.com, to serve as president of Peloton in 2018. Peloton also brought in Wall Street veteran Jill Woodworth from J.P. Morgan in 2018 to help usher the company through the IPO process and the crucial transition to being a public company with regular engagement with investors, analysts, and the media. Both Woodworth and Lynch have become faces of Peloton through investor days, earnings calls, and investment conferences, representing the company and building their own professional brands.

Peloton, with roots in fitness, media, technology, and production and a New York City home base is attempting to create a workplace that allows all employees to be who they are fully. This celebration of people's true selves plays out on the consumer side when special Pride Rides or Women's History Month classes or similar events are offered. I believe these special rides and celebrations (and the badges members earn for participating) are just as much for the company's internal team as they are for the member community. Peloton is trying to get the best out of a diverse workforce in some of the most diverse and competitive cities and labor pools in the world. An inclusive culture is a strategic and moral imperative for a company that is about connecting people through fitness and "empowering them to be the best versions of themselves anywhere, anytime." We have to assume this means while working for Peloton as well.

A LINKEDIN WORLD

In addition to the thousands of hours of classes and the formal interactions of interviews, in-person classes, and events, there have been many pedestrian and unexpected, but meaningful moments for me with the instructors, exchanges such as the Instagram-enabled one I experienced with Denis Morton.

For example, the first time I met cycling instructor Christine D'Ercole (aka CDE) was on the street in front of the original Peloton bike studio in Chelsea. I was waiting for my wife to finish an Alex Touissant class. Like a total fanboy, I stopped CDE as she walked by to thank her for her classes and her inspiring words. (I love her quotes "What's at your finish line?" and "I am, I can, I will, I do." I always feel better after she says "drop your shoulders, drop your baggage," at the beginning of a class—just a simple reminder to focus on the here and now.)

In that moment, when D'Ercole was clearly done teaching (she was showered and dressed beautifully for non-fitness activities) and on her way somewhere else, she did not hesitate to stop and talk with me for a few moments.

When I finally took an in-studio class with CDE a few months later in May 2019, we chatted a bit after class and the moment she learned we had a mutual friend, she gave me the biggest hug I've had in over a decade. That is no joke; I have the picture to prove it. Her embrace was natural—she came in for the hug; anyone who knows me knows that I am not a hugger. I loved it even though we were both super sweaty from the class (pre-Covid).

The chat on the street and the sweaty hug were what I knew of CDE, based on the brand she shares in class and beyond. She is inclusive and supportive; "hands on your back," being another of her regular phrases. My own interactions with her were physical embodiments of her encouraging and supportive brand, which she proudly displays at Peloton and beyond on social media, in the press, and via her own commercial endeavors, from her branded apparel to the word workshops she teaches. While I do not really know CDE, my time in her classes and the micro moments I shared with her have established a warm and embracing brand in my mind that is distinct from Peloton's overall brand and the brands of the other instructors.

All of the instructors have a social media presence and media exposure through interviews, features, and Peloton-generated content (blog posts and videos). When you watch them teach for Peloton and communicate through other means, it's clear that each instructor has their own unique voice and approach to building their brand and career. JSS and Wilpers have very different approaches when compared to Ally Love and Robin Arzón. This LinkedIn world side of the instructors' careers highlights the reality of today's labor markets and the complex relationship between institutions and their value-creating talent.

Although the instructors teach for Peloton and promote its platform, they have far more hours off the platform. They make great use of social media, personal networks, agents, corporate networks, and more to enhance their personal brands and opportunities.

While first reviewing basic notes for this chapter in the summer of 2019, I learned that Emma Lovewell, a Peloton cycling instructor with a green thumb, signed to be an Under Armour athlete.[40] It amazed me that an indoor cycling instructor is an official athlete in the same stable as NFL GOAT Tom Brady, Olympic swimmer Michael Phelps, former WWE wrestler Dwayne Johnson (The Rock), and Notre Dame University. In mid-2020, a year later, while going through further edits, I noticed Emma doing sponsored posts on Instagram for Secret Deodorant, a traditional brand of Procter & Gamble, and also partnering with Birds Eye Vegetables, a leading consumer brand of food conglomerate Conagra.

By February 2021, Emma would appear in a Super Bowl commercial, titled "Keep Growing" for Scotts Miracle-Gro. Others in the commercial included DIY legend Martha Stewart, NASCAR driver Kyle Busch, Carl Weathers of *Rocky* fame, Leslie David Baker (Stanley from the sitcom *The Office*), and John Travolta. Leslie David Baker would refer to Emma by her name in the commercial and Emma's phrase "crush your core," was used. The Peloton platform and Emma's talent and grace put her onto the biggest stage in consumer capitalism with the most established people, brands, and characters of the last 50 years.

Emma, with an understated brand relative to others, is not the first instructor to have an affiliation with a major athletic brand or consumer products, but her actions highlight the nature of talent in today's creative economy.

We have moved beyond the idea that someone will have six or seven *jobs*; it's possible that a person entering the labor market now will have six or seven *careers*. Robin Arzón and Matt Wilpers and JSS are examples of this concept with their ability to create their own brands and succeed in new industries. Robin's "Sweat with Swagger" and Matt's "Train Smart" have allowed them to grow their connections with members and achieve opportunities well beyond Peloton.

It's obvious that Peloton instructors will continue to have many opportunities going forward and many will end up in places well beyond Peloton, if they choose, just as Justin Timberlake, Britney Spears, and Ryan Gosling soared from *The Mickey Mouse Club*. Peloton instructors are an extreme and vivid case of the LinkedIn world, the personal brand element of the economy, but that's what makes them worth learning from.

WRAPPING IT UP

Peloton's instructors are major drivers of the company's value through the classes they create and deliver and their ability to attract customers and keep them engaged. This customer contact element is crucial to Peloton's stated value to "Put Members First." There are countless others at Peloton, from sales and customer service to delivery that are also tasked with this role, but the instructors are the most prominent.

The diversity of the instructors also matters because it impacts the content the company can create and illuminates the range of backgrounds and pathways talent can take to the top of creative and growing industries. When I interviewed instructor Jenn Sherman she told me she loves that Foley is "rooting for his talent." Building the right culture and company to support their diverse and growing workforce was a theme that came up in my research and in the company's messaging repeatedly. From the company off-site that Foley mentioned to his stated goal to build the best company in the world for employees, time will tell if Peloton can find new models of occupational well-being for its employees.

Peloton's instructors highlight the unique position of talented people in today's world. The talented have the reality of not only managing their own brands and careers, but also balancing it with and growing the organizations they work for. Personal brand building is the name of the game for talent, and organizations need to build structures and cultures supporting these efforts.

CHAPTER 5

PHYSICAL SPACE IN A DIGITAL WORLD

In 2005, *New York Times* columnist Thomas Friedman, a three-time Pulitzer Prize winner, wrote an award-winning book titled *The World Is Flat*. Friedman argued that after the Cold War, the global economy evolved to a point that anyone could do anything from anywhere using modern tools, from the internet and software to international logistics and supply chains. Dell, Microsoft, United Parcel Service (UPS), and countless other giants helped make this work possible.

At first glance, Peloton's core value proposition, access to world-class fitness content when and where you want it might suggest that Friedman's thesis is correct: the world is flat, and I can ride, run, and do yoga anywhere with their world-class content, software and hardware—bike, tread, laptop, tablet, TV, and more.

With Friedman's World is Flat thesis and Peloton's massive library of fitness and well-being classes, it has been easy to toss out the basic analogy that Peloton is "the Netflix of fitness" and believe that sums up the model that Foley and team have put into place.

However, digging deeper reveals that retail showrooms, production studios, massive warehouses, special events, manufacturing facilities, customer-led meetups, and sprawling back-office technical and logistical and field operations are central to Peloton's digital successes. Physical, in person, human- to-human contact, activities, and interaction have become essential to Peloton's growth and differentiation.

In early September 2018, as my Peloton riding reached a fevered pitch, I found myself nervously waiting outside of a new Peloton showroom near my home, hoping to meet instructor Jess King for the first time. I had never gone to any grand opening or stood in line for an autograph or movie release, but because of the Peloton bike and their business model, I considered myself incredibly lucky to join the celebration opening a Peloton showroom within walking distance of my home. Physical location mattered in this case. The new showroom was less than a mile from my home and I could walk to meet Jess King. The world was not flat as Friedman argued. I could not be anywhere to meet Jess King.

Physical space and engagement turn out to be a pillar of the Peloton success story and confirms that the idea of a "pure play" digital business that does not need physical assets is a fantasy. From the notion that Amazon is eating up every local retailer to the concept that people don't need friends and can survive on social media alone, the digitization of life is not as extreme as people fear. Peloton is one of many recent high-growth ventures to highlight the central role of physical space in the digital economy.

THE PELOTON MOTHERSHIP

In February 2017, when I observed the Peloton rider in Minneapolis, Minnesota, sharing the news that she was traveling to New York to ride at the Mothership to celebrate her 200th ride and her 40th birthday, the contradiction of wanting to physically travel and meet people from a distanced-based digital product really stuck in my brain.

I learned quickly that riding live in the studio at scheduled times with the instructors and other members was the ultimate experience for many in a customer base that loved the ease and control of riding at home and taking streaming classes at any time.

It would take a while, but by June 2018, when I was addicted to riding our bike and was using the bike and non-bike content nearly daily, I would become that member from Minnesota.

Once again, prodded by my wife, we planned to visit and ride in the New York studio to celebrate her July 1 birthday. Emily had already visited a couple times and raved about the experience. As luck would have it, my main Facebook Peloton subgroup was meeting up at the Peloton studio that same day. The group, The Peloton Monthly Challenge Team, created by friend Sam, was having a Home Rider Invasion (HRI) that coincided with Emily's birthday.

An HRI is basically a meetup organized by a group of riders who pick some dates and come to New York to work out together in the Peloton studios. Countless HRIs take place each year, and I have since participated in multiple with the Peloton Monthly Challenge Team. My wife has participated in at least three with her main Peloton subgroup, composed of physician moms. Her group is based on Facebook and known as The Physician Moms Peloton Group (#PMPG). In addition to workouts in the company studios, HRIs typically include group meals, Broadway shows, group-based SWAG and favors, and other social, New York activities. (This was all pre-pandemic.)

For my first trip to the Mothership and my first HRI, I arrived the day before Emily because my work schedule was more flexible, and my HRI was starting. I was not sure what to expect as I had never been in an indoor cycling studio or a boutique fitness class of any type. I was clueless, alone and in New York City for the first time in over a decade.

The Peloton studio, my first boutique studio experience, would be filled with people that I had been riding with virtually and posting with and talking with on Facebook and Instagram for six months; I had joined the PMCT group at the end of 2017. Many from the group would now be physically together in the Peloton cycling studio in NYC, taking our digital relationship to the physical world. We were leveling up and it was going to be sweaty.

In this case, about 50 people (out of a group of a couple hundred) were in town for two days to ride together, have a few meals, and do some New York City activities. Also, importantly, for many of us, we were going to ride live with some of the instructors we had worked out with at home for months and even years. This was nerve-wracking and exciting at the same time. I imagined this would involve post-ride selfies with the instructors, just like the pics I had seen all over social media, and I was sure to be a sweaty, red-faced mess after the studio rides.

BACK AFTER A DECADE

The truth is that I was not a big fan of New York City. I had not spent time there in more than a decade when it was decided I would visit Peloton's studio and meet up with some other riders. I passed through the city often on my way to Long Island, where my wife's family had a vacation home, but now I was like the Minnesota woman on Facebook. In reality, I was lucky to be living just outside of D.C. in Montgomery County, Maryland, as it made the journey to Manhattan pretty easy logistically.

Mid-morning on June 30, 2018, I took the business-class Gold Bus run by a service called Vamoose, from a stop less than two miles from my home and reached Penn Station in Manhattan about four hours later. From there I walked eight blocks and checked in to the Hampton Inn Hotel on 24th Street, a block or so from the original Peloton bike studio. I put my bags, which contained my size 15 Giro cycling shoes, in the hotel room, then walked a few blocks to the Peloton studio. I made a few passes trying to see inside, but there was a retail showroom visible in the front window and I was far too nervous to walk in. I took a couple of quick selfies outside with the studio and its neon Peloton sign in the background, but did not dare go in as I was not registered for any classes that day.

Instead of continuing to loiter outside of the studio, I next grabbed a quick snack at the Whole Foods around the corner and returned to my room. I was really amped up and had energy to burn. Fortunately, Peloton had recently introduced its outdoor running content, so I chose a Matt Wilpers' audio running class and went for a run on the Highline (too crowded) and down to the Hudson River. Feeling a bit more relaxed when I returned to the hotel, I grabbed a quick shower and then dinner, and went back to my room to rest up for my early morning Country Ride with Matt Wilpers; the instructor I had just run outside with on demand. I did not know at the time that I would end up interviewing Matt the next year as part of this project.

The next morning, I arrived at the studio for class with Matt and immediately recognized some people from my Facebook group. I awkwardly introduced myself to a few, and everyone was more than civil, but we were meeting for the first time and waiting to go into class and it was 7:15 in the morning. Most members in the group were women so I had plenty of space in the locker room to change and put on my shoes. I gingerly wandered around the loungy lobby area of the studio as it is not easy to walk in cycling shoes and my energy would not allow me to stand still.

We were called to class from the small lobby and walked to the studio through a narrow hallway and set of doors. Upon entering the actual bike studio, I grabbed some towels and Peloton-branded bottled water from carts near the door and I quickly located my bike, #19. I believe there were about 40 in the studio.

I immediately realized the monitor differed from the one on the standard at-home bike. I logged into the much smaller monitor. It did not have many buttons or speakers and the user interface on the small screen lacked choices of classes, my history, or a full Peloton leaderboard. This made sense for visual reasons. We were there in person so we did not need a screen to see the instructor; there was no reason to block the faces and bodies of the in-studio riders. There were also operational reasons. We were only there for live rides so we did not need speakers, libraries of on-demand classes, and so on. For riders in the studio, only the studio leaderboard is visible. I adjusted my seat and handlebars, clipped in, took a few deep breathes and prepared to ride live in the Mothership. I was nervous and my heart was racing before the class even started, there were also a bunch of strangers and new friends all around me. More deep breathes.

I looked up and saw instructor Matt Wilpers at the front of the class getting ready and slowly I moved my eyes to the ceiling and noticed a small video camera on a track. It dawned on me: this was not just a boutique cycling studio, but a media production studio, and since I was in the Peloton studio in Chelsea, I was part of the production. I was an extra for the home riders and the instructors. I was so hyped up about actually taking a real studio class that I had forgotten my researcher's mindset! I was in the production—time to pay attention.

The truth is, only a handful of studio participants are visible to home members; most look like nothing more than shadowy blobs moving to the music and the instructor's cues. Some riders, sitting in the handful of visible spots, have become mini-celebrities and taken social media by storm on occasion due to their in-class antics or apparel choices. Some members do work hard—logging in the minute reservations for studio classes become available or showing up super early to walk-in classes—to get front bikes and class spots that are more visible. Other participants choose positions that are not visible to streaming participants.

That first in-studio class with Wilpers was a 45-minute blur. There was so much to take in. From being so close to Matt to being so close to other riders—remember I had never been to a traditional boutique class before. Riding in a NYC studio surrounded by 40 or so perspiring classmates I had never met before made it all just kind of a fun, sweaty, adrenaline-fueled fog.

After the class, we headed out to the lobby for pictures with Matt and a few sweaty PMCT friends. About 10 of us PMCT members huddled around Matt, barely knowing one another, but full of endorphins and grinning from ear to ear after enjoying a real-life sweat together with Matt at the Mothership. From there, I reclipped in for the 8:30 am class with even more PMCT members and Ally Love for a 45-minute "Feel Good" ride. As Ally welcomed us and we clipped in, our crowd was excited and raucous as the Ally Love class was the official start of our PMCT Home Rider Invasion; those of us that took the Wilpers class were just getting extra classes in. My legs were already tired from the first class, but the studio was now packed with group members and it would turn out to be a ride I would always remember.

Normally I would not have done back-to-back, 45-minute rides, but when Peloton members visit the studios, it is common to take several classes in a day, sometimes even for a few days. Many members want to have as much face time with instructors and other members as possible and soak it all in, even if overdoing it a bit. You might consider it a health-based version of bingey visits to Vegas or Amsterdam.

My wife arrived later that day and took an Alex Touissant class to celebrate her birthday. Emily was over the moon meeting Alex and getting a shout-out live in the studio. I got to meet Alex in the lobby as well, even though I did not take his class. Meeting the instructors and riding live and taking pictures with them, my Peloton friends, and my wife was a blast. I did not expect sweating with semi-strangers to be so much fun. I also was fully aware that I would never have done any of this twelve months earlier. Not the group exercise in studio or the trip to NYC or the sweaty selfies or dinners with people from around the country. I knew it was happening because of the Peloton bike and community, and that first trip to the Mothership only made me love it more.

The post-class picture line and the opportunity to meet the instructors and chat, however briefly, deepens the connection between the Peloton members and instructors. The sweaty picture line is the physical continuation of the breaking down of the fourth wall between talent and audience. This ability to interact with the instructor after a physical experience (the class) creates immeasurable value for the members who are there and even for those who are not because the pictures and stories make it to social media and get shared at meetings and meals, bringing lots of smiles to the broader Peloton community and sometimes even to non-members. Peloton members often live vicariously through other members' experiences when it comes to instructor interactions. Pictures, videos, and stories of friends, and even strangers, with instructors and other members at the studio impacts the overall experience. The photographic and video evidence of physical moments at the studios and real member faces in the classes at the Mothership makes the content more than just fitness classes streaming to customers. The real, attainable opportunity to physically interact at the Mothership brings an unexpected and welcoming element to the Peloton experience.

Brad Olson, Peloton's chief business officer, explained that the company had no idea that studio riders would want to hang around after class and take pictures with the instructors. A makeshift photo line after class became the norm, and instructors and riders posed in the front entry hall of the studio in Chelsea. In the summer of 2019, the original studio finally dedicated a space with graphics on the wall for pictures. At the time of the completion of this manuscript, the new mega studios in New York and London had not been opened to the public so it is unclear how much space is dedicated to member interactions before and after class. Moreover, Covid will have clearly impacted whatever the originals plans may have been.

I have traveled to New York nearly 10 times since that first Peloton trip in the summer of 2018. Each time spending money on transportation, hotels, food and drink, entertainment, and goods. My visits to NYC and Peloton in less than three years exceeded my previous 20 years combined. I have also met and become friends with new people in the studio as most there are self-selected and excited about fitness, community, and Peloton. As we often hear from instructor Jess Sims, "You don't have to; you get to." That ethos permeates the studios and entices members from near and far to visit and enjoy physical time with one another sweating and having fun.

SHOWROOM OUTPOSTS

By September 2018, as the Peloton retail showroom was preparing to open less than a mile from my home in Bethesda, Maryland, I'd been really hooked on the Peloton bike for about eleven months. Having instructors physically on hand for store openings was the norm for Peloton at that point. Jess King was coming to launch the store and I was excited to meet King in person, as I had spent many grueling hours streaming her classes live and on demand in my basement.

The store close to my home was not Peloton's first in my region; in fact, it was replacing a micro, pop-up type of store in a local mall. There was also a store in the high-end Tyson's Corner Galleria Mall in Virginia, about six miles from my house. I am fortunate to live and work in the D.C. metro area, an early successful market for Peloton. My wife bought our original bike in the Virginia store. It is worth pointing out that the Tyson's Corner Galleria Mall was the location of the first Apple store.

The store upgrade in my neighborhood, from a mall-based pop-up to a high-traffic, main-street retail storefront, was part of a mass of retail showroom openings by Peloton as it looked to an initial public offering (IPO) in 2019. Peloton's aggressive opening and upgrading of showrooms highlighted the increasingly hybridized physical and digital business models that many of the most successful consumer firms in the world are putting into place.

Far from dead, physical space has assumed new roles and responsibilities in a digital economy, and top companies are leveraging retail spaces to achieve their strategic goals. Although Peloton's flagship offerings are connected digitally and have been limited to a couple of models of bikes and treads, the company's local retail showrooms have been crucial to its continued growth. From customer acquisition and onboarding to brand and community building, physical retail space has been fundamental to Peloton's success since its earliest days.

PHYSICAL SHOWROOMS TO SELL PHYSICAL PRODUCTS

First and foremost, Peloton stores are showrooms for the hardware (bikes, treadmills, and future products) that the company produces. As with Tesla cars, Apple devices, or Maytag appliances, potential customers can inspect, touch, and learn to use the products in the showrooms, even scheduling test rides on the bikes and runs and walks on the treadmills. The machines are sleek and beautiful, representing the style and culture of the New York–based Peloton, and the clean, open showrooms remind potential buyers the products need not be hidden like most exercise equipment. Between launch of its bike in 2013 and mid-2021, Peloton opened more than 100 retail showrooms in the United States, Canada, the UK, Germany, and Australia.

Since the Peloton team realized, in 2013, that selling an expensive, new concept online was challenging, showrooms have been central to selling bikes and later treads. In my interview with Foley, he explained to me that he spent countless hours in the early days selling bikes. He understood that riding with good music produced endorphins and that became part of the retail experience. While talking to prospects, Foley would probe potential customers on their interests and music tastes while adjusting the bike fit for them. He would then get them headphones and choose a class with their favorite type of music and vibe in mind and get them on a test ride. Foley said this process yielded him a sales success rate of 50 percent and it speaks to the interactive nature of the sales process for Peloton hardware. Test classes and use of the hardware in the stores is still the norm for Peloton, though the company is more sophisticated in its scheduling and planning of test classes. It is not yet the norm for most of the industry at this point, though in my research I went to see competitive products in their retail channels and many are learning from Peloton's success with branded showrooms, micro-stores, and retail teams, oftentimes next to Peloton showrooms.

For many Peloton customers, the showroom is the beginning of the brand experience. Samples of talented instructors and their heart-pounding classes and playlists give visitors a taste of the studio fitness experience that will stream into their homes if they purchase and subscribe to Peloton.

The design and layout of the stores has evolved to include private rooms for testing the products and as the number and reach of showrooms has grown, the staff has taken on a bigger frontline role in the sales and brand experience that potential and new customers receive. Moreover, because of the cost of the hardware, this is not always a simple one-visit sale. Phone calls, texts, and email follow up are part of the process. While not as flashy as the content or as sexy as the hardware side of the business, retail showrooms and teams have become central to capturing and engaging customers, the number-one job of any business. For many members, including me, the local retail team members become friends as we stop in often to check out new apparel lines, talk about the latest classes or discuss needed maintenance or upcoming products.

POSITIONING THE BRAND

The light, airy showrooms also serve as brand outposts. After creating a profitable, premium product and service and attracting a boatload of investment capital, Peloton is choosing prime retail locations to reach customers and position itself.

The company is choosing strategic locations and retail districts and malls that communicate quality, luxury, and cool. In the case of the new store in my neighborhood, Peloton's neighbors include Warby Parker, Apple, The North Face, Lululemon, Bonobos men's clothing, Georgetown Cupcake, Indochino menswear, a Sweetgreen restaurant, and an Amazon bookstore. All are ventures bringing innovative business models and experiences that wow growing lists of customers. The Peloton stores I visited in Denver, New York, Pennsylvania, Illinois, and Arizona had many of those same neighbors.

A BOUTIQUE TOO

The Peloton showrooms are also crucial distribution points for branded items such as leggings, hats, tanks, hoodies, and other goods. As the company is positioned as a premium provider in the fitness and well-being space, its apparel and other offerings have often been produced by established athleisure brands such as Craft, Lululemon, and Nike and newer entrants like Rhone and 4Laps. As the company has grown, the pace of new collection releases has appeared to pick up, often matching seasons and Peloton heritage celebrations, Artists Series, and other events.

Early on in my Peloton experience, when I saw Emily purchasing Peloton branded gear in place of Lululemon, a brand she had discovered in the early 2000s when we lived just a few blocks from its first U.S. store in San Francisco's Marina neighborhood, I knew Peloton apparel had big potential. I had been a Lululemon and Under Armour shareholder for periods of time and a Nike shareholder for my entire adult life. My gut told me to keep my eye on this side of Peloton's business and Peloton has continued to grow in this area.

The focus on athleisure, trucker caps, backpacks, and other soft goods may seem odd for a venture breaking a fitness paradigm (going to the gym) that has existed for thousands of years (the Greeks and Romans went to the gym to work out), but in reality, the merchandise serves a few important purposes.

First, the gear extends the brand. Most Peloton riders who own swag work out in it and often post it on social media while posting selfies and in studio pics. They also wear it proudly to Starbucks, other fitness studios and gyms, hockey rinks, vacations, and back-to-school nights. I've had interactions with strangers while wearing the merchandise on the street and at work.

The first piece of Peloton merchandise I bought myself was a black and grey, nylon track jacket made by athletic brand Ogio. It has a hood, great pockets, a Peloton logo on the front right chest and PELOTON printed across the shoulder blades. Within weeks of wearing the coat out and about, a middle-aged guy in Arlington, VA, stopped me at an ice rink to ask if I rode. I said yes, we exchanged pleasantries and leaderboard names (though I forgot his!) and that was it. But, it was clear to me by 2018, wearing Peloton merchandise "in the wild" would likely become the norm, just as people wearing team gear—college and professional —is a regular fashion choice across society. Oftentimes, as it has for me in hundreds of instances, the Peloton swag serves as a conversation starter.

Second, the branded merchandise brings in revenue to the retail showrooms. On the day of the Bethesda store opening, my wife and I spent more than $250. I bought a zip-up hoodie and a Peloton trucker hat, while Emily chose a pair of leggings and a wool baseball cap. We didn't need any of the items, but we were excited to be at the grand opening, seeing merchandise up close (rather than online), meeting Jess King, and we clearly loved Peloton. It felt no different from returning to visit the University of Michigan (our alma mater) and buying shirts, jerseys, hats, and just about anything else that a block M or "Go Blue" could be stamped on. The money we spent on branded swag during that one grand opening visit was more than six months of subscription fees to the Peloton service. This was serious revenue, and I began to think this could be huge down the road.

In Peloton's fiscal year 2020, the company reported almost $30 million worth of apparel. In February 2021, during a Goldman Sachs investor presentation, Foley remarked that the company had sold $45 million worth of apparel in Q2 2021. While that revenue is small relative to device sales and subscriptions, I am confident that this revenue stream could reach the hundreds of millions and billions annually as the membership swells and the brand grows.

The revenue of athletic apparel and soft goods relative to Peloton's monthly subscription fees is large, and the historical sales of Adidas, Nike, Lululemon, and others make the opportunity appear almost endless. In early 2021, Peloton and Adidas announced a collaboration including gear designed with Peloton instructors Cody Rigsby, Robin Arzón, and Ally Love; special classes; and more. The Adidas by Peloton campaign of March 2021 points to an enormous potential in apparel and other categories. Not much later, in September 2021, Peloton announced its own private label called Peloton Apparel.

In addition to the direct revenue that Peloton derives from apparel sales, Peloton has been awarding $100 boutique credits to Peloton members that refer others to buy a bike or tread. As my experience and others on social media illuminate, many members bring in new customers and take advantage of the $100 boutique credit.

I do not think that the original business model expected so much revenue or impact from merchandise, but it is a pleasant surprise and an indication of the strong community that Peloton has built around its members, instructors, and content. The use of boutique credits as a reward for referral has also become important in customer acquisition and branding.

COMMUNITY HUBS

When I entered the grand opening celebration for the Bethesda store at 10:45 am on a Thursday in early September 2018, there were already many customers inside (at least 30), most wearing branded merchandise they had purchased at other Peloton stores, in NYC at the Mothership, or via the online boutique. Some proudly sported their Century Ride T-shirts.

I was not the only home rider coming to meet instructor Jess King, check out the store, and mingle with other Peloton members and store staff. By that point, members were driving hours and crossing time zones and state borders to meet instructors at store openings and special events, so I was lucky to have Jess within walking distance.

When I entered the store, I was nervous about meeting Jess. I loved riding with her and was a regular viewer of her fun Instagram stories featuring commuters racing for commuter ferries to get to work in the NY metro. Through these stories I learned about Jess, her family, her dogs (Zeus and Chicken a la King), and many of her quirks.

Jess was scheduled to help open the Bethesda store at 11 am, but before I could figure out what I planned to say to her, some Peloton staff members I knew from the Virginia store welcomed me and ushered me to the back of the store to meet Jess. I mumbled how nice it was to meet her and how much I loved her classes. As with my first Matt Wilpers' interaction, I had no idea I would eventually interview Jess at Peloton headquarters a few months later. In that initial meeting, before the official store opening meet-and-greet began, when I was just another tongue-tied, shy home rider, Jess could not have been kinder and more welcoming.

When I returned in the official meet-and-greet line with my wife and some real life and Facebook Peloton friends, Jess was even warmer. Being with the people in that showroom seemed to be lighting her up.

My wife chatted with Jess about her time on *So You Think You Can Dance*. I lauded her Instagram account and the burpee exercise challenge she was leading on social media at that time—100 burpees per day for 30 days! She challenged me to join her, and within a few days I even posted a video of myself doing burpees on Instagram, something I never would done without a supportive Peloton community and King's challenge. I started to feel as if I was leading a secret double life. I had my regular life, but also a Peloton life, which included behaviors like standing in line to meet an indoor cycling instructor and posting awkward video selfies of myself doing burpees.

At the Bethesda store opening I met two Peloton members who have since become my friends online and another few that have become IRL friends. I also met more Peloton staffers, and they subsequently helped deal with our tread delivery and other questions that have come up related to Peloton products and services.

Pre-Covid, many Peloton members worked with store teams to celebrate their milestones of 100, 250, or 500 rides in the showrooms. The staff set up bikes, towels, water, and balloons for the celebrating member and their friends. Facebook and Instagram searches turn up pictures of the fun from all across the Peloton showroom universe. When the pandemic hit, the showroom teams shifted gears and began doing digital celebrations for members.

Nine days after the Bethesda showroom opened, my wife was invited to join two local riders and the store manager, Haley, before the store opened on a Sunday to ride live together in the store for a Jennifer Schreiber Sherman (JSS) ride. The other two riders were active in the JSS Tribe. That Sunday ride in the showroom was not a special occasion other than a way for those friends, and the showroom manager, to spend time sweating together enjoying Jenn Sherman, each other's company, and the bike. BTW, when people ride together in the showrooms, each rider wears headphones or earbuds.

A few months later, in February 2019, I would join some of those same JSS Tribe members in the showroom for a Sunday morning, pre-open live Jenn Sherman ride, and I used the bike in the street-facing window of the Bethesda showroom. It was an organized group ride named the JSS Showroom Showdown across more than 15 U.S. showrooms. A Maryland-based member named Miriam Feffer (#Feffer) came up with this friendly intra-JSS Tribe competition. It was another reason for

Peloton members to celebrate, and showroom managers were allowed to support members in this celebration.

When Foley and his co-founders created Peloton, they knew a challenge would be recreating the community feeling that many love in group boutique fitness classes such as indoor cycling, Orangetheory Fitness, Barry's Bootcamp, and others. With smart technology, talented instructors, and engaged customers, the company has managed to match those studio experiences with the majority of participants at home.

What the founding team did not expect was that the members would build a community off of the bike. The showrooms have played an important role in that growth, something not expected when the company began building them as part of the sales and onboarding experience. While not planned as part of the showroom strategy, it is no surprise the company has used retail showrooms to deepen community bonds and networks because that's how the members used the stores.

NEW YORK CITY STORY

As we are discussing the role of physical space in the rise of Peloton, it has to be noted that the Peloton story is a New York City story. The city has a great history in the industries of fashion and beauty, media, fitness, and especially boutique studios, with innovative indoor cycling brands such as SoulCycle and Flywheel coming out of New York. John Foley has repeatedly referred to New York city has the "Mesopotamian Valley of Fitness."

The company has committed to a massive headquarters of 350,000 square feet in Midtown. "New York City is where Peloton started, and it will continue to be our home as we scale our business globally," Foley said in the press release announcing the new headquarters. "For a long time, New York was considered to be an afterthought for tech startups, but it's now the second-highest-performing startup ecosystem in the world. As our brand lives at the intersection of fitness, technology, and media, this city is where the best talent can be found across all three of those industries."[41] In my conversation with Foley, he explained that being in New York would allow the venture to build to most talented, diverse, and creative workforce and workplace in technology.

The deal to move Peloton into new headquarters helped its commercial real estate brokers, Benjamin Birnbaum and Ben Shapiro, from Newmark Knight Frank, win breakout brokers of the year in 2019. Shapiro stated, "John Foley has a vision about what type of environment he wants to create. He wants to create the best office space in Manhattan to attract and retain top talent."[42] Physical space and place-based well-being are clearly seen as a competitive necessity as Peloton attempts to build the best company in the world to work for.

Peloton's mega studio, known as Peloton Studios New York (PSNY), with four production studios in Midtown Manhattan was slated to open to the public in March 2020, but due to Covid had not hosted any members or guests in classes when this book went to print. I was scheduled and booked to take four classes on the opening day and two classes on the second.[43] All of the classes were cancelled as mid-March 2020 was just when the United States was realizing the severity of the pandemic. The company began producing content in PSNY on an adjusted basis due to the pandemic later in 2020.

The nearly 40,000-square-foot PSNY is in a massive mixed-use development, Manhattan West, also slated to house a 60,000-square-foot Whole Foods. The development, with retail, office, and housing, will serve as a haven of health and well-being in the middle of Manhattan for employees, neighborhood residents, tourists, and others dwelling the tri-state area.

Brad Olson, chief business officer, made it clear during our interview that the members' full experience in visiting the studios was taken into consideration as the space was developed. The specifics were not shared with me and PSNY was not open to the public as of late 2021, but in an age of meetups, social media, smoothies, corporate retreats, the experiential economy, and branded athleisure, one can imagine that great spaces for a range of activities, including pics and vids, will be available when post-pandemic norms are established. Peloton opened a mega studio in London in September 2021 that will serve similar purposes for European markets.

From small family trips to group HRI's to the Official Peloton Homecoming hosting more than 3,000 members, the studio experience in New York is important to the Peloton community. Visiting the New York City studio space is aspirational, but very attainable for members and becomes part of the physical business model that makes Peloton such an engaging product. While the Mothership and the New York City DNA of Peloton were put on pause by the global pandemic, their role in Peloton's growth should not be overlooked.

Another simple reason that a physical New York City location matters to Peloton's success is that the city is a global media and entertainment capital. A New York location has made it easy for media outlets and journalists to access Peloton as a story, for the business and popular press as well as financial and technological outlets. On a day I was riding in the original cycling studio in 2019, there was a *Wall Street Journal* reporter in my class completing research for a story.

Also, on the talent side of the media business, famous personalities and entertainers have become big Peloton fans partly because the company came out of New York and media members and entertainers were physically located in the right place to become early adopters. This includes television figures such as NFL retiree Michael Strahan, talk show host Ellen DeGeneres, and *Good Morning America* anchor Robin Roberts. This has meant coverage for Peloton and its instructors via their media outlets and lots of social media love from these influencers.

HOTELS, CLUBS, APARTMENTS, AND MORE

Another way that Peloton has leveraged physical space to grow its revenues and community is placing bikes in shared spaces such as country clubs, apartment buildings, hotels, and office buildings. Peloton started doing this in 2017, and according to a January 2017 press release timed to the Consumer Electronics Show, it was a reaction to what the community of members wanted. "The launch of this new category for Peloton is truly a reaction to the demand of our dedicated rider community," Foley said. "Our community of riders love the experience so much that they want to engage with our products and our content wherever they go. Whether that's traveling to a hotel, going to their fitness club, or at their office gym, our riders want to continue enjoying the Peloton experience wherever they are. Launching this new commercial-grade bike with specialized hardware and software made perfect sense as the next step in the Peloton journey."[44]

Peloton partnered with Westin Hotels to start, but the bikes soon appeared across a range of hotels and families of brands. When this occurred, the Peloton community was excited and started using social networks to share locations of bikes. A Facebook group, Peloton Hotels and OntheGo, formed in February 2018 and offered a crowdsourced directory of bikes available for use. In June 2019, Peloton posted a Hotel Finder feature on its website for members to locate hotels with bikes.

While I have not yet chosen a hotel or resort based on whether it has Peloton bikes, my wife has phoned ahead multiple times and located bikes. She also has ridden at friends' homes, whether they were there or not. When we visited Chicago, Emily secured her friend Angie's (#willride4vino) garage code so she could ride; it did not matter that Angie and her family were out of town. Multiple postings show that whether a hotel has bikes does matter to many members, and they want the full details.

Beyond hotels, Peloton has sold bikes and group memberships to shared spaces such as apartment buildings, country clubs, and office buildings. I've met members online who ride at their offices and post frequently from their office and apartment gyms.

In March 2019, while visiting a college roommate in Denver, I learned that his apartment building had a Peloton bike in the gym. Of course, I could not resist trying the bike out and took a few short rides. I also visited the gym a couple of times to see if anyone was riding and ended up chatting with a guy in his mid to late 20s who had moved to Denver from New York to get involved in the cannabis industry. He had used the bike regularly since moving in.

The number of Peloton connected devices in shared facilities is minuscule relative to those in private homes; this market is large and potentially offers more consistent cash flows over time. In late 2020, Peloton acquired Precor, an old school U.S.-based fitness equipment maker. Precor has deep roots in commercial sales and will be used to help Peloton gain market share.

In discussing the Precor acquisition on the February 5, 2021, earnings call, John Foley stated, "Precor's product portfolio and sales team will also accelerate our commercial business where we see a significant opportunity to grow Precor's franchise while introducing the Peloton platform to an even greater number of fitness enthusiasts and channels such as hospitality, multi-unit residential buildings, corporate campuses, and colleges and universities."[45] In fall 2021, Peloton announced the creation of a single platform allowing commercial buyers access to both Peloton and Precor products.[46]

What makes this potentially even more interesting is that I have observed many, many Peloton connected products being purchased by customers who discover the product in a shared facility. In 2019, while I was riding in the Peloton showroom in the King of Prussia Mall outside of Philadelphia, I witnessed a woman explaining to her husband that she could no longer share the Peloton in their building's fitness room and needed her own. It is not hard to imagine millions of office workers, apartment renters and students, and faculty and staff across higher education having access to the Peloton platform; many will eventually decide they want their own hardware.

VERTICAL INTEGRATION: DESIGN, PRODUCE, WAREHOUSE, AND DELIVER

While I missed the delivery of our initial bike because the purchase was done behind my back, once I started researching, I quickly learned how big and heavy the bikes were and that delivery could be challenging. Co-founder Tom Cortese, in a 2017 speech I watched online, explained that small items were easy to deliver in our economy, but large items such as furniture and appliances often came down to brawn at the expense of customer experience.[47]

Because of the challenges inherent in delivering large items, Peloton had to rely on third parties for delivery, installation, and member onboarding initially. If one looks back at the Peloton Kickstarter campaign in 2013 and views the comments section, it was clear from the start that delivery was going to be hard. Comments communicate much confusion as USPS was handling those earliest deliveries and even Peloton itself conceded that shipping partnerships were challenging,

By now you should have received a form from the Kickstarter site asking you for your shipping address. We're feeding this information to our shipping partners to begin setting up for nationwide delivery. The total, packaged weight of the bike shipment is around 150 pounds. Because of the weight, traditional carriers like UPS, FedEx, and USPS are not able to deliver the bike through their regular routes on their "small pack" trucks. This is a "freight" shipment. There is a ton of cost when moving large, heavy boxes around the country and we've been very busy setting up relationships with the most efficient and reliable carriers to deliver bikes to everyone at the lowest cost with the greatest ease. We'll continue to send more shipping details as we learn more.[48]

While Peloton moved from USPS to larger, commercial logistics firms such as XPO, the team realized that Peloton needed to control the delivery and onboarding process as much as possible because their brand identity demanded a premium experience from purchase through usage. Having a third party deliver hardware was a hole in the process and potentially could sink the brand identity and hurt the member experience. It made no sense to buy an expensive, cutting-edge, beautiful bike in a showroom and then have a third-party, appliance delivery team show up to drop it off and try explain to the new member how to use it.

Peloton has spent hundreds of millions of dollars building out warehouse and distribution facilities across the United States, deploying Peloton branded Mercedes delivery vans, and hiring and training teams of operations and service people across the world. This logistical network of warehouse and distribution centers, fleets and teams is beginning to provide Peloton more control over direct contact with its customers and provides strength and flexibility as their model grows and evolves.

In 2020, Peloton was making great headway on logistics and pre-pandemic was delivering more than 50 percent of its products with its own fleets and people.[49] The pandemic changed all that as demand spiked and Peloton had to go back to relying on third-party logistical firms such as XPO and JB Hunt. This put Peloton back into a position it was in in its early years and may again take them years to recover from. While the increased demand was surely welcome, the loss of control and the logistical stress caused by the pandemic brought Peloton challenges it had hoped to build out of years before. In 2021, Peloton announced it was building a factory in Ohio, highlighting once again the focus on controlling the physical and logistical side of its business model.

THE CENTRAL ROLE OF PHYSICAL SPACE IN A DIGITAL WORLD

The Peloton experience, including retail showrooms, studio visits, factories, warehousing and fulfilment, and sweaty, physical community engagement is further evidence that the most innovative organizations in our economy, from Nike and Tesla to Airbnb and Apple, leverage location and physical and digital assets to attract, retain, and strengthen their relationships with their customers and talent. From producing and selling hardware and content to building and hosting community, physical spaces have helped Peloton differentiate itself, create value and illuminate a path to growth, success, and customer well-being in the twenty-first century economy.

CHAPTER 6

SEARCHING FOR SWEAT, FINDING A COMMUNITY

In the 25 or so years before Peloton, I probably made about 20 new friends, mostly through college, assorted workplaces, graduate schools, and eventually my kids and their activities. After 18 months of Peloton membership, I easily surpassed that adult new-friends total, and moreover, was in touch with countless Peloton people across multiple platforms.

As my personal experience began to look like some of what I was researching and observing, it was becoming abundantly clear that the community that I found and joined was one of the key values Peloton delivers to members. The living, breathing, sweating community of Peloton members, online groups, instructors, employees, and others that emerged amazed me as both a member and an entrepreneurship researcher.

When I first reluctantly clipped into the Peloton bike, regretting the memory of my adult hockey performance and fearing eternal boredom on a traditional treadmill, I was looking for a new sweat. That was all. Community, new friends, greater fitness knowledge, branded apparel, physical challenges, badges, and meetups were not on my must-have or wish list.

Getting deeply entrenched in the community myself meant riding before dawn with people from New York to South Carolina and Texas; congratulating people on their engagements, weight loss, and kids' graduations; and sending condolences for the loss of pets, parents, siblings, and even lost pregnancies. It was not long before I had a community stretching across the country, from Florida to Alaska, and it was connected by sweat.

I went from observing to participating, just as Jane Goodall experienced in Tanzania researching chimpanzees. I did not expect this when I clipped in and even when I started to study the community in early 2017, when the company had fewer than 100,000 subscribers and the Peloton Facebook page had a little over 20,000 followers.

The organic growth and incredible power of the community is one of the core reasons that Peloton is worthy of study and emulation by other organizations. The positive value it generates for both the members and the company is unique and massive.

INNOVATION AND THE UNEXPECTED SUCCESS: THE EMERGENCE OF PELOTON COMMUNITY

In 1985, management guru Peter Drucker published his groundbreaking book *Innovation and Entrepreneurship*. While many knew there were cracks in the industrial economy in the late 1970s and mid-1980s, Drucker was early in identifying the structural transition to entrepreneurship and innovation that was occurring. Most others were trying to protect and revive traditional corporate strategies and entities.

Drucker identified seven sources from which innovative opportunities emerge. Some, such as new knowledge (technology), are hard to predict and rely on time and countless factors to come to fruition. Others, such as demographics (women working outside the home in the 1960s) and changes in the public's tastes or preferences (to-go meals versus sit-down restaurants), are easier to spot and try to exploit.

Drucker points to "the unexpected success" as the easiest and simplest source of innovative opportunities to identify. This refers to opportunities created when customers and other participants in our economy act in unexpected ways, but their behaviors and needs can be exploited by innovators willing to follow their lead in this unplanned direction. The behavior-based concept of the unexpected is the opposite of economists who argue that people and organizations act in rational ways, a notion that history books and court systems will refute. For entrepreneurs and innovators, the key is spotting unexpected successes and behaviors related to them and creating products, services, and strategies to meet and extend them.

In his book, Drucker offers the example of Macy's department store in the 1950s observing that its customers were increasingly interested in buying appliances, which earned higher margins, hardly ever were returned, and could not be stolen. Unfortunately for Macy's of that period and later, the management ignored and even battled the unexpected customer behavior. When Drucker inquired as to why the leadership was trying to tamp down on these sales, which also brought in more customers to the fashion side of the business, the chairman of Macy's stated, "In this kind of store, it is normal and healthy for fashion to produce 70 percent of sales. Appliance sales have grown so fast that they now account for three-fifths. And that's abnormal. We've tried everything we know to make fashion grow to restore the normal ratio, but nothing works. The only thing left now is to push appliance sales down to where they should be."[50]

Why would Macy's leaders not follow their customers and expand appliance offerings? The leaders were following the traditional department store strategy of focusing on apparel and fashion. Rival Bloomingdale's created a housewares and appliances division to capture and profit from unexpected consumer behavior of the era and vaulted from the number-four department store to number two in New York on the back of its appliance success. In his analysis of the case, Drucker points out that it would take decades for Macy's to successfully get back into the appliance business.

Having a dedicated community of customers is a common attribute of many successful businesses, from marketplaces such as eBay and local farmer's markets to Microsoft programs, Harley-Davidson motorcycles, and Lego building bricks. Like many recent customer communities, the Peloton crowd has grown via social media, low-cost computing, mobile devices, and communication technology.

One important and fascinating thing in Peloton's case is that the community emerged immediately and independently from the company, and it turned into one of the company's most powerful value creators. The community truly has helped define and create the brand. Both the members and the company have become unexpectedly reliant on the growing community, from the leaderboards and Facebook groups to Etsy stores and podcasts.

THE VALUE OF THE PELOTON COMMUNITY FOR MEMBERS

The Peloton community was initially created by members trying to help each other with their new bikes and meet other members. The community provides incredible value to Peloton members in the form of knowledge, accountability, positivity, friendship, support, and acceptance. Reminder: I was not thinking of any of those things when I first tried the bike.

First and foremost, the community emerged out of the need to fill the knowledge gap for new users. The first Peloton riders between 2014 to 2016 were early adopters and found one another online to help share information, provide feedback on classes and equipment, and put more information behind the leaderboard names that they were riding with. Early Peloton riders found each other in the New York studio and online.

Over time as Peloton has grown and matured, official Peloton channels have begun to provide incredible information for members via the retail showroom teams, delivery, websites, blogs, and other methods. However, the community has done the heavy lifting since the beginning and continues to play an outsized role in the company's growth. Knowledge about the bike, instructors, classes, and other members is one of the great values that the community continues to provide.

Whether it is a basic question—how does one clip out, or what is the difference between HIIT rides and *tabata* rides—or more detailed information on past rides or long-running programming, the Peloton community can assist. The Peloton community continues to answer the newbie inquiries as well as the complex. Answers can be informative or wrong or contentious or hilarious or rude. I have heard of families splitting over the question of why there is no pause button.

The pause issue (the ability to pause an on-demand class or a live class—as if one had a DVR on the bike) has been controversial since the earliest days of Peloton. Some members believe a pause button takes away the dynamism of the leaderboard and makes the class less like a real studio class (where there is no pause). Others argue that life (kids, work calls, calls of nature, a forgotten towel or water bottle) gets in the way and the ability to pause a class is a basic feature that puts members first.

Peloton's resident community poet, member Howard Godnick (#Godnick), wrote a poem about the divisive issue years before it was resolved. (Peloton eventually announced a pause function during May 2021, promising that it would not impact the integrity of the leaderboard.) Godnick represented countless members when he wrote:

Pause

It's hardly a secret

I've made my thoughts known
When this page was two hundred
And then now that it's grown

For the stay at home parents
Caring for kids and the rest
When the doorbell does ring
And it's your neighbor, the pest

When your towel does drop
To the floor, all alone
Playing hooky from work
And it's your boss on the phone

We all have our missions
We all have a cause
I have begged them and pleaded
For a button to pause

It won't hurt nobody
So I ask again, Lord
Behoove me, remove me
From that dang leaderboard

Point out my persistence
Make fun of my flaws
But beseech me this one thing
Lord, let my bike pause

While not every argument or dispute in the Peloton community is handled creatively or demands as much attention as the pause button issue, the community shares ideas, opinions, and information rather effectively.

In many cases FAQs, PDFs, and massive Reddit repositories have been created by the community for the community.

Interesting, but not surprising is that questions beyond Peloton end up taking a portion of the community's time and attention. These NPR ("not Peloton related") questions and posts are in fact where many bonds among community members are built.

John Bernstein (#YukonJack), a well-known member of the community, bought the Peloton bike in 2015 after visiting the studio in New York with his brother. He posts frequently on Peloton social media pages and hosts a virtual Peloton cocktail party each Friday on the main Facebook page. The Friday cocktail thread draws thousands each week that typically share their milestones from the week, drink of choice, and well wishes for the community. When I interviewed Bernstein, he explained that there was a real desire among early riders to communicate and share information.

Bernstein told me that the early riders lacked knowledge about the bike, instructors, and classes, and they were excited to connect with others who had found this amazing fitness product. The early adopters had few people in their lives to discuss Peloton with, so they searched one another out online and began connecting on social media to share knowledge and their happiness. In those early days, even before the pandemic, it was hard to get non-Peloton members to want to discuss the bike, the instructors, or how much fun working out could be. The community made it much easier to scratch one's Peloton itch and often get sucked down a rabbit hole.

MEMBERSHIP TO FRIENDSHIP

Each class is a live, one-time affair like an *Oprah* episode or a drive-time talk-radio show. The instructors' personalities have transformed class experiences into events that many members want to participate in and talk about. Because Peloton members are spread across time and space, the internet, and specifically Facebook and other social media platforms, have become a vital method for them to share information and connect around the class content—before, after, and even during classes.

The uniqueness of classes is driven by structure (hard climbs, long intervals, or fun themes), the music playlist, the instructor (and their comments and stories), and the community members on the leaderboard, (live or on demand, the riders all appear on the leaderboard—which can also be hidden). Every class provides a shared experience for all who took it, no matter when, or how well they performed.

In many ways a Peloton class is similar to a sporting event or a concert, but in a Peloton class, all the members participate and have the sweat, muscle strain, and pride to prove it. While everyone can feel the drama and emotion of a dramatic sporting event, all participants in a Peloton class get to actually put in the work to get that dramatic moment of achievement for themselves. Sometimes, by the way, the experience could be defeat, where a member cannot hold the pace or resistance that is recommended or one's legs crap out for an interval or climb. Either way, the shared experience of burning lungs and swollen legs in a great cycling class or tread bootcamp deepens the community and the bonds between members regardless of whether they ever meet in real life.

A shared class, favorite instructor, or Peloton meme, is often a starting point for real relationships and awareness of people's lives beyond the Peloton leaderboard begins to develop. A relationship might go from being in the same Peloton Facebook group to becoming Facebook friends, and then following one another on Instagram. Before one knows it, scheduled rides occur with Peloton friends from across the country, meetups in New York are planned and holiday gifts exchanged.

This kind of relationship and friendship building through shared experiences mimics that of real life, but the default settings of amazing Peloton content and instructors and the shared growth mindset of members makes relationship creation easier and more positive from the start. In 2019, I met Peloton member Nick G (#SolarCoaster) when he joined a Facebook riding group I was part of. It turned out he grew up in Chicago, not far from me. From there I joined his Power Zone team and between the various groups and a group ride in New York at the studio, a friendship formed. Later in 2019, I would visit Nick and share a fun coffee session while in his neck of the woods on Long Island. In 2021, in my return visit to Long Island, I would once again hang out with Nick. I look forward to many more visits and rides with Nick. As my friendship with Nick highlights, because much of this takes place online, both in larger official groups and smaller subgroups, friendship or relationship building often occurs rather easily. A user can post an intention to take a ride and ask for people to join in. The reason could be a milestone ride, or an anniversary of something, or just a desire for more Peloton friends. It is easy to post and reply and join the class. Members respond to these calls to ride or join groups or challenges as people want to connect around Peloton and its content.

REBOOTING WITH POSITIVE VIBES

These easy-forming, digital-first Peloton relationships offer members both an escape from their reality and also a chance to redefine and reinvent themselves. The first step in this process is picking a leaderboard name and taking classes. Creating a leaderboard name and entering the Peloton community in classes, on social media, and in meetups is a fresh start for new members, like entering college or moving to a new city where no one knows you. Of course, many members have no need to redefine themselves, but for others, the Peloton experience is a reboot. Many of the new members from the Covid pandemic cohort had no choice but to reboot as their regular gyms and communities were stripped from them.

This ethos or mindset of rebirth, rebuilding, or redefining often is led by the instructors via classes—they are fitness instructors after all. It continues through the members and their postings, features such as badges and personal bests, marketing and media materials with slogans such as "Together We Go Far," hugely popular events such as the annual All for One classes and challenges, and online and real-world groups created by members.

Peloton has sold happiness and the celebration of individual strength and self-value from the minute I began riding the bike and tracking the company's progress. There is no doubt in my mind that the positivity and supportive nature of the community also has been embraced because it is such a contrast to the negativity of much of modern society and media.

It is easy to be mean and snarky online, but the Peloton experience shows it's just as easy to be kind, supportive, and welcoming. It is why I would rather scroll through a few Peloton

Facebook groups and hear about people's hard classes and progress than read another news story about divisive American politics, angry global leaders, and celebrity squabbles and misdeeds.

In my years of sweating my way around the Peloton community, I have seen teenagers battling cancer riding and celebrating life as well as middle-aged mothers, widower grandfathers, and out-of-shape former professional athletes, all sweating together to move forward. All are embraced by the community. No struggle or challenge is dismissed and those asking for help seem to find it.

The platform provides members an opportunity to redefine and rebuild themselves no matter who they are or where they come from. For many, Peloton has allowed them to call themselves an athlete or runner and believe it and live it for the first time in their life.

Also, the positivity of the Peloton platform offers everyone an opportunity to be a teammate and ally, and spread positivity in the world even if their workplace, home life, or media choices don't always do so. It costs me nothing to "love" someone's post on Facebook or high-five them while riding. So I do do those things often—whether during a live or on-demand class or on someone's Instagram or Facebook post about their milestone or personal record or fun morning class. Of course, it also makes me feel good that I might be making someone else feel good. A win-win for all involved.

ACCOUNTABILITY

A further value for members is that engaging in the community creates accountability on the Peloton platform. Community accountability, from the military to micro-financing and crowdfunding, is a feature that has worked for humans for a long time.

For community members, the accountability ranges from the specific and real, such as participating in a scheduled ride or a challenge where reporting is expected to more "habitual" accountability such as riding Tuesday *tabata* with a group or completing all the Sunday football rides with the JSS Tribe or a group of friends. People in the community begin to recognize leaderboard names and patterns, and very often this familiarity creates accountability, which ultimately leads to more successful outcomes in health and well-being.

In an interesting twist, members also begin to feel accountability to instructors to show up for their rides and series that we love so much. As I mentioned earlier, I felt challenged and accountable to Jess King when we discussed her daily burpee challenge.

When Peloton tread instructor Becs Gentry was preparing for the 2021 British Olympic marathon trials, I joined hundreds of other Peloton owners to send her off with good luck on her last live class before the race in March 2021. Many of us felt grateful to train and learn from her and wanted to show her our gratitude by showing up before she went off to compete for a spot on team Great Britain. I also woke up in the middle of the night to stream the race live and was truly proud when Becs finished fourth and set her own personal best marathon time. Of course I took Becs' first live run when she returned from the trials.

From accountability and personal redefinition to knowledge and new friends, the Peloton community connects a sizable, diverse range of people from across the United States and the globe and gives them real community benefits in a world where the loss of community has been decried for years. No more neighborhoods, local little leagues, or fraternal groups. Bowling alone indeed, as Robert Putnam wrote when observing the loss of community institutions in the United States.[51]

It is common for instructors and members to say, "Your ride is your ride." Participation in the community can be as great or as little as any member wants. As Jenn Sherman pointed out during our interview, "If you've got a bike, you do know that the community exists; it's there for you." Jenn continued, "It's your choice whether you want to go deep and really be involved in it."

To me it is obvious that millions of people want to be part of the Peloton community that the founding team, early members, and instructors identified and built. Moreover, it is a feature of the business model that makes Peloton truly different, even if it was unexpected.

THE VALUE OF COMMUNITY FOR THE PELOTON TEAM

For the Peloton team, including the founders, senior managers, instructors, and frontline workers, the community has been a surprise and an asset to be leveraged to expand and improve the business model and the value it generates for the members and others. The community, with its own mind and effort, has led the way on many different fronts.

The community created the first online groups and planned the earliest home rider studio visits for members to come together physically to celebrate. The large, annual company-sponsored version is now called Homecoming, takes place in May, and pre-pandemic, brought thousands of members to New York, much like a college homecoming brings a range of community members together to celebrate around a shared institution and spirit. Members also offer ideas and inspiration for products; features on the platform, including challenges and social impact campaigns; and class, music, and programming styles.

The choice of the company name Peloton is a clear nod to the founding team's goal to create a sense of community and group effort, like the pack of cyclists in a road race or the feel of an indoor cycling or yoga class at a local gym or boutique studio. Peloton's founders spent time in boutique fitness classes and endurance sports, and they understood the value of the group in performance and the achievement of goals.

However, the community that was created (and continues to evolve around the Peloton platform) was beyond anything the team could have imagined in terms of scale, scope, and impact on members, employees, and the company.

The unexpected success, growth, and nature of the community is something that almost all of my interview subjects from Peloton acknowledged and respected deeply. No one took the community and its role in the Peloton story for granted. The company continues to preach that the member experience is at the center of everything Peloton does. Peloton has done a good job of listening and responding to member and community feedback in order to improve.

An example of customer behavior playing out and Peloton responding can be seen in the cameras that come installed on the hardware. Bikes and treads come with cameras and the ability for members to video chat with others while taking classes. The assumption being that members might want to communicate with voice and video during class. Personally, I have only participated in a handful of video chats on a Peloton product and in each case the other party called me, before a class, and I hustled them off quickly, finding it challenging to talk as I prepared to ride and warm up.

That said, the Peloton team's instinct that members would want to communicate was correct, and a feature called the "high five" was introduced in May 2018. This allowed a member to tap a little hand icon next to another member's name on the leaderboard, delivering a digital high five to the other member during a workout.

For the recipient, a small notification appears on their screen that so-and-so has high-fived. Receiving and giving high fives is not intrusive and demands no immediate response or words, which are often hard to get out during classes. The high five in essence is a simple way to acknowledge a challenging or fun part of a class, congratulate the member on a milestone or a shout-out from the instructor, or even to try to push the person a little harder during a class.

Heck, if I see members with locations in Chicagoland (where I was born and raised), Maryland (where I live), Virginia (where I work), or Phoenix (where my parents have a vacation home), I will almost always give them a high five. If someone with a funny or inspiring leaderboard name or hashtag is near me on the leaderboard, I may throw a high five their way. Similar to a "like" or quick positive comment on social media, the Peloton high five, live or on demand, is a simple way to share a little positivity during a class—something I often crave in the dark morning hours or during hard pushes.

The leaderboard high five is a simpler communication to deliver and receive than the video chat, and it has become a great community feature that members enjoy. The high five also highlights that simple acts can build bonds and strengthen relationships.

The high five also illustrates a crucial concept that much of the value in the community comes from member-to-member interactions during the day-to-day moments that members share in classes, on social media and in real life. These simple shared moments, taking a 6:00 am *tabata* class or a Friday DJ class, slowly strengthen the community bonds across Peloton in an organic manner that some of the bigger events and celebrations cannot.

Also, by allowing the members to engage one another during classes, it takes some of the pressure off of instructors to provide shout-outs to members. As the leaderboards grow, the ability for instructors to provide acknowledgments to individual members has become more difficult. Moreover, some instructors are more prone to give shout-outs than others, and even that may vary ride by ride. By letting community members high-five one another during classes and to identify themselves with hashtags and locations, Peloton is allowing members to play a bigger role in creating value for other members and the overall Peloton platform.

Additionally, features such as the high five, here now (where members taking on-demand classes can see which other members are also taking that class at that time), simple hashtags, and other elements allow members to bring live energy to the class even if it is not live.

Again, the theme is that the community and the members are bringing life and engagement to the class even if there is no live instructor. Peloton will likely continue to develop and support activities and features that enable communication and engagement between members.

Of course, the members also let Peloton leadership know when there are issues that make them unhappy. For example, in early 2019 Peloton began stocking plus-size items in its boutique. This was because many of its most ardent riders could not purchase and wear Peloton merchandise. In fact, it all began when member Phill Powell (#Catchpow) could not fit into his well-earned Century Ride shirt. Phill created a Peloton group for larger riders. Eventually the lack of larger sizes became an issue shared across the entire online community. Peloton leadership even met member Richelle Martin (#XXLBeachMama) of Frisco, Texas, a leader of the group, to discuss the lack of items and has moved to take action and expand apparel options.[52]

PURE DATA

One of the key ways that the community helps the Peloton leadership and management is through the massive amounts of data provided through member's behavior on the platform. Many other technology firms interact with their customers through digital methods. Amazon has search and purchase histories, and Netflix has viewing history and watch lists. Similarly, Peloton has a treasure trove of user behavior that it gathers when members log in to use their membership.

Perhaps the most basic, but direct and insightful data come from the members' choice of classes, including fitness disciplines, lengths, styles, day and time, live versus on demand, instructor, and post-class rankings. According to multiple Peloton team members I spoke with, the most basic but powerful data point is: Did the member complete the class?

When I spent time with Brad Olson, Peloton's chief business officer, in January 2019, he told me that the company tracks hundreds of thousands of data points from many sources. Examples include support tickets that come in and class ratings to social media comments and email open rates. One such qualitative source of data is the "Feature Friday" thread on Facebook where members share their desires and ideas with the company and one another. Members "like" and "love" and comment on each other's suggestions to show support.

Jayvee Nava, Peloton's VP of Community, oversees the "Feature Friday" post and has become the face of the company on Facebook and an important part and point of contact in the Peloton community. Jayvee has been with Peloton since 2014, starting in studio operations. Nava's long tenure and regular presence online matters to many community members, including those that came to the studio in the earliest days.

According to Olson, the mass of data and information gets sorted and distributed to colleagues across the company, influencing everything from hardware and software features to marketing and content creation. Olson joked to me about how valuable the data reports are considered across the company because they provide so much insight into members and that drives the member first organization.

AMBASSADORS AND
SALESPEOPLE OR MEMBERS?

Probably the most important value that the Peloton community provides to the company is that of ambassadors and salespeople for the brand. Many members, from the earliest riders to the most recent digital users, fall in love with the product, the instructors, the community and the company. They fall for the same reasons I did: it's fun, convenient, a great workout, and full of choices that give the members control of their workout program and classes. This has meant a growing army of members who talk about, post about, and think about their workouts, Peloton, and the community a lot.

From the moment I began really observing Peloton, it was obvious that users were happy, and many were all too willing to talk about it. In fact, some members take this role of spreading the gospel seriously and go out of their way to share their happiness and encourage people to check out Peloton.

Whether Marketing 101 at community colleges or Advanced Marketing Analytics at elite MBA programs, everyone knows that word of mouth is the most powerful marketing mechanism there is. Companies can and do spend a great deal of money on advertising, from local radio spots to Super Bowl ads and viral videos for social media, however, at the end of the day, a happy customer sharing a positive experience is the most powerful sales tool there is.

It's not hard to find Peloton members willing to talk about their bikes, treads, or workouts to the point of obnoxiousness. I reached that point by early 2018. I was like the father in *My Big Fat Greek Wedding*, but instead of wanting to put Windex spray on everything, I believed that a Peloton membership, a bike or tread or digital, was the answer for anything that ailed almost anyone. I even got dinged in a student review for talking about Peloton too much. There was a period of time when I was a vegan and a Peloton enthusiast; a truly insufferable species.

In March 2021, *The Jimmy Kimmel Show* produced a video sketch titled "Teloton - Because You Won't Shut Up About Your Stupid Bike," in which a newbie Peloton rider becomes obsessed and prattles on incessantly about their Peloton experience. The sketch went on to promote a fictional dial in-service called Teloton (a play on telephone and Peloton) that Peloton members can call in to, to drone on about their rides, instructors, and just about any other thought they have while riding. At one point in the bit, the headband wearing, bespectacled, dadbod-owning Peloton rider vulnerably admits, "This bike hasn't just changed me, it saved me." By the end of the sketch, even the certified *Telotalker* operator finds the Peloton member too much to handle.

My exploration of the Peloton community led me to observe and meet a startling diversity of people that have used the Peloton platform to make themselves deliriously happy and much healthier, in some cases truly reinventing themselves. This means the company has evangelists of all types drinking the Kool-Aid and spreading the word. This diversity supports the company in marketing across society.

As we have seen, the community does heavy lifting by developing new ideas, providing direct feedback to each other and the company, and keeping the overall community vibrant, engaged, and positive in and beyond the classes. The massive, organic Peloton community has played an outsized and almost independent role in the company's success.

SELECT PEOPLE AND GROUPS
OF THE PELOTON COMMUNITY

Like any community or subculture, there are regular members and groups of members that you may come across if you spend some time with the Peloton community—either in classes, online, or in person in the studios, showrooms, or at special events.

As with anything Peloton related, each member will have their own experience in the community. In the following section, I share some of the people and groups I have observed, and in many cases, spent time with over my years on the Peloton platform.

PELO CELEBRITIES

One of the fascinating parts of the community's growth is the rise of what might be called Pelo Celebrities. They are different from the real-world celebrity members on the Peloton platform covered in Chapter 3.

Pelo Celebrities are members who have become well known in the community. Their reasons for being well known are varied, but in most cases social media plays a role. Presence in the studios in New York and at other Peloton events (store openings, Homecoming, etc.) also affects the achievement of Pelo Celebrity status.

In some ways, this reads like a fraternity roster or some fantasy world like Harry Potter, with nonsensical leaderboard names and alternative currencies and social norms. In the Peloton world, often times, goofy fun or hard challenges, with a load of sweat is exactly what the community wants and generates for itself.

The role that social media, including Facebook, Instagram, and Reddit, play in the creation of celebrities in the Peloton community cannot be underscored enough. It provides countless touch points for members to engage with one another and the various subgroups in the community. Instructor shout-outs during classes can create celebrity in an instant. Special events, local meetups, hanging out in the studios, participating in Peloton and related challenges—instructor and member comments and reshares and more also help create celebrities across the community.

Remember, for many, the Peloton platform and community provide an escape and a chance for people to redefine themselves in a supportive and safe environment. The Pelo Celebrities highlight this in a vivid way. In many cases, we know almost nothing about our Peloton friends and their real lives when we begin to get to know them via Peloton because there is often no physical connection or evidence that we can see with our own eyes. Friends from one of my Peloton groups continually joked to one another that they were "not an ax murderer" as they made plans to visit the studios and share a New York City hotel with other members, even though they had yet to meet in real life. It is as if we have complete faith that a person's Peloton membership makes them good people.

HOWARD GODNICK (#GODNICK)

Like Prince, Madonna, and Pelé, the first Pelo Celebrity that I became aware of was known by just one name: Godnick. I noticed Howard Godnick, a middle-aged lawyer, because he regularly posted Peloton related poems to the main Peloton Facebook page. The poems were silly and simple; with a limerick feel. Godnick's rhymes covered rides, his health conditions (including heart attacks), and news of the day that mattered to the Peloton community. His work often mentions the pause button—his full poem about the controversy was shared earlier in the chapter.

I slowly learned that Godnick was an early and devoted Peloton member and suffered some serious medical issues before becoming a Peloton rider. His mantra, "You didn't die, you have to live," is mentioned often in his posts and poems; yes, some of Godnick's work takes a serious turn. Godnick was also a regular in-studio rider with Jenn Sherman and was shouted out often, so I began to match the poems to classes and his real-life existence in the studio.

I also learned that Godnick delivered a speech titled "Wash Your Hair" at a 2017 TEDx Bergen Community College event. (Like many of the early players in this Peloton story, Godnick was based out of the New York City metro region.) Eventually I watched his talk and it was moving, and covering his near-death experience, with the tag line, "You didn't die, you have to live." The talk helps explain much of his fun and loving approach to Peloton, poetry, and life.

During one of my trips to the Mothership to ride live in the studio, I met Godnick as he was holding court in the small waiting area of the original studio on 23rd Street in Chelsea. Godnick sat relaxed on one of the worn out, leather couches and was wearing one of his signature "dad hats." Home riders were swirling about, excited to see him in the flesh and actually meet him; I was also excited to meet him. Some of the home riders requested pictures with him, wanting to document their meeting of Godnick at the studio.

While Howard Godnick is likely one of a 100,000 middle-aged lawyers with health issues, in that small indoor bike studio in New York City, and for millions on the Peloton platform, he is a point of connection and humor and hope for people from all over the world trying to lead happier, healthier, and better lives.

After meeting Godnick, I continued to read his posts on Facebook, see him on various rides, and hear his many shout-outs. I was neither a fanboy nor a friend, but in early 2020 I read the news that Godnick had suffered another medical emergency, this time in my hometown airport, O'Hare. "You didn't die, you have to live."

I eventually talked with Howard and learned about his path to Peloton, his views on its successes and growth, and how much the Peloton subgroup Jenn's Menn stuck together during the pandemic. Howard is an icon in the Pelo-world and has chosen to share his views, humor, and life with the community. "You didn't die, you have to live," is not my mantra, but it is now in my bag of tricks, and I do think of it often. Thank you, Godnick.

Unfortunately, in late November 2021, as this manuscript moved through the layout process, Howard Godnick passed away unexpectedly at the age of 63. An immediate outpouring of sadness and gratitude filled large parts of the Peloton community, with the shocking realization that such a big driver of Peloton's early community was gone. Stories, pictures, and memories flooded social media from members, instructors, and Peloton leadership. Christine D'Ercole dedicated a ride to Godnick and on November 30th, Jenn Sherman led thousands live in a tear-filled tribute ride she programmed for Howard, her friend from the original Mothership.

JOHN AND ERICA MILLS
(#RUNLIFTANDLIVE AND
#ERICAMGETFIT)

While Godnick caught my attention with what appeared at first glance to be silly poems, John Mills and his wife, Erica, flew onto my radar with a video posted by John. It showed Erica riding a Peloton in their home, with the Peloton bike class she was taking projected on a big screen on the wall, like a really big screen, like something at a summer camp. As Erica rode, John was dancing to the music from the class, moving around the room and Erica. It was obvious John was as excited about the class as Erica was, even if he was not on the bike. The short video posted to the Peloton Facebook page was just a few minutes long and was time-lapsed highlights of Erica taking the class and John moving around. The video had special effects added to it as well, the type of effects that some of my students might add to their video presentations and PowerPoints during transitions.

That first Mills video I watched hit me hard, like some of the earlier videos of people I saw riding with disco lights in their homes. The Mills video, however, was taking it to another level. There were two people in this video, and it was unclear to me who was filming. The screen where the class was projected was large, not something you just pick up at Costco or Best Buy and the video that was posted to Facebook, with special effects and text, was edited to give a real, time-lapsed taste of the class that Erica completed and the joy it provided.

It turned out that John and Erica lived in Connecticut, had grown children, and were regular visitors to the Peloton studios and public events. Most important, John produced a range of fitness and Peloton content, from little gifs to full sketches where he plays the roles of various Peloton instructors while using dime-store disguises he buys on Amazon. Mills would take storylines and clips from movies and TV shows and use them to make fun spoofs of Peloton, the company, instructors, and members. Mills was creative, technical, and passionate, and it all came through in the videos. Members loved his work, as did instructors and the company.

When I interviewed John during the summer of 2020, he told me he initially purchased the Peloton for Erica in 2016. John had watched for a few years as Erica battled to get bikes in indoor cycling classes just as John Foley had. Mills told me of occasions where people were upset that Erica reserved "their" bike. John Mills had been checking out Peloton online for a few years and then finally decided to buy the bike for Erica in 2016 to solve the problems Erica faced trying to get to her indoor cycling classes.

While waiting for the bike to arrive, John realized he could put the bike in the unused media room his grown children loved when they lived at home. John next wondered if he could cast the bike classes to the screen that they had from their kids. Some time on the Peloton Facebook page plus John's love of technology led him to *mirrorcast* the bike content onto the big screen in the media room.

When Peloton entered their life, John was battling high blood pressure and was running in order to reverse it and get himself excited about cardio. He saw the bike as maybe a better, fun way to get his cardio, blood pressure, and weight under control. As he watched Erica, who immediately loved Peloton, and the fun classes stream onto the big screen, John got excited about the technology. John hadn't ridden, but as a techy, software architect, the product was a toy and he became engrossed by the technology.

Mills also had bad knees from years of playing basketball, so the bike seemed like a great way to balance his running.

After talking a bit with John, I learned that making fun videos, parody-type of stuff, for work (makes me think of Michael Scott from *The Office*) and family and friends was something he loved to do. When Mills began running outside, pre-Peloton, to lose pounds and lower his blood pressure, he made fun videos about his neighborhood 5K runs, with a camera set up to capture him as he triumphantly returned home. From there he would edit the video and use graphics, add some hip-hop music (another of his passions) and special effects and share the video with those close to him.

John told me he had been doing these types of videos for almost 17 years and explained that it "naturally rolled right into Peloton. I didn't even really think about it." His Peloton content was the first that John shared beyond his friends, family, and co-workers. It turns out the Peloton community loved John's videos and enjoys watching them as much as he loves making them.

Between the focus on fun and fitness, John delivers insights into life, sharing his and Erica's experiences from young, poor newlyweds on the West Coast to where they are now. As an African American, he openly shares his thoughts on U.S. history, policy, and more. After George Floyd's killing in Minnesota in 2020, John's posts delved deeper into those topics as the Peloton community joined the rest of the country in facing the realities of racism in America.

In February 2021, during Black History Month, one of John's posts went viral well beyond the Peloton community. John's original post shared the story of a slave, The Man Fortune, who lived and was enslaved in Connecticut and whose body was later used for medical training for decades, after he slipped in a river and broke his neck and drowned. His owner was a doctor and used Fortune's bones to train his son. As Mill's explained, Fortune's bones were used for medical training and wealth creation for 135 years before being donated to a museum and put on display as "Larry the Slave" in Mattatuck, Connecticut. Finally, by the 1970s the display was removed and Fortune The Man was buried in 2013.

On Mills' Run, Life and Live Facebook page John would write, "On Sept. 13th, 2013, after being a slave, medical specimen, museum exhibit and archeological artifact spanning 275 years, Fortune was finally freed . . . laid to rest next to White society of his time . . . something that wouldn't have been allowed when he died."

John Mills shared the story on February 1, 2021, as Black History Month started and within days thousands of Peloton members had read the story, often sharing it with others. By the middle of the month, hundreds of thousands of others would learn about Fortune the Man and gain deeper knowledge and understanding of America's past and present because of all of the shares across social media. From there, Mills would go on to speak via the web to a number of schools to share what he had learned.

While Mills arrived at Peloton in order to make Erica's life easier, the platform sucked him in and gave him space to get healthy and share his full self with the community. The community and the company have embraced Mills and this has led to his impact moving well beyond Peloton and fitness and into historical research and social impact.

CRYSTAL O'KEEFE (#CLIPOUTCRYSTAL)

In mid 2017, another sign I noticed telling me that Peloton was worth tracking was a fan podcast dedicated to the company. It was called *The Clip Out* and it even had its own theme song. The podcast, combined with the knowledge that people were flying to New York to ride live and that disco lights in basements were a regular part of the experience, became three of my key pieces of evidence screaming to me to pay attention to Peloton and its community. The podcast was the unexpected behavior and success that Drucker talked about.

I listened to a few episodes of *The Clip Out* and learned that the creator and co-host Crystal was a rider in Saint Louis. Crystal's co-host was her husband, Tom, who did not ride the bike or use any of the Peloton offerings or work out or eat healthy. When I interviewed Crystal and Tom, Tom told me that he eats like an eight-year-old at a theme park. Tom had hosted a movie podcast for years, and when Crystal bemoaned the fact that she had no real Peloton friends like the people she saw online, the idea for the *The Clip Out* podcast was born. Tom reminded Crystal that all of the necessary equipment was there in the basement of their house for her to create a podcast. When Crystal wondered what she would talk about for an hour a week, Tom, immediately replied, "Sweet baby Jesus, like, I would pay cash money if you would only talk about the bike for an hour a week, you know?"

From that moment, Crystal couldn't stop thinking about the potential podcast. She wanted to meet and interview the people she was seeing on the Facebook page, which numbered around 8,000 when Crystal purchased the bike. Tom, with a full-time job in live entertainment and his own podcast, agreed to help Crystal with the radio elements and serve as co-host, but made it clear she had to line up guests, prepare scripts, and do all of the heavy lifting to get the podcast launched and running.

Since launching, Crystal and Tom have broadcast from Homecomings and interviewed instructors, Peloton CEO John Foley, and hundreds of members of the community. Crystal and Tom have established a network of informants that deliver them key information and insights, and they also have created a vibrant community on social media. Over time their podcast has become a reliable and entertaining source of news about Peloton.

In 2019, I spoke with Crystal and Tom and learned what a labor of love the podcast is to produce and how it started. In relaying the story and Crystal's early experiences with the bike and the community, Tom told me that during their first conversation about a potential podcast Tom said to Crystal, "Here's the deal, like, right now, somewhere in America, there's 10 other people thinking the same thing. And so if we're gonna do this, when we pull into the driveway and throw this car and park, we gotta get out and we gotta start it right now. We gotta start coming up with our outlines. We gotta find guests. We gotta reach out to people. We gotta work on all the elements, like we can't sit on this for two or three months because someone else will do it and whoever does it second is last." Tom's clear-headed assessment gave Crystal anxiety, but she got to work immediately.

That conversation between Crystal and Tom took place in early 2017, and they began moving right away with a first episode, featuring an interview with instructor Matt Wilpers. That first episode of *The Clip Out* aired in May 2017, not long after I began researching the company. Tom was, in fact, very correct that others would want to create Peloton-focused podcasts. By 2020 there were two other Peloton podcasts that I was aware of—

Pelo Buddy TV, which was posting video podcasts on YouTube and other platforms, and *The Spin Up*, another U.S.-based Peloton podcast. In early 2021, a podcast focused on Power Zone (PZ) training—not surprising given the massive community of riders that love PZ training—called *The Empower Hour with Katie and Sarah* was launched and I also came across shows called *Pelotalk* and *Peloton People* that interview riders from across the Peloton community. While it is impossible to know how many podcasts and other media outlets will eventually focus on Peloton, I look at Apple, Tesla, Nike, and Disney media coverage and have no doubt Peloton's community and others will be hungry for more.

The Clip Out has been an enormous success in terms of sharing information and strengthening the Peloton community. The beauty of *The Clip Out* is that it highlights the welcoming and inclusive community ethos and how the community supports those who help bring people knowledge and connections. The podcast has grown and has become a commercial entity with sponsors, contests, correspondents, and more.

The Clip Out podcast-creating experience has also been a huge game-changer for Crystal. When we talked, she explained that interviewing all of her amazing guests on the podcast made her realize she had no excuses for not challenging herself and she began to wonder why "she wasn't doing more of this." Since I interviewed Crystal and Tom, she has completed a half Ironman race, become a certified trainer, and started another podcast in the fitness space. Crystal is a true dynamo and an example of what might happen if member decides to really participate in the Peloton community.

While Tom still had not taken a class on the Peloton platform at the time of this book being submitted, I know Tom improved his diet and started moving more, but most importantly, is happy because of Crystal and *The Clip Out*'s success. When I interviewed the two of them, Tom told me, "It's fun to watch her take on this thing that she didn't think that she could do and that she thought was still out of her wheelhouse. And it was just such an alien concept to her and she really knocked it out of the park."

JOHN PREWITT (#KENNY_BANIA), THE HOLTS, BRIAN A (#BRIANA), AND MANY MORE

Kenny Bania, the name of a minor character on *Seinfeld,* has taken a new meaning on the Peloton platform. A member named John Prewitt from suburban Detroit chose #Kenny_Bania as his leaderboard name, showed up in the studio often, and turned himself into one of the chief high-five evangelists on the bike.

Prewitt is a regular contributor on many Facebook pages, including the Official Peloton Member Page and many of the instructors' tribe pages, especially social media around Cody Rigsby and Jenn Sherman. Before the pandemic, Prewitt frequently visited the studio, including attending Homecomings in May. I randomly met John when my wife and I were visiting the bike studio in 2019. This means I receive at least 20 high fives from him each time we are on a ride together. It is addictive and a nudge; when #Kenny_Bania high-fives me I return the favor and pay it forward.

In addition to riding often, high-fiving, and spending time in New York City, Prewitt also often compiles and edits instructors' comments from classes and their pre-ride banter. His compilations of instructor Cody Rigsby get thousands of comments and reshares across social media. Like Peloton co-founder Cortese, Prewitt embraces that this fitness platform is also culture and entertainment, and he has done his part to welcome members to the fun with high fives in class, memes, and laugh out loud clips from classes that he captures and shares.

In addition to Prewitt, other regulars out there include the Holt family from outside of Baltimore. Melissa Holt (#arthritis_doc), Kelly Holt, and Lindsey Holt are a mother-and-daughters team that are super active on their bikes and treads, and also social media. I first found the Holts on instructor Jess King's social media pages. I then learned that my wife, Emily, knew the Holts from a physicians group, PMPG, on Facebook. The Holts have taken thousands of classes between them and all used Peloton to get healthier and have fun; from doing Jess King Experience Classes and DJ rides to traveling to New York City to workout at Peloton's studios. The health journey of the Holts has been embraced by so many different groups and instructors across the Peloton community that they have become well-known ambassadors for Peloton, health, and wellness. Though I live within an hour of the Holts, I actually met Melissa and her daughter Lindsey, randomly on the street, near the original studio. We recognized each other from social media and had a quick hello.

Beyond Prewitt and the Holts, there are countless others that I have met from the Peloton community that keep it vibrant and engaging. Brian Albright, known as #BrianA on the leaderboards, is a University of Michigan superfan in Northern Ohio who caught my attention on social media with his posts on instructor pages and his incredibly high outputs (power created and mileage). From what I could tell, he was a super fit guy who spent hours a day working out and posting to social media.

Eventually I would catch up with Brian on the phone and learn about his path to Peloton (he bought the bike in 2016) and deep engagement with the broader community. I would discover that not only did Brian provide constant posts and motivation for the Peloton community pages, but his wife, Olivia, was in the logistics business in the Midwest. After Brian and Olivia met some instructors while visiting the studio, Olivia's venture began to provide fulfilment services for some of the instructors and their personal brands. That led to a massive chuckle on my part as I had purchased a Matt Wilpers branded hat that came from Olivia's venture.

Brian also described all the friends he had met through Peloton, traveling to Green Bay to watch his Detroit Lions play the Packers and staying with a Peloton member, who also picked Olivia and Brian up at the airport. A visit to the home of another Peloton member, met through social media, brought Olivia and Brian to the Bahamas. Brian and Olivia bought the Peloton tread upon release, share their memories and pictures across social media, and support the instructors as they grow their brands. Brian, as an early member, has helped build the Peloton community and spread the ethos of support, engagement, and encouragement.

Members like #BrianA and the Holts are active, engaged, and constantly sharing their experiences with others. They inspire, teach, learn, and gain notoriety. What is crucial to note is that they receive positive feedback from countless members grateful for their efforts and inspiration. I always smile when I go on Instagram in the morning and get inspired by Brian's kick-amazing 6 am workout results.

#BradNeedsAbs #FirmCheesecake #PositiveSpins

#JoeyB #FrannieB #ProsecutorMom

#LauraPug #FSUSeminoleGirl #RobinRa

#JasonD #GingerBeardJedi #SashaSlays

#danica_nyc #Go_Blue_Fencer #SeeJaneSpin

#JasonR #HappyRunnerChic #SkinnyVanilla

#Horse1970 #healthycityboy #Spin4Endorphins

#Moonchild #IClaimJoy #SuperMac

#MILFMoney #IsabodyMichael #SmartCookie

#dpgeezy #JudgeSpin #Stimey

#AKLiz #Laurapug #STSukovich

#BamaGuy #LuvHuntingElk #TantrumBoss

#ClippingIn #OnAJourney #TougherThnILook

#CubsFanBudMan #OregonDucksgirl #TrailRunJenn

#CupcakeForPRs #QueenofDonuts #TwinMomPlus2

#DrMeMe #PalpablePulse #WhatIsLife

#d_flecha #PittieMom13 #willspin4queso

#EscapedFromNY #Pocket_Nurse

These listed and millions of others have found a place in the sweaty community that has grown with Peloton. These homegrown Pelo Celebrities are akin to the local celebrities you might find in college town or the Naked Cowboy tourists run into in Times Square. I am sure a sociologist could provide an academic explanation of our celebrities, but to me it shows that a shared sense of history, storytelling, characters, and more add up to a vibrant, healthy group.

THE UNITED NATIONS OF PELOTON

In early 2017, as I began to explore Peloton social media, I spent a good amount of time on the main Peloton Facebook page. This is where I witnessed disco lights while riding and learned about magic pants, *tabata* Tuesdays, squeaking pedals, and the pause button debate. The official page in many ways serves as a Peloton town square, where anyone can and might show up. Some just stop by as they check their Facebook account, while others set up camp and spend hours there talking, joking, sharing information, producing content, and meeting others. This is where I first met many of the aforementioned Pelo Celebrities.

I quickly learned that beyond the main Facebook page, there were countless other pages that Peloton members created and followed. The first Peloton subgroup I joined was the Peloton Plant Posse in September 2017. I was experimenting with a vegan diet and figured I might learn a few things and meet other vegan riders. The group was not very active, and it didn't have the bike-related vibrancy that the main page had. There were posts about vegan recipes, nutrition, and supplements, all very useful, but not enough to engage me. While not much happened for me in that group beyond finding a few folks to follow on the leaderboard, it helped me get my feet wet in the world of self-organizing, non-official micro groups or tribes.

As with the general social media environment, accounts and pages and movements can be created by virtually any one individual, group of people or organization. Moreover, these accounts can coalesce around almost any theme, lifestyle, or idea. There are mom Peloton groups and regional groups; pages and accounts dedicated to specific instructors and others based on age, music, ride type and food, drink, and drug preferences (#pelostoners).

PELOTON MONTHLY CHALLENGE TEAM (PMCT)

In late 2017, about a year into my Peloton experience, I found a posting on the Official Peloton Member Page calling for Peloton riders to join the Peloton Monthly Challenge Team (PMCT). PMCT was a group of people dedicated to "setting and crushing goals." Each month there were specific challenges for the group as well as the option for members to set their own goals for the month. Members had to share their goals and post at least once a week on their progress. The core feature and value that the group offered was accountability. I had enjoyed 2017 with Peloton and had worked out a bunch, but my workouts lacked focus, and like Crystal from *The Clip Out* podcast, I knew there was a lot more out there in the Peloton community. My time with the Plant Posse hadn't yielded much; I hoped that the PMCT group might bear some fruit.

Samantha (#ThePugMother), the successful New York litigator and mother of two we met when learning about Health Buyers, started the group as she vowed to lose weight and regain her health in August 2017. Sam posted on the main Facebook page looking for accountability on her goal of riding for one month straight. When willing participants answered Sam's call, she created a Facebook group called the August 2017 Thirty-One-Day Peloton Challenge.

By September 2017, the group name changed to the Peloton Monthly Challenge Tribe as the initial members and new arrivals were interested in an ongoing space for fitness accountability (eventually the word tribe was replaced by the word team). The early members were also aware that daily riding was not sustainable or wise and new challenges were needed going forward.

In addition to requiring members to post on their successes or failures in meeting their goals each week, group rides are scheduled, often meeting up at 6 am to complete stacks of classes or to celebrate a PMCT member's milestone ride. By February 2018, the group had its own HRI, with more than 30 members meeting to ride together in the New York studio, share meals, sing karaoke, and walk around and enjoy Manhattan.

In July 2018, PMCT held its second HRI, the one that coincided with Emily's birthday, and I attended. Over the next 18 months I would attend two more PMCT HRI events in New York and would make friends with people from all around the country leading all kinds of amazing lives. Most of our interactions took place through the accountability posts, group rides, and commiseration around challenges that different members, other groups or Peloton put together.

Forty PMCT members participated in one non-Peloton challenge, for example, during the summer of 2020. We took part in a virtual 245-mile summer running challenge put on by events company NYCRUNS. While the challenge was organized and operated by an outside entity and was not directly related to Peloton, almost 25 percent of PMCT members participated between Memorial Day and Labor Day 2020. The event, called the NYC Subway System Challenge, required its participants to run 245 miles as that is how many miles there are in the NYC Subway System.

Relative to many of the Peloton groups on social media, PMCT is small; capped at just 250 members. The small size of the group is likely one of the reasons it has been effective in helping me and others keep track of goals and stay engaged and accountable. While there has been much churn and a good amount of drama (250 people might be the size of a decent high school class) in my more than four years with PMCT, it has been crucial to keeping me learning, excited about new challenges on Peloton and most importantly, the source of new friends. In addition to all the triumphs and happiness, the group has experienced much sadness, including losing a member to cancer, the death of a member's family members, accidents, illnesses, and other real-life tragedies that cannot be escaped on a bike. That said, the comfort and support delivered by PMCT in those moments has been meaningful to the members in need and helped many of us learn about resiliency.

THE JSS TRIBE

The JSS Tribe is a Facebook-based group that brings together fans of instructor Jennifer Schreiber Sherman (JSS). As discussed, Jenn was the first instructor hired by the founding team, and in some ways Jenn, being born and raised in New Jersey, represents Peloton's early East Coast and tri-state roots in New York, New Jersey, and Connecticut. The JSS group celebrates Jenn's friendly and fun spirit and loves her music, often a soundtrack for those born in the 1960s, 1970s, and 1980s.

The tribe organizes many group rides and spends a lot of time marking members' milestones, which they almost always ride with Jenn. While I rode with Jenn early in my ride count with

Peloton, I did not become involved with this tribe until a physical event; the opening of the Bethesda showroom in September 2018. I met some JSS Tribe members after I met instructor Jess King. By the time I met the group, it had members across the country. It even had a subgroup called Jenn's Menn, many of which were in New York when I met Godnick in the studio after the JSS Valentine's Day ride in 2019. #MaxsDad, #JasonR, #MichiganMan87 are a few of Jenn's Menn I've met.

Not long after meeting D.C.–based JSS Tribe members at the store opening, I was invited to ride in the Bethesda showroom as part of a group-sponsored challenge taking place across the country. The challenge was created by JSS member Miriam Feffer (#Feffer), and pitted members of the group against each other based on their local showroom affiliation. The ride was set for the Sunday before the Super Bowl, as Jenn was known for her grueling, hour-long football rides on Sunday mornings during the NFL season.

The JSS Tribe formed teams across the country, choosing names such as the Windy City Warriors, Motor City Magic, Short Hills Shermanators. In the lead up to the ride, the teams posted videos to social media, created swag, and competed for five awards. I joined the Bethesda Beasts, the team that Feffer led, on January 27, 2019. I rode the display bike in the window of the busy main retail street in Bethesda during Sherman's class. It was really fun and I waved to people grabbing bagels and drinking coffee while sweating and grinning like a fool on the Peloton bike in the showroom window.

All six of the demo bikes in the Bethesda showroom were in use and 14 other showrooms, including Chicago, Denver, Minneapolis, and Short Hills, hosted more than 200 riders that morning of the Showroom Showdown. This meant Peloton showroom teams had to open early and host groups of sweaty riders and their friends while preparing for a Sunday sales day. It highlights the member-first approach of the Peloton organization and their willingness to follow the lead of their customers, even if it's a little offbeat and goofy and unexpected.

There are Peloton groups dedicated to all of the Peloton instructors. It has become the norm for groups to be created within minutes of the announcement of new Peloton instructors being hired. When I first began exploring the community in 2017, instructors engaged with the Facebook groups directly, somewhere the policy changed and instructors no longer posted on the pages or engaged directly with the instructor groups on social media. Direct communications between instructors and the members and public generally has occurred on instructors personal Instagram and social media accounts, and through official Peloton channels, including showrooms and studios. I am not sure exactly when or why this decision was made by Peloton to pull instructors off of their fan pages, but it appears not to have dampened the enthusiasm of Peloton members for instructor-based groups. This is because so much of the value creation, even around the instructors, is member to member. The instructor groups serve as modern-day fan clubs, celebrating one another's milestones, keeping all informed of instructor's class schedule and life events, and serving as a touch point around a shared passion—in this case, the instructor.

PHYSICIAN MOMS PELOTON GROUP (#PMPG)

My wife Emily is part of the Physician Moms Peloton Group, which is exactly what its name describes. This group is a Peloton offshoot of a pre-existing non-Peloton Facebook group called the Physician Moms Group (PMG). Dr. Hala Sabry started PMG in November 2014 to bring together women physicians who are also mothers; it had nothing to do with Peloton. PMPG (the Peloton Facebook group) was started by PMG members that had bikes and wanted to ride together; the new group had no official affiliation with the PMG group.

Emily has built strong friendships through PMPG and has attended three of its Home Rider Invasions in New York City. I have gotten to know many of these women, and when I take live runs or rides, I almost always find some PMPG members and share high fives with them. I also engage with many of them on Instagram and Facebook as many of her friends and I have favorite instructors and class types in common. I end up working out live with some of them (#ladyDrG, #arthritis_doc, #Gynomite, #MsMarvel, #MellOnWheels) more often than Emily does.

I highlight the PMPG experience on Facebook because it shows how organizations and groups from the real world have jumped into the Peloton community and are using the platform to connect their members, improve their health and well-being, and even bring in new recruits. As Peloton has grown, especially in the wake of Covid-19, the importation of existing groups to the Peloton platform has occurred at a dizzying pace. From high school and overnight-camp alumni groups, to consulting and law firm groups, the Peloton platform lets any community bond through fun and sweat.

PMPG also displays a common theme of Peloton groups forming around demographic traits, personal interests, or career interests. As mentioned, the first group I joined was the vegan group, which mainly shared recipes. I then joined a few geographic groups around the District of Columbia Metro, including Peloton Maryland (members often refer to one other with the crab emoji) and NoVA Peloton (I work in Northern Virginia).

POWER ZONE PACK (PZP)

The Power Zone Pack group is one of the largest in the Peloton community with more than 50,000 members in early 2020 and almost 100,000 in February 2021 (not long after Peloton's first billion-dollar revenue quarter). Power Zone training is a well-known method in endurance sports that provides each athlete their own specific training zones (seven zones for each person) that translate to quantifiable output numbers during their workouts. The numbers are visible on the Peloton bike's screen so a rider knows if they are riding in the proper zone (1–7) called out by the instructor. By riders having their own personal zones, with matching output numbers on the Peloton bike, each power zone class, during which instructors call out zones, presents the same challenge to each participant, no matter their personal level of fitness. In some ways it is like a golf handicap leveling the challenge for all participants in a round. Periodic tests allow participants to track their progress and watch as their power zones improve over time. This size of the movement and high participation rates in power zone rides is evidence of the endurance roots of indoor cycling and of the legions of members who like a data-driven, technical approach to their training.

The group features regular multi-month challenges, with different participation level options (three, four, or five rides a week) and prizes and draws tens of thousands of participants. Each week during the challenges, the intensity picks up and the assigned rides become more grueling. This is a training-first approach to fitness and it is clear that a huge percentage of Peloton bike owners like having this option available. Many find the consistency and intensity fun. Matt Wilpers brought this approach to Peloton and its growing popularity has meant more instructors have been engaged to offer these classes. Denis Morton, Olivia Amato, Christine D'Ercole, and London-based Ben Alldis all teach classes intended for power zone riders.

I have been a member of the Power Zone Pack Facebook group for years but never became active until members of my PMCT group made it look like incredible fun and their performances visibly and dramatically improved on the bike, meaning their output on the bike rose and their place on the leaderboard improved. Participation in the challenges also provides members multiple on-demand opportunities to ride together each week as well as countless opportunities to discuss the rides, share data and graphs, and enjoy getting stronger and sweating together. The PZP group focuses on the instructors who offer power zone classes on the bike. Associated software and apps have been produced by small firms and challenge organizers (not Peloton) and upgrades are available for purchase. Participation in these non-Peloton organized challenges is free; the premium versions offer more data and other features.

Like many elements of the Peloton community, Peloton subgroups such as the Power Zone Pack are creations of members who want to have fun, grow, and connect. Some, like PMCT, aimed to gain accountability and achieve fitness and health goals; others sought members to ride with around specific instructors or training methods or times of day; and still others came from existing groups within regions, careers, or demographics and want to share the Peloton experience with birds of a feather.

PELOTON COMMERCIAL ECOSYSTEM

Often, when high-growth innovative companies arrive and reach some scale, other entrepreneurs take notice and begin to produce products and services related to the new venture. In some cases, entire ecosystems and regional economies can sprout up. Think of Dell Computers and its impact on Austin, Texas, or FedEx in Memphis, Tennessee.

While Peloton is not yet 10 years old, the makings of a commercial ecosystem around its offerings and community have begun to emerge. I realized this was happening when I noticed a product called the Spintowel that was designed to fit over the Peloton handlebars and collect sweat that was producing "Pelo puddles" and also making the handle bars slippery. In the ensuing years, Drip Accessory (the maker of Spintowel) has added other products for Peloton bikes and treads and started producing custom fitting towels for other indoor bikes.

Another small business, named Top Form Designs, developed a product called the Spintray which basically turns a Peloton bike into a desk, with space for a laptop or tablet and even a drink. Multiple product extensions related to the Spintray have been introduced since the original, and the company has started making additional after-market products for Peloton and other fitness hardware. Top Form Design has created an adjuster that allows the Peloton rider to extend the handlebars further than factory settings and also a product called the Pivot which allows an original Peloton bike's monitor to move around and pivot. Interestingly, purchases from Top Form Designs can be financed via Affirm, the same company that has partnered with Peloton to allow customers to pay for their Peloton purchase over time.

Affirm, started by PayPal founder Max Levchin, is a fintech startup that makes installment loans. Affirm has really benefited from Peloton's growth at a greater scale than the accessory makers. By becoming a financing partner for Peloton, Affirm grew dramatically with Peloton and by 2020, was able to pull-off an initial public offering (IPO) of its own. At the time of the IPO, Peloton accounted for nearly one-third of all of Affirm's revenue.[53] In the risk section of Affirm's S-1 filing for its IPO, it points out its reliance on Peloton for such a large percentage of its revenue.

Etsy has become a vibrant marketplace for enthusiasts to get their fill of Peloton-related gear. I've seen 3D printed hangers for bike shoes, wall cutouts of instructor quotes (like Fat Heads), mobile device holders that connect to Peloton handlebars, chalkboards to keep track of personal best outputs on different workout lengths, mugs, shirts, and custom leaderboard name stickers to pimp out one's bike or tread.

While participating in a secret Santa exchange with the PMCT group, I was given a wood-block cutout of a quote from instructor Denis Morton reminding me to "Take the recovery you need, not the one you want." Like many of the quotes and concepts that Denis shares, it might need a minute to percolate. My secret Santa turned out to be a Wisconsin-based PMCT member named Nancy (#PackersFan). Our connection via the bike and gift exchange highlights just how many divides Peloton can cross if it can bring a Green Bay Packers fan and a Chicago Bears fan together.

The rise of these aftermarket products is akin to the accessories market in the mobile device space or the auto market. Eventually some of these brand names may become mass market innovators and stand out like Case Logic, OtterBox, and WeatherTech have done in recent years. Many of these early Peloton-based producers used Peloton to get themselves into fitness more broadly, developing products for other fitness hardware and activities.

Since I started noticing Emily buying Peloton apparel in lieu of Lululemon, I have watched the Peloton boutique closely. In my eyes the company has constantly and consistently upgraded the scope of and pace of release of collections and athleisure in its online and physical stores. This is a highly profitable category that Lululemon, Nike, Athleta, and a handful of others have been able to grow beyond anything the apparel and fitness industries could have imagined just a few decades ago. As with the growth of the aftermarket segment, Peloton's apparel ecosystem has some power to it and can be beneficial to other ventures.

When I began to shop the Peloton boutique, both online and in showrooms in 2018, I noticed unfamiliar brands. I bought zip-up jackets and sweatshirts from Ogio and Craft, shorts from Fourlaps and Vuori and Outdoor Voices, and shirts from Rhone and Solfire. All these companies were new to me, but all were branded Peloton and that is how these brands were introduced to me.

I really grew to love the Peloton shorts and shirts and hoodie I had purchased that were designed and made by men's athleisure company Rhone. On one of my trips to the Mothership in New York, I learned that Rhone had a pop-up store in Times

Square. I ended up spending nearly $500 on two pairs of their "Commuter" style pants (tapered, athletic cut and made of a breathable, comfortable nylon-like fabric) and a clean, well-designed navy-blue zip-up hoodie, nicer than anything I've seen Zuck wear. The pants were nothing like the jeans I typically wore, they were comfortable like sweatpants, but clean cut like a nice pair of tailored slacks. Within a few months of buying them, I would wear the grey pair of Rhone pants with a sport coat to teach a university class and a week later would hike eight miles in them on a cool Wisconsin day. I have become a Rhone devotee just as my wife became a Lululemon fanatic when she discovered how comfortable and versatile their pants were when we lived in the Cow Hollow neighborhood of San Francisco, just blocks from their first U.S. store.

The Spintray, Affirm, Drip Accessory, and Rhone experiences show how Peloton's broader commercial ecosystem has grown with its sweating, committed community and been able to support a range of newer entrants. The bigger firms, like Nike and Lululemon and Under Armour, dipped their toes in with some branded merchandise in the Peloton store in the first few years.

In early 2020, while we were all starting to hunker down during the first months of the coronavirus pandemic, Nike announced that it was releasing its first-ever indoor cycling shoe. This was fundamentally different from just slapping a logo on some shirts or shorts for Peloton. This was research, time, and investment in a new category of footwear.

Nike is always paying attention to which fitness activities consumers participate in, what top athletes and sports organization are training with, and how customers might be brought into Nike's orbit and siphoned from other brands and products. Through the eyes of Nike, it might be interesting that in the first 44 years of my life, I purchased zero pairs of clip-in cycling shoes. In years 44–47, I bought three pairs. My wife also bought two pairs, and we bought a pair for our oldest child. Nike is too smart not to have noticed that trend.

Nike was correct to take action. When the Nike SuperRep Cycle (the name of their indoor cycling shoe) was released in May 2020, I preordered a pair on the Nike App and shoes were delivered the first day they were available. This was my first shoe drop! While this did not make me a sneakerhead, it was another new experience brought to me by Peloton.

I only had the Nike app on my phone because I downloaded it while visiting the Nike store on 5th Avenue in Manhattan after riding in the Peloton studio with our oldest son, Levi, in late 2019. He turned 13 years old in November 2019, making him old enough to ride in the Peloton studio. He knew how much fun we had when we visited, so he asked if riding with Alex Touissant could be part of his birthday gift; Emily and I were more than happy to oblige! We headed to NYC and the Mothership with Levi and our daughter Sari in late December 2019. On that trip we went to the flagship Nike location and I downloaded the app to help with customer service in the extremely crowded, chaotic store (pre-Covid). By May 2020, as Nike entered the indoor cycling market, the app came in handy for me as I could get the shoes immediately.

Peloton's incredible success means the commercial ecosystem around digital and in-home fitness communities will continue to grow with more apparel, accessories, footwear, and countless other ventures rushing to exploit the opportunity and improve the experience. Not only does this mean more opportunities for

Peloton members and Peloton, but also for entrepreneurs and innovators at other firms that can bring value to the fitness and well-being marketplaces.

CONCLUDING THOUGHTS ON COMMUNITY

People behave in unexpected ways each and every day. When unexpected successes occur, opportunities are created. Peter Drucker believed so much in the power of these unexpected successes in capitalist societies that he pointed to them as one of the seven sources of innovative opportunities, right up there with technological advances, demographic shifts, and societal changes in perception.

For Peloton, the unexpected success of the community was an accelerant on top of the convenience and quality created by its talent and technology and retail strategy. In fact, the community creates value for members that is not possible for the company to create. The company and its offerings are the platform on which the community was born and is anchored to. From there, the community has headed in thousands of fascinating directions, with value accruing to both members and Peloton.

The Peloton community makes significant contributions in customer knowledge, branding and sales, and product innovation. Different members are drawn to different parts of the community and contribute to it through activities as simple as likes on Facebook and high fives on the leaderboard, or as intense and commercial as creating Peloton-focused podcasts or designing and selling accessories and hardware for the bike and tread. The community has been generally open access since the first members began contacting one another and creating online happy hours and meetups. The unexpected, organic, and growing Peloton community has become one of Peloton's most important strengths, if not the single largest strength.

As Jenn Sherman and I discussed the Peloton community, she was amazed by how it had grown and its impact. Jenn even said that the community "is what makes us different." I could not agree more with Sherman about what a differentiator the Peloton community is and how much it has driven the company's growth. I also believe the community is likely to be a key strength for Peloton as it faces challenges on its road ahead. In the next chapter we will take a look at some of the issues and players that might make Peloton's next stage of growth much more difficult than its amazing start.

CHAPTER 7

COMPETITORS, HATERS, AND HUBRIS: POTENTIAL BUMPS IN THE ROAD

Experienced endurance athletes and entrepreneurs learn and accept the ebbs and flows that accompany their undertaking, especially if their goal is something of scale or their path is untrodden. From preparation and start they go to the grind, valleys and peaks, and the finish, then to repair, recovery, and planning for the next challenge or summit. Good times and bad times come to those setting and pursuing hard goals.

From my perspective as both a customer and a researcher who has followed startups for years, the Peloton story has been pretty smooth sailing. For CEO John Foley, co-founder Tom Cortese, and other team members, it's been a struggle much of the way. Foley recounted the challenges of the early years in many of his media interviews.

While the day-to-day and quarter-by-quarter struggles were real for the Peloton team and early investors, when one reviews timelines and milestones, Peloton is a special company that has traveled a funding and growth path few others have ever achieved.

Peloton's initial public offering (IPO) in September 2019 was one of the best in class for the entire year of IPOs in the United States. Peloton's IPO took place as the IPO fiasco involving WeWork, founded by Adam Neumann and backed almost single-handedly by billionaire Japanese investor Masayoshi Son, was rocking Wall Street. Because of WeWork's size and quick loss of tens of billions of dollars in value, the IPO window was slamming shut for high-growth, money-losing ventures such as Peloton. As the WeWork IPO disintegrated, it sucked others down. Endeavor Group, the entertainment venture created by super-agent Ari Emanuel with the Ultimate Fighting Championship (UFC) and other strong assets in its portfolio, was forced to pull its IPO the same week that Peloton went public. To me, the fact that Peloton was able to pull off its IPO in such a choppy market was a sign of strength.

In the eight years leading to the IPO, Peloton experienced a string of successes and invented a market for connected products that has changed the entire fitness and well-being category. When we think about how big the fitness market has been, whether viewed through health club memberships, equipment sales, technology purchases, and accessories, it is clear that Peloton was rewriting the rules well before the Covid-19 pandemic began to wreak havoc on the health club industry. Peloton's success, and the value it has created, has only grown in the face of the global virus.

Peloton's ride has truly been extraordinary, but there are likely to be many unexpected tests ahead. This chapter is broken into three sections exploring potential challenges to Peloton as it tries to scale and bring its offerings to the masses around the world. The first looks at some of the competitors interested in the burgeoning fitness and well-being markets. Next, we will explore haters and others that might target Peloton and attempt to knock it off its pedestal and take it down. Third, we will consider the damage hubris might cause. Any of these challenges can take down a firm, and failure still is the most likely outcome of any venture.

When I think of Apple, Nike, Patagonia, Amazon, Tesla, and a host of other recent, world-changing firms, their histories reveal many stormy and dark periods, sometimes including layoffs, founder departures, threats of bankruptcies, and private buyouts. We don't know what the road ahead holds for Peloton, but its enormous early success has overwhelmed the challenges faced thus far; however, there are surely more extraordinary challenges to come.

COMPETITORS CRASHING PELOTON'S PARTY

The gym and health club industry traditionally has been fragmented, with a range of players and segments, from community fitness centers and national nonprofits to massive chains, franchises, high-end clubs, and the boutique studios that presented problems that factored in the Peloton team's initial concepts.

The marketplace for fitness equipment (from Bowflex, Life Fitness, and Nautilus to Italian fitness giant Technogym) and at-home personality-based brands (Jillian Michaels and Billy Blanks to Tracy Anderson and Shaun T) is just as fragmented and diverse as the health club side of the business.

Traditional players in both the gym and health club space and the hardware space are attempting to follow Peloton and the massive growth of connected fitness. Pre-pandemic, Planet Fitness ran ads mocking Peloton and working out at home (kids, laundry machines, and stationary bikes as clothes hangers were all featured), but later created its own online social network and began moving to a streaming model to complement its physical locations. Countless brands are distributing fitness content across platforms including private networks, Instagram, Facebook, and more; even Weight Watchers has made fitness classes available to its members. Covid made streaming fitness an obvious necessity, whereas it had been ignored and mocked before the pandemic, even as Peloton doubled in size year after year.

In 2017 and 2018, as I realized the power of Peloton and how many customers it was earning and delighting, it was clear that owners and operators of traditional fitness spaces had a problem. My wife, a Peloton early adopter, had agreed to drop her Equinox membership after our initial conversation about the cost of the Peloton bike. From years of experience, I knew that if my wife was doing something, other hard-working, professional women might also. A full-service gym had been a necessity in her life for decades, but Peloton ended that four years before Covid arrived in the United States. The pandemic made it clear to millions beyond the initial Peloton community that life without a gym membership was possible, and in many cases a much better solution.

When the Peloton bike arrived in our home in 2016, we had two pieces of cardio equipment, a 15-year-old Precor treadmill and an even older Tectrix stationary bike. Both had served us well and had traveled across the country with us. That said, the Tectrix bike had become the clichéd clothing hanger years earlier, but disposing of it always seemed more challenging and costly than keeping it. We were able to keep the equipment so long because the two machines represented the old model of fitness industry sales: pay for it once and keep it. Sure there were some service revenues and maybe financing dollars, but the core business model of the equipment industry was very straightforward: sell machines, most often through a third-party retailer. The challenge for existing equipment makers that attempt to replicate Peloton's equipment model is that it is multilayered, including hardware, constantly upgraded software, content, talent, community, culture, media, retail sales and production and distribution, and brand.

Replicating an innovator's business model is by no means the only path to profits and value creation, but when a winner develops a stunning and disruptive model, others try to copy it. Fast food restaurants chased McDonald's for decades and Starbucks' reinvention of coffee has changed the morning routines of billions of people; consider Amazon's impact on retail and Musk's reinvention of transportation (both terrestrial and extraterrestrial). Peloton's stunning success has led existing and new players to take and adjust pieces of its business model and try to grow into the expanding market Peloton has opened.

Flywheel, one of the first to popularize boutique indoor cycling at a national scale, announced a Flywheel at-home bike in late 2017 and was testing by 2018. The company eventually left the at-home space and ran into serious studio challenges (pre-pandemic) and eventually fully shut down its operations. However, Flywheel Sports' brief pursuit of Peloton is worth reviewing.

An at-home option theoretically allowed Flywheel to leverage much of its talent, brand, locations, existing customer base, and years of knowledge in a battle against Peloton. The Peloton bike had only launched in 2014 so Flywheel, with its 40-something studios across the world was well positioned to counter punch and take big shares of the connected digital fitness market as Peloton grew it.

A short time after announcing its home bike, Flywheel signed a distribution deal with Best Buy, the home entertainment and electronics retailer based in Minneapolis, Minnesota. This would allow Flywheel to use Best Buy's massive retail footprint to sell its products via physical space just as Peloton had done.

From the Flywheel press release from June 2019:

"We are extremely excited about our partnership with Best Buy. Best Buy has long been a destination for consumers to discover the newest and most innovative technology solutions, and their expansion into the booming connected home fitness space is a savvy move," said Matt O'Connor, GM of Flywheel's At-Home Business. "We are delighted to bring the

Flywheel Home Bike experience to life inside Best Buy stores and on BestBuy.com, and we look forward to the opportunity to bring Best Buy customers into the Flywheel community of home riders."[54]

Additionally, by partnering with Best Buy and perhaps eventually employing its Geek Squad home delivery and installation team, Flywheel gained access and expertise in delivering large items and installing consumer technology in homes. On paper, the partnership with Best Buy seemed to make sense and give Flywheel important pieces of the Peloton model: retail stores and fulfillment (delivery and installation).

By bringing Flywheel into its stores, Best Buy got a foot into the lucrative health and well-being space. Other products that Best Buy offered during its promotion of "fitness stores" within its stores included the Hypervolt, a popular massage device, and the Hydrow, an at-home, connected fitness rower that some consider a rowing version of Peloton.

It never worked out for the Flywheel–Best Buy partnership. Flywheel ran out of money and went bankrupt by 2020 after trying to work out a deal with Town and Country Sports, the operator of nearly 100 traditional health clubs in major markets such as New York and D.C. Eventually, with the added pressure of Covid in 2020, Flywheel had to close all of its locations and cease operations.

In 2020 and early 2021, I went to visit a range of fitness retailers to better understand their responses in the face of massive Covid demand. Best Buy at the time had a small selection from a range of brands, including the Hydrow and a connected bike and treadmill from NordicTrack as well as the Hypervolt percussive, massage device that many in the Peloton community (including multiple instructors) were buying and using and posting about. My wife Emily purchased a Hypervolt massager online in 2019 for around $350.

Sidenote: Peloton cycling instructor Alex Touissant, who started his career mopping floors at Flywheel, would become an ambassador for Hyperice, the maker of the Hypervolt and other recovery products. During my tour of fitness retailers in early 2021, I saw many low-priced percussive massage guns at Walmart that sold for one-quarter the cost of the Hypervolt.

Another major pioneer of indoor boutique cycling, SoulCycle, is part of a private equity-backed high-end-skewing fitness conglomerate with Equinox and other brands. Real estate developer and operator Related Companies owns these brands. Originally a real estate operator in leading markets, Related Companies began investing in fitness because of the benefits it brought to its real estate holdings; including the value of high-quality, on-site fitness to potential tenants. When I began to research the industry, I learned Related Companies, majority owned by billionaire Miami Dolphins owner Stephen Ross, had Equinox, SoulCycle, Pure Yoga, Blink Fitness, and other fitness and health brands. Rumble Boxing, which had a studio down the street from Peloton's first bike studio, also joined the Equinox stable when I was getting to know Peloton in 2018 and 2019.

The Related Companies' goal was to focus on high-end, membership-based fitness spaces and brands that made use of its real estate knowledge and assets. So while Peloton was disrupting Equinox and its related brands, there were many customers in city centers and other dense areas that were not ready to let go of boutique fitness spaces and gym visits as part of their daily rituals. Many of these, including some in my family, were holdouts and loyal to these brands. From my perspective, SoulCycle, and its brethren, including Equinox, seemed to be banking on loyalty, ritual, and the exclusivity of their offerings.

Covid-19 changed rituals for everyone and made loyalty to a gym brand or instructor virtually impossible, and that changed reality for all fitness industry participants, including Equinox and SoulCycle. The Equinox family of brands cobbled together a range of offerings, but had no clear path forward by mid-2020 as the reality of the pandemic sunk in. A SoulCycle At-Home Bike was launched, running on an app called Variis (later renamed Equinox+) that aggregates content from across Related Companies' fitness brands. The overall response to Peloton, before and after Covid has been reactive. Moreover, as Peloton has ascended, SoulCycle has had a range of brand and PR issues that appear to have hurt them.[55]

Traditional fitness hardware brands such as NordicTrack and Life Fitness, one of the many brands owned by Utah-based ICON Health and Fitness, have been upping their smart fitness offerings and experimenting with many things that Peloton has popularized. While nowhere near as deep on the instructor focus, existing brands have been making their way into the market with a range of offerings, most of which were inching along until the pandemic and Peloton pushed fitness to its next, connected act.

NEW PLAYERS JOINING PELOTON

Beyond the offerings coming from legacy clubs, content makers, and hardware producers in the fitness space, there are new entrants (often backed by venture capitalists) such as the aforementioned Hydrow connected rower, that are attempting to follow Peloton's basic model of hardware sale plus monthly subscription. Now that Peloton has proven it is possible, the model is far more attractive, and many new makers of hardware with subscriptions have been introduced to the public. There are cardio machines, strength machines, boxing machines, and more. Peloton's success has ushered in an era of innovation, creativity, and investment in space that has been stale for decades—a fact Foley has pointed out often.

In addition to the Hydrow connected rower, new connected brands including Tonal, Tempo, Forme, JaxJox, and others have entered the strength space. FightCamp offers a connected heavy bag and classes for those who want the boutique boxing experience. The hardware race is still in its early phase so it is very possible these and other firms will end up being acquired or becoming part of the roadkill from the surge of innovation in health, fitness, and well-being that Peloton has ushered in.

Another of the recent hardware offerings that has met with some success is The Mirror. This product was created by Brynn Putnam, a ballerina turned fitness instructor whose husband is an engineer and the son of a mutual-fund king.[56] The Mirror offers instructor-led classes on a large wall-mounted mirror in your home. The Mirror is connected to the internet, and its screen is a little over four feet tall and a bit less than two feet wide. To me, it looks like a large digital fast-food menu turned on its side, so it faces the user vertically. The Mirror offers a range of classes including yoga, cardio, stretching, strength, tai-chi, and more. Like Peloton, it comes from the boutique fitness side of the industry with added technology and highlights the deep roots that boutique fitness has in the dance industry.

During summer 2020, Lululemon purchased The Mirror for $500 million in cash. The move by the super-successful athleisure brand highlights the range of players that have raced into the connected fitness space as all witnessed Peloton's meteoric rise. The Mirror has gained a following, been validated by venture capitalists (wink wink), and attracted some Healthy Wealthy customers similar to Lululemon devotees and many Peloton customers.

No doubt Lululemon's leadership, like Nike's, observed Peloton's success and realized some of their customers were becoming rabid Peloton customers. Many like my wife, were even shifting their spending to Peloton merchandise. Lululemon leadership also was keenly aware of Peloton's retail success as many Peloton and Lululemon stores are neighbors in prime retail neighborhoods.

Lulu leadership clearly viewed their nearly 500 stores as a way to massively scale sales of The Mirror and bring the Lululemon brand and lifestyle into customers' homes in a dynamic engaging way. How selling and producing expensive fitness hardware and delivering content compares with designing and selling seasonal collections of athleisure and casual wear is yet to be determined.

Though The Mirror attracted a fitness giant and a happy exit, for me, Echelon, a 2019 entrant, is the most fascinating of the new hardware competitors that have entered the connected fitness market. The company first came to my attention because it produced what appeared to be a clone of a Peloton bike, minus the built-in tablet. Users for the early Echelon bike models were meant to connect their own tablets and place them on a tablet holder above the handlebars of their Echelon bikes. Echelon products color schemes have generally been the same black and red as Peloton's and the logo looks eerily similar to Peloton's. I went out and looked at multiple versions of Echelon bikes in person, and to someone with no prior knowledge, it would be easy to confuse the brands.

Echelon set up a production studio in Tennessee where live and on-demand classes are produced, following the Peloton model. I find Echelon's emulation of Peloton fascinating, from the logo, user interfaces, programming, the name (*Ech-E-Lon* versus *Pel-O-Ton*), and even the black T-shirt awarded when an Echelon rider completes 100 rides. I'm not a lawyer, so I don't know how elements like that play out in the courtroom. Peloton and Echelon have become entangled in a number of lawsuits on issues including patent infringements and false advertising.[57]

Tennessee-based Echelon has quickly developed many fitness products, including a connected rower and a connected personal trainer similar to The Mirror. Echelon calls its product The Reflect, and has described it as a "fitness mirror." In September 2020 Echelon claimed to be working with Amazon to produce a Prime bike, which would be for sale exclusively on Amazon. Amazon denied this and asked to company to remove the product from Amazon's website. There is no doubt, Echelon leadership knows how to put chutzpah into high gear.

Echelon is the brainchild of a consumer electronics and hardware entrepreneur named Lou Lentine and his company, Viatek. Lentine has been making and selling products that exploit consumer trends for decades. Lentine has appeared on QVC, HSN, and other sales outlets with products such as the Hurricane Spin Mop, Night Stars (outdoor laser lights for Christmas decorating), and the Mighty Jump Car Starter.[58, 59]

Lentine, a New Jersey native, has done so well riding the connected fitness trend intelligently that his Echelon brand, which he released in spring 2019 after success with some basic Bluetooth-connected exercise bikes, appears in Walmart stores and Dick's Sporting Goods and Costco. Lentine and Echelon even attracted an investment at a $100 million valuation from North Castle Ventures, the backer of boutique fitness ventures Barry's Bootcamp and Equinox. In October 2019, it was announced that Lentine had signed a partnership with Villency, the design firm Peloton used for its original bike.[60] By late 2020, investors from Goldman Sachs Growth were leading a group putting another $65 million of capital into Lentine's hands.[61]

While Peloton is the obvious connected fitness innovator with the most developed model and sophisticated offering, the fitness and well-being space is burgeoning and has always been fragmented. Covid has created both more opportunity and the need for accessible products and services that improve people's lives. It's no surprise that a motley crew of entrants such as TV salesman Lentine, consumer retail giant Best Buy, newbie Tonal, traditional home fitness giant ICON Health & Fitness (NordicTrack brand), and apparel innovator Lululemon are trying to capture segments at all price points and with offerings from strength to smart punching bags and beyond.

BEYOND THE HARDWARE

Beyond the hardware makers, there are digital-only producers, ranging from Strava, a venture capital-backed app created in 2009, allowing participants in virtually any fitness activity to post and share their results in a community of nearly 50 million, to

Obé Fitness, an app streaming boutique-based sculpting classes targeting women, and countless others. Digital-only fitness plays are not new. Baltimore-based Under Armour spent nearly $600 million in 2015 in the fitness app space, eventually exiting most of those investments at a loss, and Nike has dabbled in the smart and connected space for decades, as have Garmin and others. Peloton's success has meant the non-hardware side has also seen an explosion in fitness content and tools that do not demand a hardware purchase.

In fall 2020, technology hegemon Apple turned its attention to the fitness space and announced the creation of Apple Fitness+. This suite of workouts and fitness apps would gather data from the Apple Watch and feed content through Apple TV and other platforms. While no specific hardware was announced or created at the time, a monthly subscription model was offered and varied depending on which other Apple subscriptions were in a customer's basket. Apple's entrance just a year after Peloton's IPO validates what Peloton users have known since 2014; fitness can be fun, engaging, and convenient, and provide consistent cash flows, even through digital-only subscriptions. Amazon followed a similar path in fall 2021, announcing Halo Fitness and Nutrition centered around streaming classes, data, and its Halo wearable.

Digital fitness and wellness content will continue to flow fast and furious across the media landscape; from Weight Watchers to Chuck Norris and hundreds and thousands of independent fitness pros and content producers, the content market is crowded.

In early 2021, using a financial innovation called a SPAC (special purpose acquisition company), the infomercial fitness and supplement company Beachbody, with home-based brands P90X, Insanity, and others, went public, merged with a bike maker, and grabbed the ticker symbol BODY.[62] Former Peloton cycling instructor Jennifer Jacobs joined Beachbody as a trainer just a few months before their public offering. It is only a matter of time before more giant organizations and media firms, perhaps Disney, Netflix, or Facebook, chase the cash flows and valuations that fitness and well-being can offer. These companies have decades of experience developing and distributing content across a range of channels. The fact that Peloton has been able to sell streaming content memberships for $39 a month and members think it's a steal has not been lost on existing content makers.

The next 10 to 20 years will see incredible innovation, creativity, and growth in the fitness and well-being space. The trend was accelerating when Peloton gave it a supercharge, as evidenced by its growth between 2014 and 2019. Covid-19 lit an even bigger fire in the market. Peloton has built walls and moats, but hordes of competitors will come, trying to differentiate with hardware, brand, software, celebrity, streaming, and options not yet invented or imagined.

HATERS, DOUBTERS, AND OTHER TROUBLEMAKERS

Haters are going to hate. Sadly, that maxim is especially true when it comes to successful people and organizations. This section focuses on people and institutions that already have or soon may put a target on Peloton.

Many successful firms, whether measured by reach, profits, employee count, or cultural impact, find that the limelight often brings some unexpected pain. It could take the shape of policy or legislation, court actions, or backlash to the disruption they are bringing to existing markets and ways of life. Consider how Uber, Airbnb, and Virgin were received as they entered industries.

Peloton already has been involved in range of lawsuits, some as plaintiff and others as defendant. Perhaps the most potentially damaging thus far was an intellectual property lawsuit around music rights. It began in 2019 with a group of music publishers representing tracks from artists such as Taylor Swift, Lizzo, Ariana Grande, and others. The claim was that Peloton was using the music but not paying proper royalties.[63] The group sued Peloton for $300 million, forcing the company to pull down many on-demand rides because their playlists contained so many of the songs at issue. This massive, unexpected alteration of the Peloton on-demand library became known to many as "the great purge" and would be the first of many. Purges of old classes would become a regular occurrence as Peloton's library grew with new instructors, new disciplines, and the passage of time.

Members have complained about the periodic purges. And although thousands and thousands of classes were still available, and the instructors continued to produce new rides, members were truly upset because of their lost memories. I lost a 90-minute climb ride from 2018 with former Peloton cycling instructor Jennifer Jacobs that was one of my proudest achievements. I wish I could take it again! Some members blamed Peloton, others blamed the music industry and their lawyers.

Soon after the playlist purge and many complaints on Facebook pages across the Peloton universe, ads appeared in my feed (and other members' social media feeds) from lawyers attempting to get members to join a class-action lawsuit against Peloton because classes had been removed. The last time I checked, that lawsuit was slowly working its way through the courts. In addition to the music-related litigation, many other lawsuits have emerged, including entanglements with players in the fitness space such as Madd Dog and ICON Fitness. Peloton's success will continue to attract a range of legal antagonists. Disruptive companies always experience the constraining nature of lawsuits and regulations as common tools that some haters employ to slow them down or extract financial gain.

THROWING SHADE

While many haters come after Peloton for strategic and direct financial gain, others have arrived as part of the contentious media hordes looking for clickable content. In 2018, my serial-entrepreneur friend Raymond Rahbar, was thinking about developing a cutting-edge new fitness-hall concept in downtown D.C. Ray and I would continually discuss the future of fitness, sending texts and articles about innovators and leaders as well as missteps we observed.

In early 2019, Ray sent me a hilarious thread of tweets from an Arizona-based online personality named Clue Heywood.[64] Each tweet featured a picture of Peloton bike in a gorgeous, expensive location with a beautiful owner on the bike and an obnoxious post from the Peloton owner that supposedly owned that bike and over-the-top setup. One, for example, showed the bike and rider on a balcony and stated, "I took my Peloton bike to Europe and used it on the balcony of $2,000/night Airbnb and honestly felt like I was flying over London, you should try it." Another in Heywood's thread features a more haggard looking female rider, in black yoga pants and a black T-shirt. She is riding in a garage, with a Specialized brand mountain bike high up on the wall and a small child sitting facing that same wall. The text with this tweet states, "Sometimes I let the nanny ride my Peloton. But the solarium is my space, so she can only ride in the garage and only when disciplining my children." The entire Heywood thread had me rolling on the floor, but it's existence and popularity highlighted the image that Peloton held in many people's minds: elitist and super expensive and not for "normal people." This was not the first time or last Peloton and its members would be mocked.

Just after Peloton completed its IPO in September 2019 and started to gear up for another big Christmas sales season, the company's best time of the year, Peloton ran what I and many others considered a harmless ad. The commercial depicted a wife-character sharing a selfie-based video blog documenting her year of empowerment since receiving the Peloton (wrapped with a red bow) the previous Christmas. The commercial included clips of her nervously taking her first class, waking for a pre-dawn ride, and rushing home from work to keep a five-day streak alive.

The commercial, titled "The Gift That Gives Back," reminded me of holiday advertisements that Lexus ran for years, an aspirational product for hard-working, driven people. Moreover, the social media documentation of Peloton progress depicted in the commercial is something that members were doing all over social media, so the ad represented reality for many Peloton customers. The message of a hard-working mom, striving to become a better, stronger version of herself was a basic message repeated in many commercials and deemed true to Peloton's meaning for hundreds of thousands of members.

For some reason, the media horde latched onto the slim build and sheepish expression of the actor in the ad, Monica Ruiz. The media labeled Ruiz the "Peloton Wife" and pointed to her "Grace from Boston" character as proof that Peloton was sexist, elitist, and out of touch with daily life in America.

Outlets from CNN and the *Today Show* to *Inside Edition* and the *New York Times* picked up the story and roasted Peloton for weeks during its most important sales season of the year. A December 2019 *New York Times* headline referred to the ad as cringe-y.[65] The stock price took a pounding and lost over $1.5 billion in value according to some media sources.[66] Actor, comedian, and investor Ryan Reynolds quickly hired Ruiz and produced and distributed a commercial featuring Ruiz at a bar with her friends gulping down Aviator Gin (a brand Reynolds invested in) with the storyline that she left the awful husband who gifted her the Peloton.

The scale of the wife-commercial dustup was surprising; Peloton was a health product suffering a pile-on when many other expensive but popular consumer products such as iPhones, Teslas, and home electronics don't appear to suffer the same scorn. My interpretation of the "Peloton Wife" incident was that it merely showed how culturally relevant Peloton was becoming if its simple holiday television spot could lead to national headlines and debates around marital roles and choices.

Just two years after the "Peloton Wife" brouhaha, Ryan Reynolds would once again play a role in a Peloton media controversy. In the December 2021 case, Reynolds and his marketing firm would team with Peloton to produce a rebuttal commercial after the HBO *Sex and the City* reboot show used a Peloton bike and instructor Jess King to end Chris Noth's Mr. Big character via a post-ride heart attack. Peloton was clearly caught off guard by its product and instructor placement gone awry and quickly hired Reynolds. Within 48 hours, Peloton had a viral online commercial featuring pajama-clad Noth and King in front of a fireplace, enjoying one another's company and planning to ride a set of Pelotons (visible in the commercial) together to celebrate healthy lifestyles.

BUSINESS IN A DIVIDED CULTURE

In my years on the Peloton platform I have found that even within the Peloton community there are haters to be found. Some members choose to post inflammatory statements on Peloton social media platforms, trying to treat it like your everyday, ordinary internet. Others will shame people for asking basic questions, including some of the same ones the earliest Peloton members asked, leading to the community's creation and growth.

Members and potential customers that are not happy with the products, customer service, or statements made by instructors have not been shy about their feelings. The launch of a new instructor may lead to openly negative and hostile reviews as well as tales of old instructors. Covid delays, delivery and service mistakes, class purges, and other Peloton actions have been often met with repeated postings, calls, and outreach to media outlets, and emails to Foley and other members of the leadership team. Some of these have been effective in bringing solutions and more value to the platform, whereas others have lacked clear objectives or desired outcomes.

Businesses are actors in society and are created, operated, and run by people for the benefit of others and society broadly (more choices, better standards of living, etc.). Commerce is a social activity and it is not uncommon for the politics and debates of the day to impact ventures of all types. Peloton is no different and the leadership is aware of the divided society and culture in which it operates.

The Peloton leadership team knows that leading companies, especially consumer technology and media firms, play important roles in the social dynamics of American culture and economy, and global trends also. There is no doubt that Peloton considers this reality in their strategies, communications, and actions.

Less than 10 trading days after the September 2019 Peloton IPO, which was seen as a weak offering at that point, I received an email asking if I was available to attend a dinner with CEO John Foley, some other Peloton members, and a few of Foley's colleagues from Peloton.

On the eve of its IPO, Peloton's stock price was set at $29; when it opened for its first trade on September 26, 2019, the price was lower than $29. Peloton's stock (ticker symbol PTON on the Nasdaq) closed at $25.76 that first day, down 11 percent. Peloton's slide continued for days, and on October 2, the stock touched $21.76 in trading. Just a few days later, I was contacted about the dinner. Luckily my calendar was open, and Emily and I planned for cocktails and dinner with Foley, company staff, and about 20 other members. We did not know why we were invited or what to expect, but we grabbed the invite.

Emily and I excitedly headed down to Georgetown; a dinner in the city was special treat given the ages of our three kids. On top of that, of course, it was a Peloton dinner with founder and

CEO John Foley! I interviewed John earlier in 2019 and was really impressed with his intelligence, determination, and confidence. I wondered if the rough IPO had shaken him or the team and whether the dinner would answer my question.

When we arrived at 1789 Restaurant, a classic Georgetown eatery in a Federal-era home with period décor, hidden doors, and a truly historic Washington feel, the host welcomed us. A Peloton team member led us through a maze of small dining rooms, up narrow flights of stairs to the third floor, and then to a private room. I had never been to the restaurant before, but the tiny colonial-era dimensions of the building made it ooze historic D.C. charm, and the confusing route to the Peloton private room only increased the anticipation.

We entered the room and it was full of Peloton members and staff chatting and enjoying drinks. The walls were covered with horse-themed art, as if we were at the summer residence of a colonial-era aristocrat. There was barn siding (from an eighteenth-century New England barn) and wood beams (from a home in Vermont) on the ceiling and I remember a polo mallet catching my eye as I looked for Foley. There was a built-in bar with special Peloton-themed cocktails being served. We spotted Miriam Feffer (from the JSS Tribe) and chatted briefly, then met a few other members, all of us excited for the evening with Foley. After enjoying light hors d'oeuvres and drinks and meeting some of the other member attendees, we were instructed to find our place cards, which were set up around a large rectangular table.

As Emily and I searched for our names, others sat. We searched more as others sat; it became a game of musical chairs. The empty places were disappearing quickly, and I became concerned we had been left out. Maybe we were late additions to the guest list, and they forgot our spots. Moments later I would be a bit embarrassed to find place cards for Emily and me were on either side of Foley. I assumed that the Peloton team figured the devil they knew was better than the unknown, and we ended up with prime seats for the evening.

As the dinner began, we learned that Washington, D.C., was the first stop on a member listening tour that Foley was undertaking. He said he was interested in the capital because of its focus on policy, and he expressed interest in using Peloton to bring people together and to be a force for unity. I believed him and still do. Foley noted the diverse range of members in the room, including a married couple who met through Peloton, as if indicating that the company could create the ultimate union if given the chance.

My highlight of the evening was when the dinner conversation covered the challenges that the NBA faced in China due to an early October 2019 tweet by the Houston Rockets general manager, Daryl Morey about democracy and Hong Kong. For the NBA, the episode became a catastrophe that led to the most populous country shutting out the organization, canceling events, and destroying goodwill in a market the league had spent decades cultivating. For a point of reference, Chinese-born NBA Hall of Famer Yao Ming was drafted by the Rockets in 2002, bringing hundreds of millions of Chinese fans with him over the years. The irony of a destructive tweet from the Rockets GM could not be missed.

The discussion of the NBA case in China highlighted that Foley was well aware that Peloton or any other company could suffer heavy blowback from its corporate actions or something one of its team members might say in a class or do on social media. Foley also believed that his company was a tool that could be used to change the world by bringing people together, but it would demand a point of view. Nike, Chick-fil-A, and Salesforce are examples of high-profile companies that have been targets of detractors for declaring their values and taking actions in line with their stated values. These organizations have weathered storms, pressed forward on their missions, which often evolve over time, and continue to deliver value to their customers and shareholders.

STATED VALUES AND ACTION

Peloton's *"Our Values"* - *Together We Go Far* section of its mission is the company's attempt to state its values and realize them. The company's mission reads, *"Build a diverse and inclusive community. Uphold the obligation to dissent and listen. Presume trust and be transparent."* With these values, Foley's drive to build the best place in the world to work, and its reliance on a creative based talent pool from fitness, technology, theater, television production, design, and more, it is no surprise Peloton celebrates segments of society that have been traditionally underrepresented.

For as long as I have been a member, Peloton has celebrated heritage months such as Pride Month, Black History Month, Women's History Month, Asian Heritage Month (changed to Asia and Pacific Islander Heritage Month in 2021), and Latino Hispanic Heritage Month (changed to LatinX in 2020). The company also has held special events and challenges focused on children's health, hunger, and other social issues.

Through these special classes and events and online media, instructors and other team members and members speak their minds and share their experiences and thoughts on social and cultural topics that often have histories of pain, struggle, and division.

It is as if the United Colors of Benetton campaign evolved to a point where the models in the ads are real people (Peloton instructors, team members, and customers) and they are sharing their views. Peloton's YouTube channel and social media are full of company-produced videos highlighting community and team members sharing how empowering Peloton's values are and what it means to have an organization supporting them.

When 2020 brought the United States the pandemic in March, the killing of George Floyd in May, and a contentious American election in November, the Peloton community suffered through a great deal of pain and fear and anger with the rest of the world.

Peloton, as would be expected from its history of acknowledging social challenges and from Foley's comments at the dinner in Georgetown in late 2019, leaned into the moment. In response to George Floyd's killing and protests for racial justice, which Nike had spoken out on for years, Peloton pledged $100 million to fight racism and to make greater opportunities available for those that had been kept out of technology, media, and other burgeoning segments where Peloton has influence. In a statement released by John Foley on June 23, 2020, he wrote,

---

To be clear, I haven't been blind to injustices and inequality in our society. They've been plain to see my entire life, and these same calls for justice have been made for decades, centuries even. What has also been true for decades is that we must proactively reduce inequality, with a particular emphasis on reducing the persistent disparities experienced in our Black communities. This is the work of anti-racism, and the journey for Peloton begins NOW.[67]

Foley and the company announced The Peloton Pledge. The Pledge commits the company to concrete action over four years in five specific areas, including addressing inequality by raising pay and creating more career pathways for hourly workers through the use of data, audits, and tracking career outcomes. Peloton also dedicated itself to supporting others battling institutional injustice and democratizing health and wellness by ensuring more underserved communities have access to its content. Not surprisingly, data and measurement will be part of this effort.

In November 2020, not long after the $100 million commitment, Peloton made waves by partnering with Beyoncé on a series of classes. More importantly, as part of the work with Beyoncé, Peloton made two years of app membership available to students at 10 historically black colleges and universities (HBCUs) and committed to "building our relationships with each of these schools to pursue long-term recruiting partnerships at the internship and undergraduate levels."[68]

Beyond using its size and financial might to secure institutional partners and fund social programming and efforts it supports, Peloton has taken an additional step forward into the divided spaces of culture and politics by allowing its instructors and employees to share their thoughts and feelings about events of the day. In fact, in the wake of Floyd's killing in Minneapolis, Peloton invited African American instructors to share their feelings and program classes taking on racism directly.

On June 3, 2020, I rode live with cycling instructor Tunde Oyeneyin on her "Speak Up" ride not long after George Floyd's killing. It is hard to describe the emotion of that ride and I can only imagine how difficult it was for Oyeneyin, an African American instructor of Nigerian descent to teach it. In communicating the pain and emotion of life in the United States for African Americans, Tunde quoted her colleagues of color from Peloton to communicate her points. In well under a year, that class was taken over 110,000 times.[69] In addition to Tunde's "Speak Up," ride, Chelsea Jackson Roberts, a PhD-holding Peloton yoga instructor and HBCU grad, who joined Peloton in early 2020, hosted a "Breathe In, Speak Up" meditation immediately after the ride.

While the killing of George Floyd brought Peloton's culture of social engagement to the forefront and saw it intensify with the announcement of the Peloton Pledge in June 2020, it was not necessarily new. As long as I had been on the Peloton platform, the corporate culture appeared to allow and even encourage instructors and other team members to be their full selves at work. While this may sound new agey, it was always clear from the statements, styles, and classes, that instructors were generally able to be themselves on camera, whether that was JSS dropping F-bombs during classes or CDE sharing tales of past struggles and pain. With Floyd's death, the opportunity for Peloton team members to share their full selves at work was much more painful and raw, though not unexpected.

Peloton's culture and approach to social engagement and impact was crystalized for me just months before George Floyd was killed. In May 2020, I learned the tragic story of a 25-year-old African American man named Ahmaud Arbery who was chased down and killed while out running in Georgia on

February 23, 2020. Many Americans, including me, had no idea about the killing of Arbery, and that the suspects had not been apprehended and no charges had been filed. In early May, as Peloton began broadcasting classes from its instructor's homes due to the pandemic, I learned of Arbery's death on the Instagram feed of Chase Tucker, a Peloton tread instructor. Tucker, a low-key, earnest, Muay Thai practitioner from Chicago caught my attention when he joined Peloton in 2018 due to his demeanor, Chicago roots, and thoughtful social media posts.

Chase's deep thoughts, meditations, words, and writings on Instagram revealed that there was more than just physical well-being in his bag of tricks. When Chase, as a proud young Haitian American man, shared the story of Arbery on social media and asked Peloton members to run one of his classes on demand on May 8, 2020, I was more than willing to do it, and I was appreciative of the opportunity to learn from Chase. It turned out, May 8th was Arbery's birthday and the broader running community across the U.S. was running 2.23 miles in his honor and to bring attention to his killing (on 2.23) and the lack of progress investigating his death. I took the run outside on my phone, using the Peloton app, while Emily took the class on our tread in our basement. There were over 700 people on the app when I took the class that morning. Thousands more were on the tread with Emily and Chase.

Because Peloton's approach is to let their talent be themselves in the workplace, Tucker was able to present an opportunity to learn about the Arbery injustice to the Peloton community. Thousands joined Chase and then many members, including me, posted the runs to social media with the hashtags #RunwithMaud or

#IRunwithMaud or other variations, amplifying Chase's message and more importantly, public awareness of the Arbery case.

On February 23, 2021, the anniversary of Arbery's killing, I chose to run on demand with Chase by taking his 2021 Black History Month "Icons Run." In that class, Chase played music by artists from the South Side of Chicago, where he grew up, and told the story of one of his heroes, President Barack Obama and his impact on the South Side.

While I enjoyed the chance to learn more about Chase, his worldview, and the impact Obama had on him while taking a great running class, there are likely as many who find this gratuitous and don't understand why this has any part in fitness.

The challenge for Peloton is that not all of its members and potential members (customers) agree with the corporation's engagement or approach to social issues. During the summer of 2020, I witnessed many law enforcement officers and their family members disagree with Peloton's approach and step back from participating in the community. There were others that just wanted to work out and did not want to mix their sweat with the news of the day, Peloton being their escape from the stresses of real life, both personal and societal. It was as if their nirvana had been spoiled by reality.

Media and entertainment companies, from radio and television producers to movie studios and sports leagues, have faced these issues in the past. Peloton's intimacy, community, and instructor focus make the potential for intensity and cleavages in a divided culture era a real and ever-present possibility for the company. The Peloton team was aware of this and accepted it before 2020, in statement and deed, but the events of that year made it evident for all to see.

A SUNDAY COMPROMISE

As the year 2020 highlighted, there are many times when the main social media pages and the Peloton community are impacted by the same racism, sexism, body shaming, political schisms, religious intolerance, and damaging forces of broader society, no matter how much Peloton members share the overriding goals of health and well-being.

Members and instructors have their own minds and social media accounts and are free to share their views, periodically displeasing other members in the community. So, no matter how much the company repeats "Together we go far," and people flock to Peloton for happiness, health, and escape, the fears and pressures and trolls of the real world and social media do appear within the generally positive community that has carried Peloton.

In my years on the Peloton platform, I have watched the request for Christian music rides come up for discussion repeatedly. Oftentimes the requests are met with scorn and ridicule; it's truly unfriendly and disappointing when it happens.

For some members, their requests for these rides appear to be a reminder that many members do not want explicit lyrics with their fitness. (Classes are marked when their playlist songs have explicit lyrics.)

In fall 2019, in what appeared to be a compromise, Peloton began a ride series with instructor Ally Love titled "Sundays with Love." And while there are not clear references to church, the Bible, or Christianity, the themes discussed are those that might be covered in houses of worship. In announcing these rides on Facebook in October 2019, Love wrote, "Every Sunday join me at 11:45 AM ET for a 45-minute ride for an inspirational, spiritually grounded, thought provoking ride! Every week we will be focusing on a different virtue, creating a space to celebrate one another."

None of this surprised me. One only has to follow Love's social media to know that she is a spiritual person and regular church attendee. Moreover, Love's public LinkedIn profile highlights that she studied theology/theological studies at Fordham University, a Catholic institution in New York City.[70] The series appeared to be pretty popular and returned for a second season in 2020 and does not appear to be letting up. Why Peloton has not programmed Christian music classes has never been openly stated, or if it has I missed it.

SHORT SELLERS, ANALYSTS, AND WALL STREET

The last broad group of haters to discuss are those found in the stock market. These are investors and traders who will bet against Peloton, speak negatively about it, write research reports questioning it, and post disparaging information on message boards. They could be invested in competing companies or trends and opposed to Peloton thriving, or they can be short sellers who need the Peloton stock price to decline for their investment to be profitable.

At the members dinner with Foley in 2019 just after the IPO, Foley and I had a brief side conversation about the fact that more than 80 percent of the Peloton shares available were sold short in early October, not even two weeks into the stock's existence. Selling short is basically a bet that a company's shares are overvalued, and the price will decline. To take advantage of this belief, investors can sell shares that they do not own with the expectation they can buy them later for a lower price. Short sellers sell high and then buy low instead of the traditional buy low and then sell high. This means short sellers borrow shares in order to sell before they buy. Selling short received major news coverage in 2021 when Reddit traders and short sellers battled over game retailer GameStop.

When Foley and I discussed the massive short position, Peloton ranked as one the five most-shorted stocks on the Nasdaq. That meant there were a ton of haters when Peloton first went public; those short sellers must have believed it was just a bike with an iPad.

During its first six months of trading, Peloton had much higher short interest than the average Nasdaq stock. One group called Citron Research put a $5 price target on Peloton in December 2019, which got many people excited and floated the notion it was another GoPro or Fitbit.[71] How prominent shorts will be in Peloton's existence going forward is impossible to know, but it is an old tool for financial haters to make their feelings known. There is nothing illegal about it, though there are many investors who find the idea of selling short immoral because it is investing hoping for negative outcomes. Tesla, Amazon, and many other high-flying stocks have regular bouts with short sellers.

From short sellers on Wall Street and in chat rooms, to Twitter hacks and talking-head academics such as New York University's Scott Galloway, Peloton's success has made it a target for a range of haters. Some fundamentally don't agree with the sustainability of the model and others just make their money off of destruction and negativity. Perhaps these folks need to clip-in and sweat it out, or take a mediation class.

It should be noted that there has been a strong community of Peloton believers on Wall Street, such as J.P. Morgan Internet Analyst Doug Anmuth. In February 2021, with the pandemic rocketing Peloton forward, Anmuth put a $200 price target on the stock (this would be soon be lowered after the company faced challenges). There are also a range of social media supporters (#OCshree and #bluehousebro) on Twitter and Reddit, many who own Peloton products as well as stock shares.

HUBRIS BEFORE THE FALL

As an 18-year-old, in my first semester at the University of Michigan in 1991, I took a course called Great Books. We read *The Iliad*, the *Odyssey,* and other classics. As the semester ended, the teaching assistant offered a trick to those of us exposed to Homer and other such works for the first time: if you do not know why a character is behaving in a way that leads to catastrophe, blame it on hubris.

Like the great problems among gods and mortals, the business world is full of companies and leaders that faltered and failed because of their hubris. Excessive pride and arrogance stop many in their tracks, either combusting quickly or leading the firm to run out of steam and slow down.

High-fliers like Peloton, Beyond Meat, and others that exhibit rapid growth, attract venture investors, and gain legions of customers are rare indeed, and celebrated far and wide in our economy. A sense of confidence and importance can settle in to teams, investors, and others associated with such firms.

The WeWork venture is a case study in hubris, with the players wrapped in pride, arrogance, self-importance, pretension, vanity, and greed. The We Company IPO document opened with: "We dedicate this to the energy of We—greater than any one of us but inside each of us." It also stated, "We are a community company committed to maximum global impact. Our mission is to elevate the world's consciousness."[72] CEO Adam Neumann's arrogance had him trademarking the term "We" and selling it back to the corporate entity that he and main investor Masayoshi Son were trying to take public. A *Wall Street Journal* piece exposing some of Neumann's behavior in September 2019 read like the movie *Almost Famous* with international flights on private jets, illegal drugs, lots of tequila, and strategic decisions infused with the Kabbalah mysticism that has also been practiced by Madonna and Ashton Kutcher.[73]

The public market sniffed out the hubris of Neumann, Masayoshi Son, and WeWork and refused to take the IPO. It did not matter that Goldman Sachs, J.P. Morgan, and Wells Fargo were leading this IPO. The world smelled the BS they were hustling and told them all to take a walk.

If you read the S1 filing that Peloton released to go public, Foley's letter to prospective investors and members states, "It is no secret that exercise makes us feel good. It's simple science: exercising creates endorphins and endorphins make us happy. On the most basic level, Peloton sells happiness."[74] Was selling happiness and belief in endorphins enough of a strategy to go public and change the world? Elle Woods, played by Reese Witherspoon (a Peloton member), from *Legally Blonde* might agree, but many may find this a bit delusional for a billion-dollar technology venture.

Peloton is led by a hard-charging CEO and leadership team who are open about their belief in current possibilities and their huge plans for the future. During the 2020 Peloton Investor Day presentation, Foley shared his oft-stated goal of 100 million subscribers—nearly 100 times larger than the 1.09 million connected devices Peloton reported at the end of fiscal year 2020, and 50 times more than 2 million subscribers on board midway through 2021.

In early 2017, when I realized the incredible impact Peloton was making on its members, I began to imagine that the company could become one of the biggest in the world. At that point, the company did not yet have 100,000 bikes sold and the Facebook page had just over 26,000 members. Four years later, with over 2 million connected fitness devices sold and more than 6 million members, Foley, Cortese, William Lynch, and others have not been shy about how impactful Peloton plans to become. When I interviewed Foley in 2019, he explained the massive pressure he and the team feel daily because, as they believe, "this is going to be one of the special companies of all time." The line between confidence and arrogance can be a fine one.

HUBRIS AND LOGISTICS

Peloton has made growth a central theme in its strategy; inventing a category, expanding, and controlling it. In less than a decade, Peloton has developed a global supply chain (buying manufacturers and building distribution, manufacturing, and fulfillment assets across the globe), established a network of more than 100 retail stores, designed and built massive production studios in Manhattan and London, developed additional premium hardware, completed an IPO, and, most importantly, improved millions of lives. This kind of growth, including massive head count increases, and expansion, obviously leads to confidence, but might also lead to excessive pride, bloat, and blind spots.

Logistics, for example, have been a challenge for Peloton as bikes, treads, and other large pieces of technical hardware are not easy to produce, deliver, install, or service. Peloton is proud of the work it has done investing in the physical side of the business, but this was a necessity as third-party delivery partners, including the publicly traded XPO, were not doing installation and onboarding befitting the beautiful $2,200 indoor bike and the more than $4,000 treadmills customers were buying.

Co-founder Cortese's 2017 public speech at a PSFK sponsored event highlighted the company knew it needed to own the process of installing and servicing its products from end to end.[75] Cortese's remarks emphasized that it was crucial to control the member experience from the online inquiry, to store visit, through the installation of the product, and into the classes and social media engagement. This vertical integration was necessary to the experience. The company invested hundreds of millions of dollars building more than 20 fulfillment centers across the United States by 2020, replete with Sprinter vans and teams of Peloton-uniformed field operations specialists.

Even after seven years of learning and investment, Peloton still must rely on outside partners because of demand, in both the gross number of products purchased and the places where Peloton cannot reach eager customers with its own infrastructure. The challenges with XPO and other fulfillment partners were known, but they were a small issue until the pandemic hit and demand and wait times grew. As the pandemic became the new normal, the fulfillment side of the business was crushed, as customer service was overwhelmed with excited but unhappy customers waiting for their bikes.

During the initial phase of the pandemic, Peloton brought in more third-party help and increased production, but demand could not be met. Social media began to fill with complaints against Peloton and its partners. Perhaps the ultimate irony was when a Facebook group called Peloton Delivery Discussion Group was created in late 2020. The group was created so new customers and potential customers could discuss the nightmare delivery and rescheduling issues they were experiencing. My old Peloton friend #SunshineKnight became a contributor on that page as his Bike+, an upgraded version of the original bike, was delayed multiple times. We exchanged a few messages and I even inquired with my local sales team to see if they might have a clue. His original order was placed on November 2, 2020, and the bike was finally delivered on April 27, 2021. Throughout his 176-day wait, people in his region that purchased months after Chris were receiving their Bike+ orders. Chris had been a huge and loyal advocate of Peloton since I met him in 2018. By spring 2021, he was openly angry and beyond disappointed with the company, feeling lied to by multiple customer service agents. Years of goodwill and a true customer ambassador were lost, due to poor logistics and even weaker communications. This hubris, such as overlooking early customers, in a race for scale can become a problem, especially for a company that has relied on its community to do so much of the heavy lifting.

While Peloton began tackling the issues of pandemic demand and delivery during 2020, even using air freight to move product from Asia, the gross physical size of Peloton's products, their weight, and the fact they must be brought into members' homes has always been a pain point for Peloton. Logistics has been a challenge since inception, and many of the comments on the Kickstarter campaign from 2013 revolved around the difficulty of delivering bikes and the reliance on partners pressed into service to help. Peloton's delivery issues continue to be a challenge and serve as an example where unbridled growth has potential to undermine the goodwill that Peloton built in its early years.

HUBRIS AND HARDWARE

While Peloton bikes and treads have been lauded by reviewers and owners alike, producing and delivering new-to-world, high-end fitness hardware at scale has not been without its problems. After a couple years of owning the bike, my wife didn't feel that it was pedaling as smoothly as it once had. Emily called Peloton and they sent out a service team. The service team replaced the bearings.

We got back to riding. Within a few weeks, it was clear Emily was not happy with the fix and she called Peloton again. Once again a field ops team came out and serviced our bike. Once again Emily was not happy. At that point, Peloton offered us a refurbished, yet newer bike. I assumed they figured that was cheaper than coming out frequently to service our bike. (I am convinced that my copious sweat from riding thousands of miles in 2018 killed our bike, but Peloton never pressed me on that.)

In reality, it is not super hard to find users whose bikes have had failures, from tablets and incorrect outputs, to pedals that snap off while riding. In fact, pedals snapping was one of the first Peloton failures I learned about via social media in 2017. I am lucky that I learned about this problem (it has something to do with how the pedals are installed) as I experienced this while riding live in the studio in NYC in the summer of 2018. Yes, a Peloton pedal snapped off while I was at the Peloton Mothership riding live!

I was in the early part of a live Ally Love class during a PMCT Home Rider Invasion (HRI), and the pedal on the bike I was riding felt wonky from the start. Because I was aware of the pedal failure issue from social media, I pedaled gently, fearful of what might come. My caution was warranted because the pedal snapped off loudly during the ride. The pedal was now stuck to my shoe (remember, I was wearing clip-in bike shoes). #SunshineKnight was on the bike next to me and took a picture with his phone, with the flash on, breaking a cardinal rule of taking live classes in the studio: no phones on during classes. I pedaled gently with one leg the rest of the ride and wondered how I was going to get the pedal off of my shoe.

Fortunately, I was not hurt, and after the class the Peloton studio team removed the pedal from my shoe quickly and easily. We watched as the bike was wheeled out and then we hustled to get in line to take our picture with Ally. We apologized to Ally for disrupting the class with the pictures, but explained the pedal snapping caught us off guard and Chris couldn't help himself from taking a picture as he is a trained photographer and loves documenting his life. It would take until 2020 for mainstream media outlets to cover the pedal problem and Peloton to issue a recall.[76]

Another troubling hardware issue appeared not long after Peloton began delivering its first treadmills in late 2018. Complaints began to appear almost immediately regarding both delivery (members often blaming fulfillment partner XPO) and performance challenges with the product. Pictures of nicked walls, scratched floors, half-assembled treads, and boxes left behind were shared across Peloton social media.

By far the most dooming posts were of non-performing tread bases, and videos of loud, angry-sounding treadmills came to dominate dialogue on the Tread Group on Facebook throughout 2019. Many many members told stories of multiple tread base replacements. At one point in April 2019, a non-scientific poll of tread owners on the Facebook page found that about 20 percent of the treads delivered had been serviced or had major parts replaced.

Our tread ran into problems after a few months, and we had to have a major part (the crossbar) replaced. For some reason the crossbar was not recognizing the safety key, and our tread came to an immediate stop during classes while I was running because the machine thought that the safety key had been removed. It happened to me twice and the sudden stop did not feel good on my lower back.

While waiting for our major part replacement, we lost the use of our tread for nearly a month, and our family was totally bummed. However, we were fully aware that we had purchased the first generation of a large piece of technical hardware. We were also so happy with our bike that there was no question we were going to trust the company and grow with Peloton, so the crossbar failure on our treadmill did not bother us too much. We have not had a problem with our treadmill since the crossbar issue, and our family has completed thousands of classes on the machine. There was in fact, as of early 2021, one Facebook poster and Peloton member that claimed to have had five base replacements. I reached out to this person multiple times via social media and they never replied. I have seen them on leaderboards and social media since. They have a long record of complaining about Peloton on social media, yet continue to run and ride regularly. Haters are gonna hate, even members.

In spring 2021, the Peloton Tread+ (the larger of their treadmills), became a problem when news came out that a child had been killed in an accident with the massive piece of equipment. This was a type of tragedy few, including myself, even considered when bringing a treadmill into our home. Peloton, with Foley taking the lead, put out some statements and an email addressing the reports. On March 18 I received an email that stated, "Hi David, I am reaching out to you today because I recently learned about a tragic accident involving a child and the Tread+, resulting in, unthinkably, a death. I can't tell you how much this news and horrible reality has hit me personally and our entire team at Peloton."[77] The email was signed by Foley and went on to remind all recipients about Peloton Tread+ safety procedures and age limits and that the company would work with members to make their experience as safe as possible.

A short time later the U.S. Consumer Product Safety Commission (CPSC) announced that it was aware of dozens of incidents, including the death of a child, related to "being sucked beneath" the Peloton Tread+. The CPSC recommended a recall of the Tread+ and shared some strong warnings, including advising users to:

Stop using the Peloton Tread+ if there are small children or pets at home. Incidents suggest that children may be seriously injured while the Tread+ is being used by an adult, not just when a child has unsupervised access to the machine.[78]

Wow, the language was vague, yet broad and incredibly vivid; almost suggesting Peloton's world-class treadmill might be as dangerous as, I don't know, a woodchipper or chainsaw.

Peloton immediately pushed back against the CPSC recommendations (which were voluntary and not directives) and issued a press release stating:

> Peloton (NASDAQ: PTON) cares deeply about the safety of its Members and one of its core values is putting Members first. The company is troubled by the Consumer Product Safety Commission's (CPSC) unilateral press release about the Peloton Tread+ because it is inaccurate and misleading. There is no reason to stop using the Tread+, as long as all warnings and safety instructions are followed. Children under 16 should never use the Tread+, and Members should keep children, pets, and objects away from the Tread+ at all times.[79]

A class action lawsuit soon followed. Like the class action lawsuit when the music purge occurred, calls to join this suit soon showed up in my Facebook feed in late April 2021. In early May, just days before its earnings call, Peloton announced a treadmill recall (with various remedies available), a pausing of all treadmill sales, and a corporate commitment to safety. The company also admitted its initial response to the CPSC was hasty.

While Peloton has warnings on the machine and makes it clear the Tread+ is large and potentially dangerous, the child fatality is a reminder that even the most well-intentioned ventures cannot control or foresee everything, and scale and high-growth can often come at a cost. In the wake of the incident, Peloton vowed to improve safety features going forward.

How long it will take for the Tread+ and the new smaller Tread to become defect-free products is unknown, and it is hard to know how long Peloton's goodwill will last if issues such as broken pedals, screens falling off, and child-safety recalls become a regular feature of the brand.

HUBRIS, MEANING, AND MEMORIES

On February 19, 2021 I took my favorite Colleen Saidman Yee (CSY) 10-minute morning yoga class for the 365th time. That was a year's worth of mornings with Colleen Saidman Yee, Peloton's original in house, part-time yogi. I had never practiced yoga before Peloton. I learned to love yoga with CSY gently and happily guiding me along in the convenience and comfort of my own home, Peloton's original and core value proposition. Some mornings I did additional classes or other classes completely.

After achieving that 365 milestone in mid-February, I considered posting my achievement to the main Peloton Facebook page (there were 400,000 people on that page at that point), sharing my happiness and love for yoga and my gratitude for Colleen and Peloton. I decided not to. Frankly, I did not want to call any attention to the stash of Yee classes that existed, concerned that the Peloton powers that be might read my post and purge Colleen and my favorite classes. I just kept on flowing with CSY. On February 26, just a week later, I took that morning yoga class for the 368th time. That turned out to be the final time

I would take that morning flow with Colleen or any class on Peloton with Colleen Saidman Yee.

On February 27, 2021, Peloton purged a large number of older classes and we lost all of the CSY classes. According to a Pelo Buddy TV post I read not long after the purge, there were 44 CSY classes purged that fateful day in late February 2021.[80]

Because there were so many new members brought in during Covid, it's likely only a handful of members were disappointed. While I mourned the loss and cursed myself for days for not having screen recorded the entire class, in reality, I knew everything was going to be okay. I had taken more than 1,100 yoga classes with Peloton at that point, and by early 2021 there were six professional, full-time yogis producing amazing classes for Peloton.

After a day or two of anger and sadness (mostly for not saving that morning class), I knew it was time to move on. I spent a week or so of searching for 10-minute yoga classes and stretches; I decided to level up and start taking the 20-minute "Morning Yoga" classes that Kristin McGee, Chelsea Jackson Roberts, and Anna Greenberg had on demand; soon after I tried 30-minute morning yoga and 45-minute morning classes. I turned the purge into a growth opportunity, but I was still sad about the lost Yee classes.

Purges of classes, like the ones initiated during the music lawsuits and the February 2021 purge where I lost my beloved CSY classes, have become regular occurrences and can wreak havoc for members. Classes in the Peloton on-demand catalog might be important because members did them in the studio with family or friends or because they reached a milestone and received a shout-out from a favorite instructor. I've lost many classes that were special because of who I was with (in person or on leaderboard) or a shout-out or a special action or comments or stories from the instructor.

Each class is unique, with different playlists, structures, leaderboards, and shout-outs, and member and instructor mindsets. Much like live sporting events or jam-band performances, each class is a show of its own. The meaning that a particular class can hold for members makes purges painful and contentious. It is as if a member's VHS tapes are destroyed or hard drive full of a family's pics are lost forever. Peloton's incredible success has meant class purges hurt.

Bottom line, with classes being produced constantly, purges are going to keep happening as storage and demand are not infinite. It is hard to know how big of a deal this will become over the long term, but it is likely to be a challenge. Many streaming and content services, including Netflix, are continually adjusting their catalogues. Will most members flow with the content changes as I did with the removal of CSY's yoga and the departure of Jennifer Jacobs? I reframed both "Pelo-losses" as opportunities to evolve, and maybe even go bigger. Although I still follow both on social media and pine for them often. Perhaps Peloton, its members, talent, or others will develop a solution to ensure the hybrid, physical, and digital experiences that occur on the Peloton platform are available over time for the people for whom they hold such deep meaning. Perhaps members could buy the rights to those classes (NFTs or some other secure version) or even short clips of their shout-outs or favorite instructor quotes or moments from rides.

STUMBLE, BUT DON'T FALL

When ventures are creating new categories and pushing boundaries, challenges will occur and mistakes will be made. This is no different from Tesla owners putting up with buggy software or Apple buyers accepting that not every iPhone or iPad release is going to be flawless. While reading about Tesla in 2019, I learned that the company was just starting to do its own body work. The first Tesla roadster came out in 2007! This means it took Tesla 12 years to get to one of the most obvious parts of the auto industry, body work, repair, and replacement. It is common for innovators to overlook some of the basics of an industry when pushing so hard on the boundaries.

From my interactions with Foley, Cortese, Robin Arzón, and others, I observed that many members of the Peloton team plan to go big and understand there will be challenges along the way. When they see a challenge or problem, they go after it, not away from it. With so much success the team is intent on building a world-changing company that can be as big as Apple or Amazon or Tesla, with hundreds of millions on its platform across the globe. Many of the instructors and talent are building their own brands and have large ambitions as well.

Beyond becoming a trillion-dollar venture, the greater hope is that Peloton can truly change people's lives through health and well-being; that is why I started researching the company in the first place. If the company achieves its goals, Peloton will have helped shift the economy further toward the business of well-being, and beyond delivering physical stuff and content to devour while sitting on a couch or staring motionless at a screen.

The team's aggressiveness and growing vision is inspiring and amazing. I just can't forget what my classics teaching assistant,

Stephen Sheehi, who is now a professor at the College of William and Mary, taught me about hubris. I hope that hubris does not prevent Peloton and its talented team from achieving their full potential. The challenge of not letting growth, fanfare, and success create arrogance or lead to mistakes and lost opportunities is real. Foley acknowledged in our conversation that no one knows how to do what Peloton is trying to do, making the bumps in the road nearly impossible to see. The great companies make it over the bumps and keep growing and creating value.

CHAPTER 8

THE TREAD, THE GLOBE, AND GROWING BEYOND SWEAT

When I spoke with co-founder and CPO Tom Cortese in 2019, I asked him if he ever imagined Peloton would be this big. The company was privately valued around $4 billion at the time. The not-yet-40-year-old Cortese sheepishly smiled and said when they started he was confident they could build a strong, profitable technology business that scaled and helped people lead better lives through fitness.

I don't know if Peloton had surpassed Cortese's early goals by late 2016 when the bike arrived at my home, but for an inconsistent jogger like me, finding the Peloton indoor bike with engaging instructors, great music, and an insane sweat in the safety and comfort of my own home was world-changing. Peloton made me want to work out, as Cortese liked to say, when highlighting why Peloton was so different from anything else the industry had seen before. Wanting to work out versus feeling compelled to work out, meant that in 2017, my first full year with the bike, I exercised more times than in any other calendar year of my life.

BEYOND THE RIDE

In January 2018, the PMCT group on Facebook introduced me to Peloton classes called "Beyond the Ride." I noticed that other members of the group were taking many of these classes, usually affectionately and efficiently referring to them as BTRs. These classes included stretches, short strength classes, cardio and HIIT workouts, and yoga. Some were as short as five minutes, while others lasted 10 or 20 minutes. The term Beyond the Ride would disappear when Peloton realized it was going to offer running, bootcamps, strength, and more. Eventually classes that did not require Peloton hardware were referred to by their discipline— stretching, yoga, strength, cardio, and so on.

My curiosity around the non-cycling classes got the best of me, and I made one of my January 2018 PMCT monthly goals to complete 12 BTR classes. That translated to three classes per week, many of which would only be five minutes. I figured this would be an easy goal for the month. I started simply by following the cycling instructor's advice to take a five-minute stretch after each ride. This would make achieving my goal of 12 classes easy as I knew I would definitely take 12 bike classes in January 2018 as I could feel my addiction to Peloton growing.

I fell in love with BTRs quickly. The five-minute stretches after rides helped my recoveries from hard rides, enabling faster improvement in my performance and endurance. Peloton kept count of my BTRs and awarded badges as I did more. (Peloton's gamification worked well with the goals I was developing in the PMCT Facebook group.) There were strength classes, for example, lots of five- and 10-minute arms and shoulders and core classes. There were even simple boxing classes, including a five-minute shadow boxing session that served as a good warm-up or to stack on top other classes when I just wanted a little more out of my workout that day.

What I realized with that January 2018 BTR challenge was that Peloton could provide value well beyond the ride, meaning without their hardware; from a business expansion perspective, this was a massive. I blew away that January goal of 12 non-bike classes, completing more than 40 that month. By the end of 2018, just two years after taking my first ever indoor cycling ride, I had completed more than 800 non-bike classes.

I fell in love with the snack-size flexibility of the non-bike classes; allowing me to stack multiple classes to create my own personal workouts. With the ability to pull up rides and floor exercises on the Peloton Digital app on my phone, I now had a virtual gym and indoor bike studio in my pocket, and it was growing each day, with new classes being produced and offered to members.

It was through gorging on non-bike workouts in 2018 that I discovered yoga with instructor Colleen Saidman Yee. I had no idea that Yee was one of the most famous yoga instructors in the

United States, but I discovered she had produced a bunch of yoga classes for Peloton's on-demand library.

Never before had I taken yoga. In the cities I lived in—San Francisco, Chicago, London, and Washington D.C.—I always felt intimidated by yoga studios in the urban neighborhoods where I worked, lived, and hung out. Yoga appeared to be for really cool people, not tall, stiff, bookish types who jogged a few months a year. My previous reluctance to try yoga was probably due to my own baggage, but Peloton's yoga with Yee, in the privacy of my own home removed any barriers. Offering basic classes in five- and 10-minute blocks allowed me to dip my toes into yoga in a safe and private environment.

By mid 2018 I was trying to take at least one short yoga class each morning. The 10-minute classes really changed the way I began my day. I ordered yoga blocks and a yoga mat from Amazon's Amazon Basics brand. I was addicted; yoga became an addiction within an addiction. I also wondered how I had missed this awesome yoga thing my entire life. Some basic research revealed that yoga was really popular across America. A 2019 report from fitness industry software maker Mindbody found that yoga was the single most popular group fitness in America.[81] I was super late to this giant global party of flow, but I loved it and Peloton had brought me there, just as it had brought me to indoor cycling.

I must not have been the only Peloton member in 2018 loving the yoga offering. In late 2018, the company announced that three full-time yoga instructors (Kristin McGee, Anna Greenberg, and Aditi Shah) would begin streaming live from Peloton's tread studio in Greenwich Village. Four years after the bike and less than a year after introducing a treadmill, Peloton was fully moving into producing content that did not involve bike or treadmill instructors!

In addition to various types of yoga (power, slow flow, restorative, and more) and various levels (beginner, intermediate, and advanced), the new yoga instructors would offer regular guided meditations on subjects from happiness and peace to sleep and performance.[82] Peloton still had fewer than 250,000 connected fitness subscribers at this point and was not a public company, but it was clear the future was getting bigger and broader.

Peloton was moving with the marketplace to a more holistic view of well-being, from the physical to the emotional and spiritual. Peloton would introduce a fourth full-time yoga instructor, Chelsea Jackson Roberts, in spring 2020, again highlighting the popularity of the full-time yoga and meditation classes.

With non-bike and non-tread classes, including yoga instructors and meditation, Peloton could provide a broader range of well-being classes. Given the size of the mindfulness and yoga markets, it is not surprising that Peloton quickly found value off the bike and leveraged its success on the bike to introduce customers to other areas. When I interviewed Robin Arzón in 2019 and we discussed Peloton's growth she told me, "We are going to be the singular touchpoint for people's association with wellness, and it's really exciting to see that happen even at this nascent stage."

Peloton's ability to create yoga, outdoor audio runs (introduced in July 2018), strength, HIIT, cardio dance, meditation, barre, family fit, Pilates, and other classes demonstrates that while the company started with hardware at home, its team could provide value in segments of fitness and well-being that did not demand purchase of their hardware and could be done outside the home. Peloton members like me loved these options, and in July 2020, a popular 10-minute core class released by cycling instructor Emma Lovewell on April 29, 2019, passed the 1 million times taken milestone. I guess we should expect to see a lot of six-pack abs in the future.

By using its instructors for disciplines off of Peloton hardware, the company has delivered even greater value to its members. Whether on Peloton apps made for phones, tablets, computers, TVs, or the hardware, members have access to expanding libraries of content. Additionally, all of the non-hardware content makes the option to be an app-only (or digital) member (using Peloton classes on non-Peloton hardware) a greater value just as it does for those that own Peloton connected devices. By mid-2021, Peloton would have more than 1,000,000 digital-only subscribers.

HARDWARE

As I rode the bike happily through 2017 and researched Peloton, I knew there had to be more to come. The success of the indoor bike and the intensity of the community combined with the size of the home fitness and health club markets made it obvious that the company would come out with something else. Peloton did come up with more and made headlines in January 2018 by introducing their version of the treadmill at the Consumer Electronics Show (CES) in Las Vegas. CES, the most influential technology show in the world, has been the place where video game makers, home electronics giants, software innovators, and media companies come to make a splash with new products.

The Peloton treadmill, originally named the Tread, was a beast (weighing over 300 lbs) and drew attention immediately for its screen, size, slatted treads (versus a traditional belt to run on), and hefty price tag (over $4,000). The machine, featuring a 32-inch HD display, would stream running, walking, floor, and bootcamp classes from a new production studio in the Greenwich Village neighborhood of New York. The company started offering and producing classes for treadmills in April 2018 and began delivering the massive piece of fitness hardware to home users in the fall of 2018.

My wife Emily, clearly the smarter consumer in our house, placed a deposit for the Peloton Tread the day it was announced, so we were in the first grouping to receive word that the treadmill would be coming our way before the end of 2018. While I wasn't sure if we needed this new treadmill, I had learned my lesson from the bike experience and did not argue.

The Tread's introduction and additional fitness modalities (running, walking, bootcamps, and more) meant new instructors and a greater chance to try new fitness approaches. For those members riding daily and addicted to Peloton Facebook groups, Reddit discussions, and instructor Instagram accounts, the new machine was like a gift from Foley and the entire Peloton team. We lined up to give them our money!

Not so many years ago, many leading consumers waited for the new iPhone or iPad and waited on the mind-blowing product presentations from Steve Jobs. The Peloton Tread Experience that I attended in fall 2018 in New York (where I met my friend #EvryBdyLuvsJery) was a launch event that felt like a Disney attraction, Peloton class, and Apple event rolled into one. Dedicated members in the Peloton community have shown similar anticipation for the company's new hardware announcements, instructors, content, and features.

In addition to bringing in new talent for the treadmill, the new platform gave cycling instructors Robin Arzón and Matt Wilpers, who both have extensive backgrounds in running, a chance to share more of their knowledge, passion, and content with Peloton members.

For existing bike owners that purchased the Peloton tread, the new hardware would not demand an additional $39 subscription fee. The treadmill content would be covered under the $39 monthly membership fee that bike owners already paid. Bike owners that did not buy the tread would have access to the content and could use it on devices with treadmills from other makers. As with the bike, no stated limits were placed on how many memberships were allowed on a tread subscription. This decision to allow the one connected subscription fee to cover the bike and the treadmill was brilliant and made it much easier for existing members to add the Peloton tread to their home. The positive reception to the treadmill by both the media and consumers led to speculation that an entire suite of hardware could be coming.

The successful marketing and launch of the tread proved that Peloton could scale beyond the bike. As important, in my analysis, was that Peloton displayed its magic by basically doubling the price of its second offering (more than $4,000 for the initial tread versus just over $2,000 for the original Peloton bike).

It is important to note that traditionally the treadmill market is twice the size of the stationary bike market, which is a reason why Peloton decided to enter. I think it is possible the initial Peloton bike and content (instructors) have been so disruptive that it may create a long-term structural change toward bikes being more common than treadmills for the at-home market, but only time will tell.

After the tread release, Peloton watchers envisioned a new rower, or a strength machine, or maybe a climber or stepper. Regardless of the hype, speculation, and rumors about future product releases, we fell in love with our Peloton tread and found ourselves constantly trying to balance between treadmill and bike content.

I traveled to New York multiple times in 2019 to take treadmill running and bootcamp classes with instructors Selena Samuela and Olivia Amato, throwing myself into the tread world and community as I had with the bike.

Many PMCT and other "Pelo-friends" bought treads and took to helping to build out the community on social media. Having cross-over instructors Arzón and Wilpers and a cast of new instructors made the tread exciting and comfortable at the same time.

Despite this, the Covid-19 pandemic impacted Peloton's ability to produce and deliver treadmills and bikes to meet demand. The pandemic massively changed the public's view of connected and at-home fitness. The pandemic led to enormous funding and experimentation around many new ventures and products in the connected and smart fitness space; some were discussed in the previous chapter.

In fall 2020, as the pandemic continued, demand for Peloton products continued to grow. In the face of great demand and limited supply, Peloton officially announced two new hardware products: an upgraded bike and a lower priced treadmill. The new hardware product line extension fit with the company's stated goal to have a "pruned" product portfolio with a "better" and "best" offering in the categories that Peloton enters. As much as I watched the company, I was not expecting an upgraded bike. Emily was not expecting a new bike, but, of course, she immediately upgraded us to the new offering, known as the Bike+. I was a supporter and had done a complete 180 from when Emily told me she purchased the original bike back in 2016.

When Peloton announced these new products, it also announced a plan whereby existing members could trade in their original bikes if they were upgrading to the new Bike+. This "reverse logistics," as Foley referred to it, highlighted the potential value of the physical logistics infrastructure Peloton had invested in and the opportunities it might pose for the company and its community going forward.

We experienced the first version of the system in action and watched as a Peloton field ops team came to our house in October 2020 to take away our original model Peloton and bring us the new Bike+. Getting our upgraded bike took longer than we expected as demand was great upon release. During the earnings call on November 5, 2020, (which covered earnings through September 30, 2020), Foley stated, "We did our best to estimate the demand for Bike+. But while we are incredibly excited about the positive reaction to Bike+, sales outpaced our internal estimates, quickly causing wait times for Bike+ to balloon. As such, we are working swiftly to pivot manufacturing capacity to Bike+."

In that same call, Jill Woodworth, Peloton CFO, later added, "We expect the growth in our supply chain to allow us to get back to normal order-to-delivery time frames for our bike by the end of this calendar year. However, we will likely be operating under Bike+ supply constraints for the foreseeable future, causing longer order-to-delivery time frames for Bike+ for a couple more quarters. We are already shifting manufacturing capacity in favor of Bike+, but continue to expect our original bike to be our top-selling product in fiscal 2021."

The introduction of the more expensive Bike+ (while lowering the price of the original bike), was met with massive demand, just as Peloton experienced with the more than $4,000 treadmill in 2018. This immediately forced Peloton to adjust its production infrastructure to support the more expensive, newer Bike+, even as the original was hitting record sales.

The massive demand for the new product innovations and higher price points plus the global pandemic meant that by fall 2020 Peloton's global infrastructure was being taxed dramatically. No matter, the market wanted more and more. Calls for strength machines, rowers, and other connected devices were coming from all corners—Peloton members, media, Wall Street, and beyond.

In late 2020, just as the calendar year was ending, Peloton announced its acquisition of fitness giant Precor. Peloton's purchase of Precor gave it ownership of two U.S. manufacturing facilities as well as a massive product portfolio and a team of designers and engineers with decades of experience in all elements of the fitness equipment industry. In one acquisition, for around $500 million, Peloton quickly expanded its infrastructure, talent, and corporate knowledge of fitness equipment design, production, and commercial sales.

In 2021, as I reflected on Peloton's progress, the booming well-being market and other great innovations, I began to imagine a day when Peloton fulfillment teams, in self-driving electric vehicles, aided by robotic dollies and lifts, regularly swap out equipment, accessories, and other well-being products (from a broad Peloton portfolio) for members at their homes or other locations (e.g., office, vacation spots).

In that potential scenario, different members with different needs and physical spaces might purchase different subscription levels with different options. What is considered a connected well-being device, and where all of Peloton's members might be in the future, will be fascinating to watch as the demand for and understanding of well-being grows.

EH HOSER, SPRECHEN SIE DEUTSCH?

Before becoming interested in startups and new venture creation, I focused my time on international politics and business. I learned Japanese in college and did a home stay with a Japanese family in the suburbs of Osaka during my junior year at the University of Michigan. After college, I moved to London to study the international politics of Asia and dreamed of being a global business leader or the secretary of state. A range of factors, including the rise of the internet, made it clear that startups would be a better space than international affairs.

Although I am no longer a regular reader of *Foreign Affairs*, I was not surprised that another vector for Peloton's growth was across geographic lines.

Peloton opened the United Kingdom with a cycling studio in London in 2018 and used that beachhead for its invasion of continental Europe. The company started with two English-language instructors (Benjamin Alldis and Leanne Hainsby; they ended up becoming a couple), added two German-speaking instructors (Irène Scholz and Erik Jäger), then added more British instructors (Hannah Frankson and Sam Yo) and German-language instructors (Cliff Dwenger and Mayla Wedekind). Thus far, all of the instructors for the UK and Germany have been based out of London.

In October 2018, Peloton expanded north to Canada, the United States' second-largest trading partner, and opened a store in the global cultural capital of Toronto. The company's first retail site was formerly occupied by Hermès, indicating the choice locations Peloton has secured in many retail real estate markets. Entering Canada was logical and likely easy for Peloton, considering stellar relations between the nations, shared language and culture for programming, and easy access for moving people and materials. The physical nature of Peloton's products, sales channels, and community can never be discounted.

By mid-2020 it was common to see riders from the UK and Germany on the leaderboards. Peloton has invested in a massive production studio in London that opened in September 2021. The new, lower-priced and smaller treadmill appeared well positioned to physically fit in markets where spaces may be smaller; heavy marketing and selling of the new treadmills began in Europe in 2021. As more members come on from Europe, content, community, and more will grow, deepening the experience for members across the platform. While sales and marketing of the newer, smaller, lower-priced Peloton treads were paused globally as a result of the recalls in the United States in 2021, the cash-cow bike and cycling content were always the keys to Peloton conquering Europe.

Germany and the United Kingdom are the second and third largest health club markets after the United States, so Peloton is simply following the data to mature markets in fitness. In 2019, co-founder Cortese told me that time zones and languages are likely to be some of the obvious and challenging impediments to scale, and he is correct on that. The opening of Australia and the Asia-Pacific in mid 2021 made it clear the Peloton is driving towards a 24-hour-a-day global fitness and well-being platform. Peloton's global expansion reminds me of the early days of CNN and ESPN.

Japan, China, India, Latin America, Africa, and the Middle East present more questions about language, logistics, time zones, culture, and local competition. If Peloton is going to reach its stated goal of 100 million subscribers, about 97-odd million more than it has at the time of this final draft in late 2021, it will demand global talent, physical spaces, technology, media, and community engagement, among other assets.[83]

FITNESS, WELL-BEING, AND BEYOND

One of the simple truths that I realized upon completing my 500th ride, a 45-minute, live '80s ride with Jennifer Jacobs, was that the best way to celebrate health and well-being is with more health and well-being. I made this observation after being so excited about my 500th ride that I "had" to go for a 20-minute Pop Fun Run with Olivia Amato later in the day. I realized that the more wellness and health I believed I had, the more I wanted. I wanted only to sweat more, see progress, and grow with each pedal stroke, tree pose, or burpee that I completed. It was another one of those "Who am I?" moments that Peloton often provides (like exercising in a store window). Why was I celebrating a 500th ride with a 20-minute run and then posting about it to my online friends?

There was an inertia to working out, eating well, stretching, meditating, and trying to manage work hours and stress. I began to wonder why I wasn't focusing on my overall well-being, and I started visiting museums, reading more books, and looking for botanic gardens when I traveled. My realization that I hadn't visited a museum in years came when I saw Peloton DJ John Michael post photos from his visit to the New York Botanical Garden in the Bronx. Inspired to get outside and engage more, I even volunteered to help clean and repair the Great Falls National Park along the Potomac River, where I liked to do some of my outdoor runs. My then-nine-year-old daughter came with me, and we spent a few hours scraping and repainting the mule pen at the C&O Canal Great Falls Visitor Center. All of the aforementioned activities were undertaken because I believed they would be fun and increase my overall well-being. My search for well-being was taking more of my time, but it was bringing new people, experiences, strength, and happiness.

I was becoming more engaged with the world around me and intentional about how I spent my leisure time. During one New York trip to visit the Peloton studios and complete interviews, I decided to visit an art museum. After googling a bit, I learned there was an Andy Warhol exhibit at the Whitney Museum of American Art. After taking a class at the Peloton studios, I quickly showered and then walked to the see the Warhol exhibit. Not only did I see iconic art and learn about social issues that his work covered (deeper than the soup and celebrity images that I knew of), but I also enjoyed a true New York experience when I encountered model, actress, and spokesperson Cindy Crawford and her husband, Rande Gerber, while browsing the multi-room, multi-floor exhibit. Without Peloton and its community supporting my drive to live well, I would not have seen Warhol or Crawford in real life!

I was enjoying a good life, with a happy family and great career before Emily bought the original Peloton indoor bike. That good life somehow dramatically leveled up with my use of Peloton's platform. Had Peloton, starting with an indoor bike, unlocked some secret to well-being for me and millions of others? Without the Peloton bike, its instructors, the Peloton community, and social media, would I be searching out and visiting museums in every city I found myself in, painting fences in national parks, or exercising in the window of a retail store in order to celebrate friendship and sweat with people from across the country, most of whom I had never met in person? I am not sure how to describe my experience other than trying to get healthier and stronger, live well, and enjoy it. I was in a zone and it was amazing.

I was not alone in this quest, and Peloton was not the only one trying to meet the market's demand for health and wellness. I noticed well-being and wellness across society, from the local branch of Walgreens to the emerging CBD and alternatives industry. I knew something was there, but I did not know exactly what wellness and well-being were. I looked up various definitions of wellness and well-being. Fortune favored me. It turned out that George Mason University had a Center for the Advancement of Well-Being (aka CWB). Even better, it offered an understandable and powerful working definition of well-being.

According to the team at Mason's CWB, well-being is "building a life of vitality, purpose, resilience, and engagement."[84] That definition is worth repeating and rereading: well-being is building a life of vitality, purpose, resilience, and engagement.

6 AREAS OF WELL-BEING

The four words in the CWB definition were strong and clear. The simple definition made sense to me when I read it. Surely, to live well, one needed vitality, purpose, resilience, and engagement. What I found most interesting was the intentional approach: the definition began with the word *building*. Peloton was helping to build my well-being. With the support of the community and the instructors, I was leading my life with more intention. I was feeling more vital and resilient, I was spending more of my time with purpose. There was no doubt I was more engaged with the world, physically and digitally, mentally and socially.

I started reading about well-being in the workplace and then learned of the supposed Blue Zones around the world, where people appeared to be living longer and better.[85] My entrepreneurship center's Associate Director Becky Howick and I began to research the concept and learned of other centers, policy makers, and trade groups exploring these ideas. There were also countless ventures being launched developing products and services with the intent of improving the well-being of groups, individuals, and segments of society.

It was obvious that well-being was a meta-concept that impacted many areas of life. For me to understand it, well-being had to be broken down and operationalized to match the observable economy. After some researching, considering my past work on innovation and entrepreneurship, my history as a consumer, and sorting of ideas, I landed on six types of well-being that we could observe consumers and organizations spending time and money on:

- Emotional (& spiritual)
- Financial
- Occupational
- Physical
- Place-based (home, office, public spaces)
- Social

Each of the six areas of well-being were massive and growing with increased demand and incredible innovation to match it. For example, occupational well-being, often in the form of corporate wellness programs, flexible schedules, or intentional corporate culture building, was a massive market with growing budgets. Physical well-being, including a range of ventures like Peloton and Nike in fitness, and Beyond Meat and WW (Weight Watchers International) on the food and nutrition side, had long been a part of the economy, but were continuing to grow and innovate into different areas and segments as the number and types of consumers swelled.

The famous Blue Zone studies by Dan Buettner and a team from National Geographic found core activities and behaviors that appeared to explain pockets in the world where more people live significantly longer, healthier lives; up to three or four times the number of people living to be 100 years old.[86] The findings, from moving regularly and drinking wine to participating in strong communities and living with purpose, are based on years of research into the cultures, lifestyles, and work in the so-called Blue Zones, such Okinawa, Japan, and Sardinia, Italy.[87]

Though many of the Blue Zones are found in traditional societies, modern lifestyles and capitalism turned well-being and related activities into a $4.5 trillion business by 2019 according to the Global Wellness Institute (GWI).[88] Since the pandemic, this number has only grown as more individuals and organizations realize the importance of investing in well-being.

In our economy, activities ranging from corporate retreats and mindfulness apps to using reclaimed materials in construction and practicing regenerative farming and eating local are viewed as contributing to the well-being of individuals, organizations, and society. Some of the market categories that GWI measures generate hundreds of billions or trillions in annual revenues. Examples include: "Fitness and Mind-Body," "Personal Care, Beauty, and Anti-Aging," and "Healthy Eating, Nutrition, and Weight Loss."

As I looked around the economy with my well-being lenses, it appeared full of ventures connecting various types of well-being to their missions, offerings, and operations. I began to view the well-being economy as being composed of ventures dedicated to thriving, not just surviving. This was an Oprah-type approach for leading your best life, and companies like Peloton were there to meet and actually grow the demand. The six areas of well-being provided a simple framework from which I could try to make sense of what different ventures were providing to their customers and also in as many cases, to their employees and the communities in which they operate.

PHYSICAL WELL-BEING

Peloton has scratched the surface of physical well-being with their hardware offerings, content creation, celebrations and events, family classes, and more. There are many other areas and segments of physical well-being for Peloton to explore, from sports- and age-specific training (imagine golf, tennis, basketball, or soccer-focused classes) to recovery, sleep, massage, skin care, and personal care. The Global Wellness Institute's Global Economy report in 2018 pointed to over $1 trillion in spending on personal care, beauty, and anti-aging.[89] No doubt many Peloton members spend on these items—in fact—for my PMCT secret Santa exchange in 2018, I sent bath salts as part of my gift to one of my teammates (another group member told me my recipient enjoyed non-scented bath salts—not easy to find, but the internet saved me). The market opportunities in physical well-being are huge, and Peloton and its instructors have developed a community and brand that consumers will follow as it presents new offerings.

For example, in my years on the Peloton platform, I have witnessed countless members use a range of meal delivery services—from Purple Carrot and Tattooed Chef to local providers—and also employ a cornucopia of eating and nutritional systems—such as Weight Watchers, StrongerU, Noom, and traditional approaches such as counting macros and calories and all kinds of cleanses. Instructors discuss their nutrition on a regular basis and even advertise various products, supplements, and foods.

Peloton members spend countless hours in various groups discussing food and nutrition. Remember, the Peloton Plant Posse was the first subgroup I joined when venturing into the Peloton community. Moreover, relative to the $39 connected fitness fee, revenues from food and nutritional services could be enormous and recurring. For Peloton and its leadership, the question on this nutritional side of physical well-being is whether, when, and how they enter, as this market is ripe for Peloton and its brand and could bring greater recurring cash flows. From sports drinks and bars to meal kits and restaurants, the healthy, eating side of physical well-being is a large and congruent with Peloton's brand and position.

When discussing Peloton's retail showroom strategy, we covered their role as sellers of branded merchandise. The revenue from apparel and fitness accessories has the potential to be another area of massive growth and strength for Peloton. After more than five years with Peloton, we have more Peloton-branded athletic apparel than any other. Some was acquired with boutique credits from referral fees, other items were purchased, and more was received as gifts, as people knew Peloton gear was an easy way to make us smile. I have a Peloton Philly shirt I bought while riding in the King of Prussia store. The Denver and Phoenix stores were sold out of shirts when I stopped in for rides while traveling, but I was able to buy Peloton Washington D.C. and Peloton Chicago shirts. We have also purchased a few items for family members and friends as they evolved into happy Peloton members; we even brought Peloton gifts to a New Year's Eve Party. Our black Peloton gift bag stood out among all the bottles of fine wines and trendy spirits. Yes, the hosts of the party were Peloton members who owned both an original bike and treadmill.

The University of Oregon's Lundquist School of Business estimates that global sportswear sales tallied over $350 billion in 2019, with the U.S. accounting for more than $130 billon.[90] Global brands such as Nike, Adidas, Lululemon, and Patagonia underscore how much of that can be captured by fitness and lifestyle brands with passionate, loyal followers and a true position in the marketplace.

The Nike SuperRep Cycle indoor shoe release in 2020, Lululemon's purchase of The Mirror in 2020, and the Peloton–

Adidas–Ivy Park collaborations in 2021 underscore just how aware existing players are of Peloton's potential to change the athleisure space forever. For Peloton members, whether digital or connected, Peloton is their community and team, and wearing the brand means something. I have often found myself wondering if apparel could ever end up being the biggest revenue line for Peloton.[91]

EMOTIONAL AND SPIRITUAL WELL-BEING

One of the basic values Peloton offers to members is a convenient escape from the stress of day-to-day life. Throw in incredible instructors, music, themed classes, and a strong community and a class can become cathartic event. I have experienced this a handful of times, and it's a regular posting on social media. The loss of a loved one, freedom from a bad relationship, or work stress are just a few of the reasons members have stated for searching for emotional and spiritual well-being with the help of Peloton and its community.

As anyone who takes classes with Peloton (and many boutique offerings) knows, fitness and movement have deep emotional and spiritual components. Great coaches, whether teaching at Peloton, leading Michael Jordan's Chicago Bulls, or instructing a high school track team, pull out great performances by connecting the mental and physical capabilities of their athletes.

Although not every class at Peloton can demand or create a deep emotional or spiritual response, the coaches and classes impact members daily as they ride the ebb and flow of life. Classes around heritage celebrations and artist series can set up both instructors and members for an experience that goes beyond just fitness. The "Sundays with Love" series, which came out of repeated requests from members, highlights how many members want their workouts to test and grow them in the spiritual, not just physical realm.

For the day to day, Peloton coaches have catch phrases that are clearly intended to support member's emotional and spiritual well-being as much as their physical. Christine D'Ercole's reminders of "You are bigger than a smaller pair of pants" and "I am. I can. I will. I do." Robin Arzón's "We don't do basic," and Hannah Corbin's "Your body is not Amazon Prime; it won't show up in two days" are just a few member favorites that are repeated often on social media and employed in life. Have I found myself sharing Peloton-inspired phrases to myself and my students? I have reminded my students "no pressure, no diamond," a phrase I picked up during a Denis Morton Power Zone ride.

A quick visit to Peloton social media pages (Facebook, Reddit, or Instagram) will find members using the instructors, rides, and community to pull through health issues and family traumas and career challenges. As I often say, the Peloton community can make you cry on a daily basis as members share their challenges. However, the stories of struggle generally end with some form of triumph and gratitude for Peloton and the community's positive role in making members stronger, more balanced, and resilient. This happened en masse during the pandemic; countless new groups emerged such as Stay Home Stay Motivated (#SHSM). The combination of the specific words and directions from coaches and the embrace of the Peloton community offers emotional and spiritual support and meaning to widowers, chemo patients, and young adults struggling with self-esteem.

Stretching, yoga, and meditation (including a range of breathing practices), highlight the opportunities that span from the physical to the emotional and spiritual. The introduction of a variety of types of meditation with new yoga instructors in 2019 shows that Peloton leaders recognized the need and demand for emotional and spiritual well-being among customers and society. The Peloton community has been eating up this content. Apps such as Headspace and Calm have been huge successes in the marketplace and with investors, and meditation and mindfulness are now regular features in public schools and workplaces. According to the Global Wellness Institute's 2019 report "Move to Be Well: The Global Economy of Physical Movement," the "mindful movement" is worth $11.4 billion in the United States and almost $30 billion globally.[92] Peloton has the platform, culture, and community to keep driving into the emotional well-being and mindfulness marketplace.

In early September 2020 Peloton announced the creation of the Peloton Health and Wellness Advisory Council. It is made up of MDs and PhDs with the stated charge of "working closely with the company as it continues to look at how it can positively impact the physical, mental, and emotional well-being of community of Members from around the world."[93]

In the press release announcing the formation of the council, Peloton President William Lynch said, "We constantly hear from our Members that Peloton has not only profoundly impacted their physical, mental, and emotional health, but also has helped them cope with issues ranging from neurodegenerative disease or cancer to PTSD or post-partum depression."[94] Peloton was witnessing the same behaviors that I observed when I began to research the Peloton experience.

Members were improving their emotional and spiritual well-being with a community around a bike. As with the treadmill, yoga, Pilates, and other offerings, Peloton was creating value where its customers were leading the company.

In May 2021 Peloton announced the release of a mood series designed to offer members classes matching their mindset. "However you are feeling when you arrive at your workout, these classes will give you the freedom and space to sit with your emotions, move through them, or come out on the other side with a different state of mind," stated the official Peloton Blog upon the release of the first Mood Classes. The five moods initially covered were happy, sad, calm, heated, and confident. I took a number of these classes in the yoga modality and really enjoyed them. There was a warning before the mood yoga classes I took telling me:

This class is not a substitute for medical diagnosis of treatment, and is not a substitute for psychotherapy. Please speak to your health provider or a mental health professional if you are having concerns about your emotional or mental well-being.

The instructors communicate the same idea when the classes start: this is not therapy, but it does target your emotional well-being.

Could Peloton one day host meditation retreats (online or physical); provide streaming therapy sessions; build physical meditation, spirituality, or mental health centers; or develop tools for use in clinical or workplace or educational settings? Peloton's brand, high standards, and early success make the company as likely as any to define, grow, and drive growth in the emotional and spiritual well-being space as it catches up to markets in physical well-being.

PELOTON AND SOCIAL WELL-BEING

As we explored, the community that has evolved around Peloton has been a secret accelerant and strength that was unexpected but is now crucial to so much of what occurs with Peloton.

By mid-2018, I realized I was actually making real friends on the Peloton platform. When I interviewed members through 2019 and 2020, I inquired about the social element. I began asking directly if Peloton produced more friends than any other part of their adult lives, including work or parenting or other social groups or neighborhoods they were part of. A majority of my respondents said yes. The great relationships that have formed, mostly between members, is something that Peloton has been building on since discovering the community's existence and its extraordinary power.

Examples of actions that enable social well-being include special themed rides with the stated intent of bringing people together, expanding studio spaces around the world, and adding technical features such as high fives, hashtags for the leaderboard, and on-demand session classes, where groups of members can schedule on-demand rides and have their own real-time, private leaderboard.

I believe the demand for more and more social features is to fill the void that many had been feeling as society became more mobile, fractured, contentious, and social media oriented. Loneliness, among young and old, has been a concern of public health officials for years, and Peloton has turned out to be an amazing social experience for so many. During the pandemic, Peloton provided immediate and positive social connectivity to the millions of new members that arrived.

As with physical and emotional well-being, the opportunities in social well-being are large for Peloton as its community grows and asks for more opportunities to engage with one another. For Peloton, the market is theirs to create, from fitness and well-being events and festivals that bring people together (such as Peloton's Homecoming event online and in person) to tours and experiences where members and others can share real-world well-being opportunities with one another. The markets for fitness and well-being travel is also large according to the Global Wellness Institute, which reports wellness tourism at over $600 billion in 2018, roughly six times the size of the $109 billion annual fitness market.[95] Many of Peloton's instructors have experience participating in, leading, and hosting retreats that bring people together.

Peloton has partnered a bit with hotels, universities, and others in the past and its acquisition of Precor gives it long-standing and deeper relationships with institutional partners of all kinds. Alumni associations and others have long served as levers to tighten bonds and strengthen communities. Peloton's strength and experience using its digital and physical assets to bring people together and deepen bonds match individual, organizational, and societal demands and needs for more social well-being. As the platform, talent base, and infrastructure grow, social well-being opportunities could be anything from private, special-event classes and trips to unique and upgraded online communities and experiences.

PLACE-BASED WELL-BEING

From the start, Peloton has been about bringing world-class boutique fitness opportunities into member's homes. Peloton has made its members' residences and offices the best places to get fit. It did not matter if a member had a beach-front property in South Beach or a split level in Peoria, the Peloton platform transformed a member's space into a world-class fitness facility.

Many members, including my family, have begun building fitness spaces around Peloton's offerings, not just space for hardware, but also for classes that do not demand a connected fitness device. As we built out the basement of our home in 2019, we focused on our new home gym, ensuring there was ample space for stretching, strength, yoga, and a new machine or two that Peloton might offer in the coming years. I even demanded laundry hookups in a closet, knowing that we would be generating a great deal of sweaty gear and towels. In the old days, our basement design would have focused around a big screen television and passive entertainment options. The idea that the home could be the locus of well-being became a novel concept for members that were new to working out or had spent years at gyms and boutique studios. Covid made the need for spaces that supported well-being even more obvious.

Will Peloton augment its initial focus on at-home fitness products and move deeper into other physical spaces? Accessories and furniture? Architecture and design? Might Peloton's studios and showrooms across North America, and globally, become sites for gyms, special events, or well-being hubs?

The acquisition of Precor puts Peloton directly in the institutional space as Precor has existing customers across higher education, hospitality, government, and other markets.

During the earnings call in February 2021, after the Precor acquisition was announced, Foley's opening remarks included, "Precor's product portfolio and sales team will also accelerate our commercial business where we see a significant opportunity to grow Precor's franchise while introducing the Peloton platform to an even greater number of fitness enthusiasts and channels such as hospitality, multi-unit residential buildings, corporate campuses, and colleges and universities."[96]

As part of the Peloton Pledge and the 2020 collaboration with Beyoncé, Peloton opened relationships with 10 HBCUs, and it is likely that relationships with more institutions of higher education, athletic teams, and organizations, and other civic institutions will help those partners improve their place-based well-being offerings for their stakeholders.

Countless Peloton members have chosen hotels, Airbnbs, and offices based on Peloton availability.[97] As Peloton has become a regular ritual for millions, they take their apps with them as they travel and move throughout their daily life. Peloton's earnings release in Q4 2020 reported that connected device subscriptions averaged nearly 25 workouts per month, almost one workout with Peloton per day.[98] With the platform becoming so entrenched in members lives, more physical points of connection outside of the home might make sense, even for a connected, at-home fitness company.

In spring 2021, while scrolling Instagram, a post from the Four Seasons Resort in Maui (@FSMaui) in Hawaii came through my feed because I follow #Peloton. The picture from the Four Seasons' post featured a woman riding a Peloton bike in one of their outdoor spaces; a lush, beautiful Hawaiian landscape, replete with palm trees, mountains, and oceans, was in the background.

The post started, "From in-suite @OnePeloton bikes to exploring Wailea's coral reef on a private guided outrigger canoe paddle, the Resort has introduced a variety of ways to stay active, all designed with health and safety in mind."[99] It was another holy-shit moment. Here was one of the elite brands in hospitality using a Peloton bike to sell its rooms in Hawaii, one of the elite destinations in vacation travel. By 2021, Peloton had the power to make a hotel special when five-star service, humpback whales, and green sea turtles could not. From Hawaii to New York to Berlin and everywhere in between, Peloton has the power to make any space the place to be.

WELL-BEING CONTENT CREATOR

From classes and social media feeds to meetups and store visits, there is an insatiable demand among the community for Peloton and well-being content. From the names of instructors' pets (I know more than I care to admit) and their favorite vacation spots and wedding photos, to rumors about new fitness products and apparel collections, the Peloton community loves to consume Peloton-related content. For the company and its instructors and many community members, developing content around classes, events, community, and well-being generally has already begun in order to meet demand.

Peloton video, audio, and even print content and programming around health and well-being could be distributed across various networks and partners. Many professional sports leagues, college conferences, and brands and creators (e.g., the Big Ten and Southeastern conferences, Oprah, and Martha

Stewart) have developed multi-format media empires to distribute their content and achieve their goals.

Many Peloton instructors are broadcasting on a variety of topics on social media and appearing on other outlets and as influencers across media and society. Jess King, a born artist, has been producing a range of content on social media, including cooking shows. In 2020, Peloton produced a series of video content around Robin Arzón and her pregnancy, and in 2021, Peloton produced a video series on treadmill instructor Becs Gentry's attempt to make Team Britain for the Tokyo Olympics.

Reality and lifestyle programming with Peloton instructors (and eventually members?) and omnichannel distribution would be congruent with Peloton's mission to use "technology and design to connect the world through fitness, empowering people to be the best versions of themselves anywhere, anytime." The opportunities are endless, from reality shows searching for Peloton's next instructors, to cooking, home décor, career, relationships, arts, fashion, music, real estate, finance, beauty, and travel. Peloton could evolve to become a true 24-hour, global lifestyle media brand producing and delivering content supporting its members, partner institutions, and society's drive to live well.

MEDIA AND TECHNOLOGY INNOVATOR

Peloton's reimagination of at-home and boutique fitness and its creation of the connected fitness market gives it a significant lead in producing and distributing world-class live and on-demand fitness and well-being content. From its initial concept of live streaming to customer's homes, to streaming classes on morning shows and from Pyeongchang during the 2018 Olympics, to producing and streaming live classes from instructors' homes around New York and London during the early part of the Covid-19 pandemic, Peloton's technical and production teams have been innovating from the start.

In the absence of televised sports during the early months of the pandemic in the United States, Peloton partnered with ESPN to produce and air two 20-minute Peloton cycling classes pitting a range of professional and Olympic athletes and ESPN personalities against one another.[100] The women's class was taught by Robin Arzón and won by Colleen Quigley, a U.S. Olympic track and field star. Alex Touissant taught a men's race dominated by U.S. Olympic swimmer Matt Grevers. All the racers were in their own homes, from California to Florida, while the Peloton instructors were in their New York homes. The races were recorded and developed into one hour's worth of programming, hosted by instructor Ally Love, that aired on ESPN in May 2020 as the depth of the pandemic was being realized. (BTW, Peloton members were able to take the two All-Star rides on demand after the program aired.)

This anecdote highlights the Peloton team's creativity and ability to develop and execute unique and interactive programming built around the company's content, talent, ethos, and community. Less than a year after the ESPN rides, in spring 2021, Peloton would announce the production of a Champions Collection of classes featuring world-class athletes from around the globe such as sprinter Usain Bolt, German tennis player Angelique Kerber, and American Paralympic champion Scout Basset; all participants were also Peloton members.[101]

Perhaps Peloton will use its software, hardware, and content production expertise and success to become a service provider for other ventures in the streaming media or health and well-being markets. In addition to its technical teams producing content in studios and remote classes, Peloton has expanded its distribution from its own platforms to others, including Apple TV, Roku, and Amazon Fire TV. Peloton's engineering and production talent, often found in theater and media hotbeds of New York and London, have expertise managing massive amounts of content and data and streaming it on demand globally, while receiving real-time metrics back from bikes, treads, apps, smartwatches, heart monitors, and more. This technical, programming, and market knowledge that Peloton has created and earned may allow the company to move in interesting directions in a world that expects well-being, loads of streaming content, and connected hardware, homes, vehicles, institutions, and cities.

Amazon, for example, has grown dramatically by taking its experience in e-commerce, hosting, warehousing, and data to create massive infrastructure businesses such as Amazon Prime, Amazon Marketplace, and Amazon Web Services. By providing services to other firms, massive and micro, Amazon has become one of the most important and dominant firms in the history of capitalism.

Major League Baseball (MLB), while appearing stodgy and slow to many, was one of the first professional leagues to stream its games. Eventually MLB.com became a de facto leader in sports streaming and app development, managing the app presence for Major League Baseball, World Wrestling Entertainment (WWE), the Professional Golfers Association (PGA) tour, HBO Plus, Fox Sports Go, and more. As its successes grew, the company, known as BAMTech, was spun out of Major League Baseball, with a value of $3.75 billion in 2017.[102] The venture was purchased by Disney and is now a major part of ESPN+, a massive streaming service.[103] Will Peloton leverage everything it has learned across community building, retail, streaming, software, hardware, gamification, media, content, and more to become a massive service provider and host for other communities? The Amazon and MLB.com cases highlight potential paths.

Because of all of the work the Peloton team, from Foley and retail managers to celebrity instructors and field operations, has put in, capital, goodwill, and opportunities abound. One of the biggest challenges for Peloton is that the company can do so many different things; the health and well-being market is massive and only getting larger; and the Peloton community and members trust the company. The key will be to leverage its strengths—convenience, quality, talent, culture, technology, logistics, and community—while continuing to put members first instead of doing things just because they can or because other ventures are taking action.

CHAPTER 9

CONCLUDING THOUGHTS OF A PELOTON ADDICT

As an entrepreneurship researcher, I lucked out in the fall of 2016; my wife bought a cutting-edge consumer product (against my will), and that gave me an up-close view of the future.

Once on the Peloton bike, I quickly saw, through sweaty eyes, that many of the most fascinating and important innovation and entrepreneurship concepts were wrapped up in the Peloton business model. In early 2017, I realized that Peloton was much more than a bike that streamed classes. Peloton was a fun and effective fitness hardware and content provider that was more convenient and better than previous and existing options. Peloton was disrupting the huge and growing fitness industry.

Beyond fitness, Peloton was part of an expanding streaming media landscape where entertainment, fashion, and pop culture could bring energy and excitement to consumers wherever they might be. Peloton's streaming of digital assets to physical assets in a member's home pointed to the future of place making in society. Throw in Peloton's engaging instructors and community, thriving and positive social media, and gamification, and the company was truly a unicorn in my eyes, drawing from emerging business and marketing playbooks and creating new ones.

By mid-2017, having spent some time on the Peloton bike and observing its community, I roughly sketched out the elements of their business model: streaming media, well-being and fitness, music and pop culture, hardware sales and recurring subscription revenue, community engagement, social media, celebrity talent, gamification, physical and digital spaces, and more. I began to believe there might be no better company for understanding the future of the economy than the New York–based Peloton.

I had no idea what was to come exactly for Peloton, but there was a momentum and energy that was felt in classes, in showrooms, and across social media, and I was gripped by it. Milestones came fast for Peloton: a treadmill (the Tread+), international expansion, media and artist collaborations, an initial public offering, social impact initiatives, 1 million subscribers, lawsuits and media storms—all validating my early observation that something was different about this company and it was about where the economy was going and what consumers wanted.

In the five years since first clipping in and researching Peloton and completing this manuscript, I have taken well over 5,000 classes on the platform. I've traveled to the company's studios in NYC for many, many classes, met thousands of members, and interviewed two of the founders and a range of corporate leaders, as well as four of their top instructors. I've spoken to and spent time with frontline showroom and field-ops team members and visited showrooms in seven states.

I've ridden bikes and run on Peloton treadmills in hotels, apartment buildings, health clubs, and other people's homes, and taken classes on mountain trails and balconies, in basements and movie theater lobbies. After all of that sweating, straining, flowing, meditating, running, and stretching with the Peloton community, I am more convinced than ever that Peloton provides deep insights into the future of economy and society.

Peloton has the potential to be as big as any other venture because it is on the path to fundamentally altering individual and societal approaches to health and well-being. This means directly changing how time and money and focus are spent by billions of people. I was not a boutique fitness member or road cyclist and I drove an F-150 pickup truck when I first tried a Peloton class. Peloton and its community changed me and my habits, friends, family, and daily actions. All of that altered my behavior, well-being, and economic impact.

People's behavior and actions, and how their time and money is spent are the truth tellers about what matters to them. I could see from my own experience, that of hundreds of thousands of others, and Peloton's financial reports that the company's offerings consume people's time, money, and thoughts, and many members only want to give the company and its community more. This was true before Covid, during the pandemic, and as the vaccines rolled out.

The result of all the time and money I put into Peloton was that by age 48, I was fitter than ever, had new friends from across the world, and shared a passion with my family about well-being, movement, and fitness. I was more intentional about how I spent my time and energy. I could not have predicted any of these outcomes when I clipped into our first Peloton bike in late 2016.

While Peloton's business model is multilayered and path dependent, the preceding chapters have explored the different elements, how they succeeded in meeting and exceeding the needs of a wide range of customers, and how Peloton has altered the growing health and well-being marketplace. The lessons from the Peloton experience can and should be mined for use in other markets, with other customers and stakeholders, and through social challenges because the results, in terms of customer satisfaction, well-being, and revenue, validate what Peloton has achieved in its first decade.

This concluding chapter will share some of the lessons I've learned from exploring Peloton and the Peloton community. While some of them are simple and known, they have been hard for individuals, organizations, and societies to execute over sustained periods of time.

POSITIVITY, HOPE, AND HAPPINESS SELL

Positivity, hope, and happiness sell. This one is simple, but for some reason people and companies forget it. And if you can actually deliver it, it sells incredibly well and people want to buy more of it. From self-help books and New Year's resolutions to summer blockbusters and political campaigns, positivity and happiness are always in demand. Hershey and Disney have done well with this basic starting point.

In Peloton's case, the company has developed a model that delivers happiness across the physical, emotional, place-based, and social sides of life for those willing to put in the sweat and work. Peloton messages strength, growth, and self-empowerment for all on the leaderboard. Positivity oozes from the instructors and the members supporting one another in classes, studios, and showrooms, across social media and in real life. While positive vibes are inherent to the consumer fitness industry, much of it is also based on exclusivity, body shaming, and activities where pain, boredom, and suffering are the core validation. Before Peloton, much of the boutique industry used those attributes to differentiate themselves, keeping the boutique in boutique.

Peloton's community and the company have evolved into a cult of positivity, with countless positive sub-cults and evangelists. This ecosystem of hope is a stark contrast to the divisive culture found across much of modern public discourse and media. It's hard to understand exactly why so much of contemporary culture has chosen to see others as content to be mocked and scorned, but it has, and institutions that offer a positive alternative often find support and loyalty.

Although the Peloton community and the media covering the company experience bouts of nastiness, and the company is engaged in the cutthroat well-being, media, and technology industries, the overall culture has been positive, happy, and forward-looking for most involved. This happy culture leads to friendships (social well-being) and can be found any place that the Peloton app can be accessed or where there is Peloton hardware. Peloton's happy, celebratory culture is there for all members.

As co-founder Tom Cortese has pointed out repeatedly: Peloton took fitness, which was avoided by a vast majority of people, as evidenced by obesity rates and poor health outcomes, and created a happy time and place for millions. Peloton members created groups, holidays, challenges, and more to keep the positivity flowing throughout the community. The happiness feedback loop of the platform is incredibly powerful and has helped push millions forward. Getting so many people to choose to work hard at this scale has never been achieved before.

One of the basic strategies Peloton has employed to bring joy and grow membership is to have the company and the community celebrate often. The use of simple gamification concepts, actual or dreamed-up holidays, special event classes, and social media means a constant stream of celebration and recognition of members, instructors, community wins and efforts, and the company itself. This keeps members coming back because celebrations, with costumes, swag, badges, and more are fun.

Bringing happiness and joy to the day to day of many businesses may seem challenging, but it can be done. When I was growing up in the 1970s and 1980s, coffee at home was scooped out of a can and coffee in a restaurant was 50 cents, including unlimited refills. Starbucks took a mundane and static product in the U.S. and helped turn it into a lifestyle product with physical locations and innovative beverages that bring pleasure and escape to the customers around the world who frequent their cafes, guzzle down *doppios,* and squeal when it is time to celebrate fall with pumpkin spice lattes.

The challenge is to listen to customers, engage them (even let them take the lead), and truly focus on making them happy, even if it's a micro moment, like a high five on a ride or a quick social media reshare or a milestone badge. Micro-moments of happiness work.

ACCESSIBILITY AND INCLUSIVITY

Before Peloton's emergence, the top brands in indoor cycling and boutique fitness were known for their exclusivity. From the high price of individual classes and the limited number of spots available to the zip codes where the studios were located, boutique-style fitness was not for the mass market.

Peloton founders Tom Cortese, Yony Feng, John Foley, Hisao Kushi, and Graham Stanton went with a totally different strategy: inclusivity and access. They believed they could use technology to bring huge numbers of people together in classes with the best instructors in the world. Jenn Sherman, the first Peloton instructor, immediately brought a sense of fun and a big NY personality that was instrumental in setting a welcoming tone. This technology enabled an accessible and inclusive approach, versus the exclusivity business model that dominated the industry. This created more value for more people from more places at more times. With accessibility and more seats in classes, more members arrive and scale can set in, allowing the company to deliver more and improved content to more members. There is a network effect to positive inclusivity.

The idea that inclusion creates more value than exclusion was not invented by Peloton; it is the ideal that democracies and free-market capitalism strive to live up to. It is strange that a consumer product with a seemingly high price tag highlights the value of inclusion in economic and social terms as well as any organization out there.

The employee culture that Peloton is trying to build, Peloton's investment and engagement in a range of social issues, its emerging bike donation program, the push to lower prices, offer more sizes in the boutique, expand its heritage month celebrations, and broaden the diverse nature of its membership and community groups highlights that inclusive community supports growth. More and more customers prefer to be on the accessible, inclusive team versus the elite, exclusive, and elusive. Peloton issued its first ESG (environmental, social, and governance) report in October 2021.

While many elite societal and economic institutions, from institutions of higher education, industries, and neighborhoods to clubs, fashion houses, and fitness offerings, will continue to brand and communicate value through exclusivity and scarcity, Peloton proves that a strategy of inclusivity and accessibility can work and impact more people. The Peloton platform has become a place where all are welcome as long as they make an effort and respect others. This openness to help all that arrive has been essential to the company's growth and success, and is a crucial lesson.

PLATFORM FOR OTHERS

Any fitness or well-being institution or offering is in the business of helping others achieve more in some way. The question, of course, is do they really deliver, how much and for how long can that platform deliver? Peloton's mix of fitness content, great hardware, community, social media, gamification, and fun have created a platform countless have jumped onto and taken advantage of.

Obviously, the platform supports members like me who are improving their physical and social well-being in a convenient and fun way. The instructors and other amazing Peloton team members are building incredible careers as the company grows and attempts to impact health and well-being all over the world.

The Peloton community, from the start, has become an open space where countless people, many that we discussed through this book, have been able to share, build, and grow—and express themselves. From Clip Out Crystal and John Mills to Sam Ettari and John Bernstein, the Peloton platform has allowed a range of people to share their ideas and emerge and grow. The commercial endeavors (e.g., after-market hardware, podcasts, swag, apps) and social groups and institutions that have grown with Peloton underscore the value of being a platform for others to build in their own, unique ways. Allowing the community to do much of the building and management has extended the platform and its opportunities dramatically.

IF YOU WANT TO DO BIG THINGS, HAVE A TEAM

Like many of the lessons from my Peloton experience, this one is not new but somehow many forget it. As the saying goes, "If you want to go fast, go alone; if you want to go far, go together."

The Peloton story thus far is full of groups of people working together to achieve positive and shared goals. It starts with Foley recruiting colleagues from his tech career to join him in launching the company to bring boutique fitness to more people in their homes.

When the founders launched Peloton, a community formed and grew, and the team mindset has extended in thousands of directions, from chasing fitness goals to members helping others fighting cancer and society grapple with racism. For many in the

Peloton orbit, Peloton's motto, "Together We Go Far" is more than just a catchphrase. It has become an operating principle and mantra.

This concept is not new. Adam Smith points to self-interested collaboration as the key to the human progress and economic growth. Social efforts like groups, wolfpacks, clubs, families, teams, and flocks work.

TIME IS A ZERO-SUM GAME; EVERY PEDAL STROKE COUNTS

As I spent more time taking Peloton classes, engaging with the community, and working on my well-being, it became clear that I couldn't do other activities. My time spent watching television and randomly surfing the web and social media dropped. I shifted work times and schedules where possible, and I even altered time and activities with my kids, to take classes live or to celebrate milestones with friends.

For example, instead of watching a movie with my son's youth hockey team during a travel tournament, I headed to a Peloton showroom to take a class (grab a quick sweat and a blue dot), meet some Pelo people, and buy a local showroom T-shirt.

For many members, Peloton has become non-negotiable "me time," for getting stronger; dropping baggage; recharging for family, friends, and colleagues; and having fun with members and instructors. Sales, member engagement rates, and social media followers prove that Peloton is stealing time and dollars from other activities, goods, and services. This Peloton time occurs when members are on the platform taking classes, but also while engaging with the community during non-class time and planning for future well-being activities and goals.

The company and its instructors continually message the importance of all efforts, big and small. It is why I have learned to love five- and 10-minute classes and appreciate the accretive benefits of small things over time. During a cycling class, I once heard instructor Jenn Sherman say, "Every pedal stroke counts." I have come to agree with JSS that every effort helps, even the smallest ones, and that they all add up to progress and improved well-being. Understanding the value of time and how much can be done with even just five minutes is a key lesson that has helped me greatly and led to incredible customer engagement and growth on the Peloton platform and off.

TURN WEAKNESS TO STRENGTH

For Peloton, its members, and many of its instructors even, the ability to take a weakness and turn it into a strength has been a strategy for success. In my own case, my legs had always been weak (relative to my upper body) and I had always lacked flexibility (stiff-tall-person syndrome). Just a few years with Peloton, cycling, running, and practicing yoga, have turned me into a kind of limber and balanced dad with legs ready to hike or carry Ikea boxes up stairs all day.

The company, since the start, has taken apparent weaknesses and turned them into strengths. Early on, when Foley and team reached out to existing players in boutique fitness they were rebuffed, leading them to build their own bike, software, content, and entire ecosystem. When rights issues with the music industry became challenging and forced major class purges, Peloton focused on music and grew its Artist Series offerings. This turned music back into a true differentiator and strength, providing more opportunities to partner and celebrate across the platform. Peloton has been battling logistics and delivery challenges since its launch on Kickstarter and will likely prevail and grow out of these challenges. Its actions include beginning reverse logistics, purchasing Precor for its U.S. factories, expanding into Europe and Asia, and breaking ground on its first manufacturing facility in the U.S. as the pandemic entered its second year. The company has been steadfast throughout.

The Peloton team, from its time as a digital boutique fitness startup through its growth into a fitness industry giant, has continued to take tricky situations and threats and turn them into opportunities and strengths. Through all the tests, I have observed that the Peloton leadership is confident and aggressive, and does not shy away from challenges, large or small.

COOL DOWN, STRETCH, AND PREPARE FOR WHAT'S NEXT

For most of Peloton's cardio offerings, whether a 45-minute cycling class, a 60-minute run, or a 20-minute bootcamp, there is never a long enough cool-down. When those classes end, I am usually red-faced, huffing, puffing, and dripping like an old faucet. Though the clock has hit zero on the session, the endorphins are pumping and I feel great, even as I think my heart might explode. I've learned from the instructors to take a five- or 10-minute cool-down class afterwards and then a stretch as well. The cool-down session and stretch allows the body to absorb the work while gently returning to normal heart and breathing rates.

The cool down and stretch also bring the body and its systems to gradual stop, rather than an immediate slamming of the breaks. Tread instructor Becs Gentry once compared a cool-down effort to using a comma, rather than a period.

The added cool down and stretch leads to a good recovery and prepares the body for the next session. In this way, all workouts are connected. Over time, as I listened and learned more, I began to add a warm-up when possible before my workouts, like warming a vehicle on a cold day. The addition of warm-ups and cool downs, which Peloton produces, added to my time on the platform, but connected my workouts by easing my body and mind into and out of workouts.

By stringing my efforts together with warm-ups and cool-downs, my move toward well-being began to feel like a continuous and evolving journey. Even as my choice of exercise, challenge, and instructors changed, the pace was always forward. In many ways, this lesson is no different from innovation and entrepreneurship and art and all other endeavors; progress demands movement and evolution and learning.

A number of years ago while teaching lean startup concepts, I began to say to my students and anyone else that would listen, "Nobody smart finishes where they started." I state this to communicate that whatever the starting idea may be for a business or product, if it creates value and the team works hard and learns, the concept will evolve and end up in places never imagined. Amazon, for example, started with books.

Consistency, evolution, learning, and a growth mentality are central to Peloton. Peloton started with the idea to bring studio-quality indoor cycling into the home through a connected bike. A decade later, Peloton is a global technology, media, and well-being innovator covering the globe, with millions of insanely happy customers and trillions of dollars of market opportunity ahead of it.

YOUR RIDE IS YOUR RIDE OR MODIFY AS NEEDED

There is no doubt that the leaderboard, rankings, instructors, badges, challenges, and groups on the Peloton platform push and pull members to places that they never expected to be. My core Peloton group, the Peloton Monthly Challenge Team, thrives on this ethos and members are required to share goals each month. However, each member of the group sets their own goals.

You will often hear Peloton cycling instructors and others remind the community that, "Your ride is your ride." I often joke that "Your ride is your ride," is the number-one rule of Peloton. You will always hear instructors, no matter the discipline, remind members to modify where and when necessary during classes. Each member has to decide each day what is right for them. It could mean staying at a resistance lower than what the instructor calls out or taking a restful child's pose when your legs are tired during a yoga session. Denis Morton often states, "comparison is the thief of joy," and member Howard Godnick's poem, *Don't Yuk My Yum* speaks to this ethos and reminds all on social media why its so important:

Don't Yuk My Yum

For those taking issue
With the 10 minute ride

Who jump on this page
With an eye to be snide

Have you ever received
A scary prognosis
A hereditary disease
Or perhaps a thrombosis

Your chest sawed in half
Or it's chemo for weeks
Each day it's own struggle
With its valleys and peaks

Have you ever struggled
To walk up the steps
Just to get out of bed
Is a nightmare of schleps

'Cause until it is you
Who has walked in those shoes
Put your egos aside
And from them take your cues

What for you may be easy
For another, it's pure pride
So please don't yuk my yum
Please don't criticize my ride

ONE LAST THING

Every day for roughly five years I have checked Peloton social
media to monitor the passion of Peloton members. Every damn
day I see something that makes my eyes tear up. This was going

on before the pandemic and before the IPO and before the expansion into Canada and Europe and Australia. Peloton was changing lives before the tread and outdoor runs and Artist Series classes. Since the beginning, Peloton has created and conveniently delivered happiness, strength, resilience, community, and hope.

In reflecting on my experiences and sharing my observations about Peloton, I've covered a range of issues that the company's phenomenal growth has exposed. Many lessons and concepts relate directly to the founders, leaders, instructors, and members who make up the Peloton community, but other themes explore technology, society, culture, talent, physical and digital spaces, and the rise of the well-being economy.

Applying the Peloton learnings to broader swaths of society and economy is why I started to track the company and its community in the first place. If a venture making a bike that goes nowhere could enable life-changing outcomes for so many types of people, how could we not want more companies and organizations to be able to do that?

I wanted to understand how and why this well-being and economic phenomena was happening and discover how other organizations and groups might create similar outcomes. As this book shows, the Peloton story has evolved in ways no one could have predicted. The team identified a problem, brought together great people and developed a product and service that was better than anything on the market. From there, the unexpected community emerged and the company, its leaders, and instructors engaged; growth and well-being flowed and more opportunity was uncovered, especially when the pandemic arrived.

The Peloton story will continue with new offerings, members and opportunities for people to become better, more well versions of themselves. I plan to continue to observe and explore the business of well-being as it expands to more and more sectors of society and economy. If you need anything from me, you can find me on the leaderboard. See you soon, #ChicagoBorn.

PELOTON'S MISSION AND VALUES

OUR MISSION

Peloton uses technology and design to connect the world through fitness, empowering people to be the best version of themselves anywhere, anytime.

OUR VALUES

PUT MEMBERS FIRST

- Design with a user-centered mindset
- Obsess over every touchpoint of the member experience

OPERATE WITH A BIAS FOR ACTION

- Challenge the status quo by continuously innovating and improving
- Take risks, fail fast, and learn from past failures
- Don't let perfect be the enemy of good

EMPOWER TEAMS OF SMART CREATIVES

- Hire the best and get out of their way
- Think and act like owners
- Stay lean, scrappy, and creative

TOGETHER WE GO FAR

- Build a diverse and inclusive community
- Uphold the obligation to dissent and listen
- Presume trust and be transparent

Retrieved from Peloton Interactive website 9/2019
http://www.onepeloton.com

THE PELOTON PLEDGE

JUNE 23, 2020

The past few weeks have been an intense time of reflection and action-planning for me and our leadership team. Frankly, while I've always believed that Peloton is a force of good in the world, and that we've created an inclusive workplace and community for everyone, I've been humbled to realize what a privilege it has been for me to be satisfied with that belief.

To be clear, I haven't been blind to injustices and inequality in our society. They've been plain to see my entire life, and these same calls for justice have been made for decades, centuries even. What has also been true for decades is that we must proactively reduce inequality, with a particular emphasis on reducing the persistent disparities experienced in our Black communities. This is the work of anti-racism, and the journey for Peloton begins NOW.

We shared this news with the Peloton team last week and would now like to share it with you: Effective immediately, we are announcing Peloton's commitment to invest $100 million over the next four years to fight racial injustice and inequity in our world and to promote health and wellbeing for all. In this pivotal time in history, I believe we have an enormous responsibility to do our part to combat systemic racism, and I am committed to ensuring that we use our resources, platform, and influence to change our society for the better—into a place where everyone can and will thrive.

This kind of important work starts from the inside out, and our highest level of responsibility in this ongoing journey is to our own team members, especially those on our frontline who are the backbone of our organization. In order to do what is right for the world, we must ensure that, at all times, we are doing right by our team who works tirelessly to foster and execute on our Members first philosophy.

In an effort to make a real impact—internally at Peloton, within our community of 2.6 million Members and with the Black community at large—we'll be investing and delivering broadly across five areas to fight racial injustice and inequity.

We commit to addressing global economic inequity, starting with investing $60 million dollars to increase the hourly wages of our own workforce. Effective July 1st, all North American and European-based, non-commissioned hourly team members at Peloton are getting a $3 USD per hour pay increase. This change brings the starting hourly rate at Peloton to $19.00 USD.

We commit to addressing our own job opportunity gap by investing $20 million in Learning + Development programs with a dedicated focus on our hourly teammates.

We commit to continuing to support the fight against systemic racism at the institutional level, by investing $20 million in third-party, nonprofit organizations dedicated to this cause. This will continue the initiative we started last month with our $500,000 donation to the NAACP Legal Defense and Education Fund.

We commit to doing our part to democratize access to fitness, and bring health and wellness to all communities. We will make our product and content more accessible to underserved communities (via our Digital and Connected Fitness platforms). In four years, it is our goal that at least 10 percent of our classes are streamed to and taken by members of these communities.

We commit to becoming a truly anti-racist organization and delivering on our robust, long-term agenda of diversity + inclusion goals, beginning immediately with anti-racism learning opportunities at all levels of the company, a review and report of diversity data, a comprehensive inclusivity audit, and the implementation of bias-mitigating strategies in all key points of the employee lifecycle (hiring, reviews, promotion, and more). We have a lot to do here, and this is our shared responsibility.

"Together We Go Far" means that we are greater than the sum of our parts, stronger collectively when each one of us is at our best. I'm looking forward to working alongside all of you to create a world we are proud of—a world that is equitable, kind, and a truly inclusive place for all.

It's time to get started.

SELECT INSTRUCTOR QUOTES

This is a selection of impactful quotes attributed to Peloton instructors that members and others have shared on social media, in interviews and surveys, and other places. This is by no means exhaustive as there were almost 50 instructors when this book went to print.

Ben Alldis
You didn't come this far to only get this far.

Robin Arzón
Do epic shit.
Fix your crown because I only ride with royalty.

You did not wake up today to be mediocre.
This is a funeral for your excuses.

Hannah Corbin
Treat your body like it belongs to someone you love.
Your body isn't Amazon Prime, it won't show up in two days.

Christine D'Ercole
Drop your shoulders; drop your baggage.
Hands on your back.
I am. I can. I will. I do.
What's at your finish line?
What if you can?
You are bigger than a smaller pair of pants.

Leanne Hainsby
Done and dusted.

Jess King
Don't let what should be get in the way of what could be.
Glitter is a strategy.
You are you and that is your superpower.

Ally Love
A crown of sweat and a soul of fire.
Are you ready? Yes or Yes?

Emma Lovewell
Work out because you love your body, not because you hate it.

Matty Maggiacomo
Inhale the good shit, exhale the bullshit.

Kristin McGee

Everything you could possibly ever want, have, or need is right here inside of you.

Denis Morton

I make suggestions, you make decisions.

If you can't be good, be careful.

Comparison is the thief of joy.

Tunde Oyeneyin

Today is a great day to have a great day.

Your mind is your strongest muscle.

Cody Rigsby

Grab your towel, grab your water, and get your life together.

If cauliflower can be pizza, you can be anything you want.

It's not that deep.

Selena Samuela

If you want the rainbow, you gotta put up with a little rain.

Hard work puts the tiger in the cat.

Stay humble, work hard, stay true to your heart and never, ever give up.

Jennifer Schreiber Sherman

Just fucking do it (aka #JFDI).

Jess Sims

You don't have to, you get to.

Make yourself strong, not small.

Never easy, always worth it.

How you do anything is how you do everything.

Andy Speer

Fight fatigue with focus.

Step into your power.

Alex Touissant

Inhale your confidence and exhale your doubt.

Feel good, look good, do better.

Smile, you woke up this morning.

This ain't daycare.

Kendall Toole

They can knock you down, but never let them knock you out.

Adrian Williams

If you need to take an emotional lap, take an emotional lap.

Matt Wilpers

Learn to be comfortably uncomfortable.

Long-term consistency trumps short-term intensity.

Milestones are consistency trophies.

Train hard. Train smart. Have fun.

Sam Yo

You don't have to reinvent the wheel, you just have to turn it 'round.

CRYING ON THE BIKE

Spend more than a few days with the Peloton community and you will likely hear about a member having an emotional, tear-inducing moment on the bike. The range of inciting incidents are as varied as the membership itself—a favorite song of a deceased parent, a major milestone achieved, or recovery from an injury.

When I first started reading the crying stories, they compelled me to want to learn more about Peloton, much like the riders with disco lights and the trips to the Mothership. Like those other behaviors, I couldn't get my head around crying during a fitness class.

Of course, as with much of the Peloton experience, I would eventually find myself in powerful, emotional state on the bike.

(I've come close on the Tread+, but the required balance and open eyes make a large emotive release much more challenging.)

There are a handful of classes that have caused me to have emotional reactions, including some tears. It happens on the bike periodically, when the combination of the physical strain from the class, cues from the instructor, the music, and the emotional build from life leads to a release of feelings—good and or bad—while exercising.

For me, Robin's challenging rides and statements can do it, as can Christine D'Ercole and Jess King. I know they are doing it, and I know it's part of the programming, but somehow, it works.

When Christine asks, "What's at your finish line?" I often get emotional, thinking of all the things I yearn to achieve (from completing this book and seeing my kids happy and healthy to owning and operating a farm and eventually providing scholarships to 300 kids). In that moment, when CDE asks that question, I often feel all the feels as I think about what could be, but is not yet, and how I can get to that finish line.

There is also a specific Aditi Shah meditation class that gives me comfort, but causes me to feel deep sadness when I take it. Shah is one of Peloton's yoga and meditation instructors, and she joined the platform in 2019 with Anna Greenberg and Ross Rayburn when the company began offering regularly scheduled yoga and meditation. According to her website, Aditi practiced a bit of yoga as a kid as her parents periodically brought teachers into the home, but it would not catch hold as young Aditi preferred running and playing sports. Shah started studying yoga while in college.

On February 20, 2019, I logged in and took a 10-minute kindness mediation Aditi had taught a week earlier. I do not remember why I chose a kindness meditation; maybe I was nasty to someone that day or was having too many unkind thoughts. I knew meditation is good for overall health and was intent on making it part of my approach to well-being, given that it was easily accessible with Peloton.

The kindness meditation class started with the basic premise that you have to be kind and have compassion for yourself if you are to be kind to others, and that our goal during the mediation was to start with ourselves and eventually, by the end of 10 minutes, create a general kindness or love and softening of the heart towards humanity as a whole. It sounded like a big task, but I was willing to try. From there Aditi had us repeat a mantra:

May I be happy. May I be well. May I be safe.
May I be peaceful. And at ease.

Simple enough, I did it and kept on meditating, sitting on some yoga blocks eyes down. I would later learn this mantra was a general meditation and used frequently.

From there, Aditi explained, we are going to focus on someone that is easy to love, maybe a kid or pet. Then we repeated the same mantra but with the intention, compassion, and hope being sent to that lovable target. And we repeat.

May you be happy. May you be well. May you be safe.
May you be peaceful. And at ease.

Next, we did it for our families and friends. Then Aditi asked that we direct this kindness to people that we have difficulty with; I thought about some of the characters that I work with for this part.

Lastly, as we neared the end, Aditi delivered what she had promised at the beginning, a chance to try to generate and share a tenderness and kindness to the world generally. She took the mantra and adjusted it one last time, instructing us to state:

May all beings everywhere be happy
May all beings everywhere be well
May all beings everywhere be safe
May all beings everywhere be peaceful and at ease . . .

When I heard Aditi lead us to dedicate those thoughts to "all beings," a deep sadness gripped me. I immediately began to think of the Syrian civil war that was raging and how many people and especially children were not safe and nor peaceful nor at ease; images from Syria that I had seen and stories I had read went rushing through my mind.

I began to cry quietly, knowing that all beings were not safe, well, or at ease, as I was on my $120 cork yoga mat. When you accept that and say it out loud, it is powerful and sad. Sitting there in my dark basement gym, with just the glow of the light from the Tread+ illuminating the room, knowing that billions of people and beings are not safe, well, or at ease is a powerful thing.

I have completed that meditation many more times and go back to it often, appreciating Aditi's ability to guide me to such emotion and to give me the space and tools to try to cultivate more love and compassion in my being.

While it may be hard and disappointing to accept that meditating via a $4,000 treadmill could bring me to tears and closer to humanity, it is true. Peloton, its instructors, and the content they program are bringing tears and emotional well-being to members around the world.

HIGH FIVES
OF GRATITUDE
FOR THE PELOTON COMMUNITY

There are so many Peloton members that helped me on my way as I joined Peloton and then began researching the company and community and the reasons behind their explosive growth and impact. Whether it was fun and inspiration on the leaderboard, meeting in person at studios, retails stores and other events or sharing lessons, jokes or videos on social media, the Peloton community is a strength I relied on throughout this entire process. A quick high five of gratitude and love to you all and so many others.

#adiosbabyweight
#ADayWithQuay
#AKLiz
#AlanM_HockeyRef
#Alejandro75
#AlwaysLiveHappy
#AngieVerb
#Arturo3
#ASHspins4wine
#Ash_Cat
#AtomicBlonde1
#BadGyal
#BabyGotBike
#BakingintheSun2
#BamaGuy
#Beachrunnergirl

#becsspins
#BeeHope
#BeerRunnerAudra
#Be_Fit_Be_Happy
#Be_Rad
#BikeForBourbon
#BikeLikUStoleIt
#BlingJunkie
#BlueEyesNJ
#bluehousebro
#BookOfSammy
#BorderlineSavge
#bossBaby711
#BradNeedsAbs
#BrazilChica
#BrianA

#BrownDogLover
#ButFirstSpin
#ByeComfortZone
#CanadaKath
#CariJay
#catchpow
#Chardonn_YayMe
#chasing_jackie
#clipclipclip
#ClippingIn
#ClipOutCrystal
#CountryLady
#Coups
#c_rob_goeshard
#CubsFanBudMan
#CupcakesForPRs

#CycleYogaLove
#danica_nyc
#DawnBreaker
#DerbyCityMama
#DCDonna
#DJJazzyJen
#DocFortWorth
#DocMomDiaz
#DoggyDocSteph
#DollarBill
#DoodleMom69
#DoxieJunkie
#dpgeezy
#DrMeMe
#DTaz
#dustyW3
#d_flecha
#Elayna21
#Elijah0626
#EmilyATL
#EmilyTX
#englishmuffin
#EpicRN
#EricaMGetFit
#EscapedFromNY
#EvryBdyLuvsJery
#EyeWillSurvive
#feffer
#Feisty_Fraulein
#FirmCheesecake
#Flash_ER
#Flubber
#FrannieB
#FSUSeminoleGirl
#GingerBeardJedi
#GinsTwin
#Gluttn4Punishment
#GoBeachGritsGo
#godnick
#Go_Blue_Fencer
#GoKateGO

#GoldnGirl
#Grey_Wolf
#Gynomite
#HannahEK
#Happy_Crystal
#HappyRunnerChic
#healthycityboy
#HeyNowLondo
#HockeyMom143
#Hockey_Meg
#Horse1970
#IChardSoHard
#IClaimJoy
#Intrepid
#iPoopedToday
#Intrepid
#IRideForSanity
#IsabodyMichael
#i_teach600
#janelmarie
#JasonD
#JasonR
#jeffinoregon
#JentleBern
#jeremytheCanuck
#Jersey_Koi
#JerseyProf
#J_Izaks
#JoeyB
#JudgeSpin
#judy_booty
#Kari_Gormley
#Kawaga93
#KenJoy
#KennyBania
#kholt20
#kilnerstrong59
#kilnerstrong66
#kimberlygeorge
#KnowsNoBoundary
#Krankin_It

#KSmitty19
#KyleeWitchey
#ladyDrG
#LadyLoveHandles
#LakeErieMermaid
#Lauradini
#LauraPug
#LBIGirl
#LewisRules
#lholt20
#LindasTherapy
#Lizaks
#LookBetterNaked
#lukekevin
#LuvHuntingElk
#LynnSweats4Fun
#MADMom31
#makesmovemandy
#MamaPomps
#maxsdad
#Marnorama
#Mdotmom
#MegBrownski
#MelBWorthIT
#MellOnWheels
#MendeP
#MichiganMan87
#MikeRidesMtTam
#Mims_IS_IN
#MILFMoney
#Modaddy99
#MollBurgher
#mommatoblueeyes
#Moonchild
#MotherTuckerOf3
#MrsMaryKay
#MsMarvel
#MSWarrior
#Mystique6
#NeverStop
#NikisRunDiaries

#NJ_Wahoo
#notoriusRPM
#NurseBetsy
#NuttyNettie
#OCshree
#OffHeGoes735
#oldfashiongirl5
#OldLadyJay
#OnAJourney
#OregonDucksGirl
#OrianaMarie
#OscillateWildy
#PackersFan
#PalpablePulse
#PaulaT
#peloridernyc
#Pedal4Joy
#Pedal4pie
#PedalsInPearls
#Peletor
#Pelobuddy
#peloridernyc
#PELOpeena
#PharmaSpin
#PhoneHomeElliot
#PinkMamba
#PineapplePedalz
#PittieMom13
#PocketNurse
#PositiveSpins
#PositiveVibes31
#Prigad86
#PRortheER
#ProsecutorMom
#PsychProf
#PTON_Gainz
#PushaT
#QueenofDonuts
#RealtorReyna
#redheadedrebel
#Resbird_Joe

#RobinRa
#RonnieHam88
#RunBeerRun
#RunLiftAndLive
#runnergirlfargo
#RunningDocSM
#runnylegs
#SashaSlays
#saskatoon
#SchweatyBetty
#SeeJaneSpin
#Seglo3
#ShariAlex
#SheDidIt
#SforSMatt
#ShadowGazer
#SillyRabbit_
#SilvaViator
#Simu
#SinOrSpin
#SkinnyVanilla
#skokiemom
#SmartCookie
#SmashPatriarchy
#SolarCoaster
#Spin4Endorphins
#SpincessOfPower
#Spinona_Rider
#SpinTowel
#statsgirl10
#Steelbike
#Steph_of_The_OC
#Stimey
#StrokeSurvivor
#StrongAFSam
#STSukovich
#SunshineKnight
#Super_Mac
#SwaggieMaggie
#Sweetpeags
#SylvieShames

#TalkPeloToMe
#Tammster
#TantrumBoss
#TeachesArt
#tenaciousTrish
#TequilaGeo
#TheGriz
#TheMeghan
#ThePugMother
#TheQueenofKings
#ThereIsNoTry
#Tiss_is_it
#ToddFather
#TougherThnILook
#TrailRunJenn
#T_runsthismotha
#TurkeyFryGuy
#TwinMomPlus2
#Up2TheChallenge
#UVGotMal
#VisionQuest76
#walshmyballs
#WhatIsLife
#WhiskeyAGoGo
#willride4vino
#WeiszAss
#WhyIPeloton
#WickdParrotHead
#willspin4queso
#WoodenShoe
#wolfymama
#wolfypapa
#XerciseUrDemons
#XXLMamaBear
#YesIam
#YouVsYou
#YukonJack
#zachys_mom
#zakerino
#ZoesPack

REFERENCES

1. Steve Blank, "Why the Lean Start-Up Changes Everything," *Harvard Business Review*, May 1, 2013, https://hbr.org/2013/05/why-the-lean-start-up-changes-everything.

2. Natt Garun, "Review: Peloton Brings Live-Stream Spinning Classes to Your Home," The Next Web - TNW, May 22, 2014, https://thenextweb.com/news/spinning-startup-peloton-cycle-brings-demand-cycling-home.

3. Tehrene Firman, "9 Cooling Weighted Blankets to Keep You Comfy on Hot Summer Nights," *Well+Good* (blog), July 7, 2019, https://www.wellandgood.com/cooling-weighted-blankets/.

4. When users register with Peloton they create a username which will appear on leaderboards across the Peloton platform as well as for logging in. Many treat it like an email or social media and use it to communicate their identities or values. Users can keep their profiles private on the Peloton platform if they choose.

5. Howard Stern discusses his 100th ride and T-shirt on the 15 February 2020 show. He also discusses following instructors Jenn Sherman and Kendall Toole in Instagram.

6. Scott Leitch, "Marathon Participation Still on the Rise," Canadian Running Magazine, May 25, 2015, https://runningmagazine.ca/uncategorized/marathon-participation-still-on-the-rise/.

7. Chris Wilson, "New York City Marathon Runners Are Slowing Down. Here's Why," *Time*, November 3, 2017, https://time.com/5007486/new-york-city-marathon-runners-slow/.

8. Melissa Rodriguez, "The 2020 IHRSA Global Report: Clubs Post Record Numbers in 2019," IHRSA, June 26, 2020, https://www.ihrsa.org/about/media-center/press-releases/the-2020-ihrsa-global-report-clubs-post-record-numbers-in-2019/.

9. Club Industry staff, "U.S. Fitness Product Sales Exceeded $5.2 Billion in 2017," Club Industry, April 17, 2018, https://www.clubindustry.com/news/u-s-fitness-product-sales-exceeded-5-2-billion-2017.

10. Preeti Wadhwani and Saloni Gankar, "Fitness Equipment Market Trends 2021: Industry Size Forecast 2027" (Global Market Insights, June 2020), https://www.gminsights.com/industry-analysis/fitness-equipment-market-report.

11. Rodriguez, "The 2020 IHRSA."

12. Ophelia Yeung and Katherine Johnston, "Move to Be Well: The Global Economy of Physical Activity" (Global Wellness Institute, October 2019), https://globalwellnessinstitute.org/wp-content/uploads/2019/10/2019-Physical-Activity-Economy-FINAL-NEW-101019.pdf.

13. Global Wellness Institute, "Wellness Industry Statistics & Facts," Global Wellness Institute, accessed September 18, 2021, https://globalwellnessinstitute.org/press-room/statistics-and-facts/.

14. Erwan Le Corre, "The History of Physical Fitness," *The Art of Manliness* (blog), September 24, 2014, https://www.artofmanliness.com/articles/the-history-of-physical-fitness/.

15. Ibid.

16. Lance C. Dalleck, M.S. and Len Kravitz, PhD., "The History of Fitness," accessed September 18, 2021, https://www.unm.edu/~lkravitz/Article%20folder/history.html.

17. Institute of Medicine (U.S.) et al., *Fitness Measures and Health Outcomes in Youth* (Washington, D.C.: National Academies Press, 2012).

18. Ibid.

19. "Read It Here: Kennedy's The Soft American," Recreating with Kids, October 26, 2011, http://www.recreatingwithkids.com/news/read-it-here-kennedys-the-soft-american/.

20. Pamela Kufahl, "Club Industry Features Clubs of the 1980s," Club Industry, December 1, 2008, https://www.clubindustry.com/news/club-industry-features-clubs-1980s.

21. Ibid.

22. "Health Clubs of the 1990s," Club Industry, January 1, 2009, https://www.clubindustry.com/news/health-clubs-1990s.

23. "Spinning: The Mind & Body Experience with Johnny G," MedicineNet, October 23, 2003, https://www.medicinenet.com/script/main/art.asp?articlekey=53946.

24. "Johnny G Biography," Krankcycle, accessed September 18, 2021, https://krankcycle.com/johnny-g/johnny-g-biography/.

25. T. J. Murphy, *Inside the Box: How CrossFit Shredded the Rules, Stripped Down the Gym, and Rebuilt My Body* (Boulder, CO: VeloPress, 2012), 1–2.

26. Ibid.

27. Glassman, always an inflammatory type, stepped down from leadership of CrossFit in 2020 in the wake of a crisis created by his statements and actions related to racism and social unrest in the United States.

28. "Boutique Gyms Part I: What They Are and Why They Are Gaining Steam," *Life Fitness* (blog), accessed September 18, 2021, //www.lifefitness. com/en-us/blog/boutique-gyms-part-I-what-they-are-and-why-they-are-gaining-steam.

29. Garnet Henderson, "People Love Gyms like CrossFit and Pure Barre Because They've Made Fancy Fitness a Status Symbol," Quartz, October 24, 2016, https://qz.com/816740/boutique-gyms-like-crossfit-and-pure-barre-are-raking-in-billions-by-making-fancy-fitness-a-status-symbol/.

30. Anthony Dominic, "Orangetheory Fitness Exceeds $1 Billion in 2018 System-Wide Revenue," Club Industry, February 4, 2019, https://www.clubindustry.com/news/orangetheory-fitness-exceeds-1-billion-2018-system-wide-revenue.

31. Jason Kelly, *Sweat Equity: Inside the New Economy of Mind and Body* (Hoboken, New Jersey: Bloomberg Press, 2016).

32. Danielle Friedman, "The History Behind Women's Obsession with Working Out," Harper's BAZAAR, February 14, 2018, https://www.harpersbazaar.com/culture/features/a14626590/history-boutique-fitness/.

33. "ClassPass," in Wikipedia, The Free Encyclopedia, July 15, 2021, https://en.wikipedia.org/w/index.php?title=ClassPass&oldid=1033718162.

34. Alex Konrad, "How a Retro Approach to Retail Is Helping Peloton Turn Indoor Cycling Into a Digital Empire," Forbes, May 19, 2016, https://www.forbes.com/sites/alexkonrad/2016/05/19/peloton-retail-strategy-is-building-an-empire/.

35. "Spinning Classes," *Well+Good,* October 2021, https://www.wellandgood.com/good-sweat/peloton-to-revolutionize-spinning-at-home/.

36. I received almost 150 responses to a Peloton Member Survey that I sent out between December 2018 and February 2019. Questions asked basics about member location and favorite classes and instructors as well as open-ended inquiries behind the why and how of discovery and purchase of Peloton and impact on life. Social media and email forwarding were the methods of distribution.

37. These new members were discussed during the Q3 2020 earnings call in May 2020.

38. RobinNYC, "SHUTUPANDRUN: Sweat with Swagger," Tumblr, accessed September 18, 2021, https://shutupandrun.tumblr.com/robinnyc.

39. Richard Florida and Jim Goodnight, "Managing for Creativity," *Harvard Business Review*, July-August 2005, https://hbr.org/2005/07/managing-for-creativity.

40. I know about Emma Lovewell's passion for gardening and more from her Instagram feed.

41. Peloton, "Peloton to Open State-of-the-Art Flagship Location, Peloton Studios, at Manhattan West in Fall 2019," Cision PR Newswire, May 23, 2018, https://www.prnewswire.com/news-releases/peloton-to-open-state-of-the-art-flagship-location-peloton-studios-at-manhattan-west-in-fall-2019-300653619.html.

42. Breather, "NKF Brokers Win Award for Guiding Peloton to Hudson Commons," *Commercial Observer* (blog), June 11, 2019, https://commercialobserver.com/2019/06/nkf-brokers-win-breakout-broker-award-for-guiding-peloton-to-hudson-commons/.

43. While I admit six classes in two days would have been a bit much, it was the grand opening of PSNY and I was willing to put my body through the meat grinder a bit to be part of the celebration. The first day, March 19, 2020, I was booked for two tread workouts in the morning. One, a 45-minute Women's History Month celebration, was going to be taught by Rebecca Kennedy, and the other with Matty Maggiacomo was a 30-minute Pop Fun Run stacked with a 10-minute Glutes and Legs Strength. Later than day, I was booked for a 30-minute ride with Christine D'Ercole and another with Emma Lovewell. Day two, March 20, 2020, I was booked for a 45-minute Pop Ride with Kendall Toole and a 45-minute running and strength class with Becs Gentry.

44. Peloton, "Peloton Launches Its First Commercial Bike, Bringing an Immersive Fitness Experience Beyond the Home," Cision PR Newswire, January 4, 2017, https://www.prnewswire.com/news-releases/peloton-launches-its-first-commercial-bike-bringing-an-immersive-fitness-experience-beyond-the-home-300384554.html.

45. Motley Fool Transcribing, "Peloton Interactive (PTON) Q2 2021 Earnings Call Transcript," The Motley Fool, February 5, 2021, https://www.fool.

com/earnings/call-transcripts/2021/02/05/peloton-interactive-pton-q2-2021-earnings-call-tra/.

46. Lauren Thomas, "Peloton Looks to Commercial Customers like Hotel Chains for New Growth," CNBC, September 20, 2021, sec. Retail, https://www.cnbc.com/2021/09/20/peloton-looks-to-commercial-businesses-like-hotels-for-new-growth.html.

47. PSFK Originals, PSFK 2017: *How Peloton Is To The Fitness Industry What Netflix Was To The Entertainment Industry,* YouTube Video (PSFK Originals), 2017, https://www.youtube.com/watch?v=zc9r8Pzatso.

48. Peloton, "The Peloton Bike: Bring Home the Studio Cycling Experience," Kickstarter, November 22, 2013, https://www.kickstarter.com/projects/568069889/the-peloton-bike-bring-home-the-studio-cycling-exp.

49. Motley Fool Transcribing, "Peloton Interactive."

50. Peter F. Drucker, *Innovation and Entrepreneurship: Practice and Principles* (New York: HarperBusiness, 1993).

51. I was inspired by Putnam's title in naming this book about Peloton, because my research showed that Peloton was recreating institutions and methods for building strong communities and bringing people together. Putnam's important work focused on the fracturing and disconnection that had occurred in society.

52. Amanda Mull, "I Joined a Stationary-Biker Gang," *The Atlantic,* December 2019, https://www.theatlantic.com/magazine/archive/2019/12/the-tribe-of-peloton/600748/.

53. Sophia Kunthara, "Affirm's IPO Filing Reveals Nearly a Third of Its Revenue Comes from a Single Customer," Crunchbase News, November 18, 2020, https://news.crunchbase.com/news/affirm-s1-ipo/.

54. Flywheel Sports, "Flywheel Home Bike Now Available on BestBuy.Com," June 25, 2019, https://www.prnewswire.com/news-releases/flywheel-home-bike-now-available-on-bestbuycom-300873957.html.

55. Related: Stephen Ross came under fire from many Equinox members for a Trump fundraiser he hosted in 2019, and in 2020, one of SoulCycle's celebrity instructors, Stacey Griffith, was deemed to have jumped the vaccine line in the early days of vaccine distribution by stating she was an educator. See Rachel Siegel, "Who Is Stephen Ross, the Billionaire Criticized for His High-End Trump Fundraiser?" *The Washington Post,* August 9, 2019, https://www.washingtonpost.com/business/2019/08/09/who-is-stephen-ross-billionaire-criticized-his-high-end-trump-

fundraiser/ and Troy Closson, "A SoulCycle Instructor Got the Vaccine as an 'Educator,'" *New York Times,* February 2, 2021, https://www.nytimes.com/2021/02/02/nyregion/stacey-griffith-soul-cycle-covid-19-vaccine.html.

56. Amy Feldman, "How a Former Ballerina Turned Mirror Into a Buzzy $300 Million Exercise Phenomenon," *Forbes,* May 28, 2020, https://www.forbes.com/sites/amyfeldman/2020/05/28/how-a-former-ballerina-turned-mirror-into-a-buzzy-300-million-exercise-phenomenon/.

57. Bloomberg, "Peloton Sues Cycling Rival Echelon, Accusing It of Free-Riding," *Los Angeles Times,* October 8, 2019, sec. Business, https://www.latimes.com/business/story/2019-10-08/peloton-sues-cycling-rival-echelon.

58. Anthony Dominic, "Echelon Fit Receives Private Equity Investment," Club Industry, July 18, 2019, https://www.clubindustry.com/news/echelon-fit-receives-private-equity-investment.

59. Lisa Denton, "Perfect Pitch: Inventor, TV Salesman Lou Lentine Grows Product Empire from Chattanooga," *Chattanooga Times Free Press,* January 1, 2019, https://www.timesfreepress.com/news/edge/story/2019/jan/01/perfect-pitch-inventor-tv-salesmlou-lentine-g/485554/.

60. PR Newswire, "Designer Eric Villency and Echelon Fitness Announce Partnership," Markets Insider, October 10, 2019, https://markets.businessinsider.com/news/stocks/designer-eric-villency-and-echelon-fitness-announce-partnership-1028590315.

61. Echelon Fit, "Echelon Raises $65 Million, Furthering Goal to Put Innovative Connected Fitness Within Reach for More Consumers," Cision PR Newswire, December 28, 2020, https://www.prnewswire.com/news-releases/echelon-raises-65-million-furthering-goal-to-put-innovative-connected-fitness-within-reach-for-more-consumers-301198643.html.

62. Howard Smith, "Why Beachbody Has This SPAC Stock Flexing Its Muscles Today," The Motley Fool, February 10, 2021, https://www.fool.com/investing/2021/02/10/why-beachbody-has-this-stock-flexing-today/.

63. Todd Spangler, "Peloton Settles Legal Fight with Music Publishers," *Variety,* February 27, 2020, https://variety.com/2020/digital/news/peloton-settles-music-publishers-lawsuit-1203517495/.

64. Clue Heywood (@ClueHeywood), "Love putting my Peloton bike in the most striking area of my ultra-modern $3 million house,"

Twitter thread, January 27, 2019, https://twitter.com/clueheywood/status/1089699762331217920?lang=en.

65. Tiffany Hsu, "Peloton's Cringe-y Ad Got Everyone Talking. Its C.E.O. Is Silent." *New York Times,* December 9, 2019, https://www.nytimes.com/2019/12/09/business/media/peloton-ad-ryan-reynolds.html.

66. Martin Belam and Joanna Partridge, "Peloton loses $1.5bn in value over 'dystopian, sexist' exercise bike ad," The Guardian, December 4, 2019, https://www.theguardian.com/media/2019/dec/04/peloton-backlash-sexist-dystopian-exercise-bike-christmas-advert.

67. John Foley, "A Message from Our Cofounder and CEO John Foley," *The Output* (blog), June 23, 2020, https://blog.onepeloton.com/peloton-pledge/.

68. Peloton, "Beyoncé and Peloton Team Up for Unprecedented Partnership," *The Output* (blog), November 10, 2020, https://blog.onepeloton.com/peloton-beyonce-partnership/.

69. Katherine Rosman, "Yoga, SoulCycle and Peloton Face Truths About How Black Lives Matter," *The New York Times,* July 23, 2020, sec. Style, https://www.nytimes.com/2020/07/23/style/peloton-black-lives-matter-ride-soul-cycle-y7.html.

70. Ally Love's public LinkedIn profile highlights elements of her professional and educational background. https://www.linkedin.com/in/ally-love-01581455/.

71. Emily Bary, "Peloton Shares Could Be Headed to $5, Short-Seller Citron Research Says," MarketWatch, December 14, 2019, https://www.marketwatch.com/story/peloton-shares-could-be-headed-to-5-short-seller-citron-research-says-2019-12-10.

72. Lee Schafer, "Will the 'energy of We' Fuel the WeWork IPO?," *Star Tribune,* August 25, 2019, https://www.startribune.com/lee-schafer-will-the-energy-of-we-fuel-ipo/558028262/.

73. Shayndi Raice and Konrad Putzier, "WeWork Founder Mixed Spiritual Group with Business," *Wall Street Journal,* October 16, 2019, https://www.wsj.com/articles/wework-founder-mixed-spiritual-group-with-business-11571232391.

74. U.S. Securities and Exchange Commission (SEC), "Registration Statement Under the Securities Act of 1933: Peloton Interactive, Inc." (No. 333, August 27, 2019), https://www.sec.gov/Archives/edgar/data/1639825/000119312519230923/d738839ds1.htm#toc.

75. PSFK Originals, PSFK 2017: *How Peloton Is To The Fitness Industry What Netflix Was To The Entertainment Industry,* YouTube Video (PSFK Originals), 2017, https://www.youtube.com/watch?v=zc9r8Pzatso.

76. Many media outlets, such as the New York Times, e.g. Jenny Gross, "Peloton Recalls Pedals on Thousands of Bikes After Reports of Injury," *The New York Times,* October 16, 2020, https://www.nytimes.com/2020/10/16/business/peloton-pedal-recall.html.

77. Peloton Interactive, "Email from Peloton Interactive to the Author.," March 18, 2021.

78. United States Consumer Product Safety Commission, "CPSC Warns Consumers: Stop Using the Peloton Tread+," United States Consumer Product Safety Commission, April 17, 2021, https://www.cpsc.gov/Newsroom/News-Releases/2021/CPSC-Warns- Consumers-Stop-Using-the-Peloton-Tread.

79. Peloton, "Peloton Refutes Consumer Product Safety Commission Claims," Cision PR Newswire, April 17, 2021, https://www.prnewswire.com/news-releases/peloton-refutes-consumer-product-safety-commission-claims-301270942.html.

80. Pelo Buddy TV is one of the fan/member created content creators that have grown. The story on the February 2021 purge was posted February 27, 2021.

81. Peloton, "Peloton Yoga Studio Opens In New York City," Cision PR Newswire, December 5, 2018, https://www.prnewswire.com/news-releases/peloton-yoga-studio-opens-in-new-york-city-300760508.html.

82. Ibid.

83. Lauren Thomas, "Peloton Thinks It Can Grow to 100 Million Subscribers. Here's How," *CNBC,* September 15, 2020, sec. Retail, https://www.cnbc.com/2020/09/15/peloton-thinks-it-can-grow-to-100-million-subscribers-heres-how.html. Peloton leaders have stated the goal of 100 million subscribers on numerous occasions. Robin Arzón mentioned that number during our interview and it has been mentioned in public appearances and media outlets.

84. For an overview over of well-being from The Center for the Advancement of Well-Being, see https://wellbeing.gmu.edu/about/well-being-overview.

85. The original Blue Zone research and books were released in 2004. By 2020 as I learned about them, it was a small movement, with Buettner and colleagues running a consulting and media venture.

86. "5 'Blue Zones' Where the World's Healthiest People Live," *National Geographic*, April 6, 2017, https://www.nationalgeographic.com/books/article/5-blue-zones-where-the-worlds-healthiest-people-live.

87. The five Blue Zones that have been identified are Okinawa (Japan); Sardinia (Italy); Nicoya (Costa Rica); Icaria (Greece); and among Seventh-Day Adventist communities in Loma Linda (California, USA).

88. Beth McGroarty et al., "2019 Wellness Trends, from Global Wellness Summit" (Global Wellness Summit, 2019).

89. Global Wellness Institute, Ophelia Yeung, and Katherine Johnston, "Global Wellness Economy Monitor, October 2018" (Global Wellness Institute, October 2018).

90. Roger Best et al., "COVID-19 Impact on 2020 U.S. Sportswear Sales," Lundquist College of Business - University of Oregon, December 2, 2020, https://business.uoregon.edu/news/covid-19-sportswear-sales.

91. When filing its S-1 to go public and in its first couple of quarterly reports, Peloton offered a revenue line called other. The last quarter reported publicly was $6.1 million in Q3 2020 (period ending 31 March 2020). After that quarter the line item disappeared. I hypothesized at the time that Peloton wanted to hide this item because it was getting so big and the ambiguity it might provide when competitors and others are trying to make sense of its revenue mix. Just a thought of mine at the time the line disappeared. Its apparel and other items becomes too large it will likely have to be broken out again.

92. Yeung and Johnston, "Move to Be Well."

93. Peloton, "Peloton Introduces Its First-Ever Health and Wellness Advisory Council," Cision PR Newswire, September 1, 2020, https://www.prnewswire.com/news-releases/peloton-introduces-its-first-ever-health-and-wellness-advisory-council-301122024.html.

94. Ibid.

95. Yeung and Johnston, "Move to Be Well."

96. Motley Fool Transcribing, "Peloton Interactive."

97. See the discussion in Chapter 5 around Peloton's partnership with Westin and the Peloton community's development of directories of hotels and other locations with Peloton equipment.

98. Peloton's investor letters report the average number of workouts per subscription. https://investor.onepeloton.com/financial-information/quarterly-results.

99. Four Seasons Resort Maui at Wailea (@fsmaui), "From in-suite @ onepeloton bikes to exploring Wailea's coral reef on a private guided outrigger canoe paddle, the Resort has introduced a variety of new ways to stay active, all designed with health and safety top of mind.[…], Instagram photo, March16, 2021, https://www.instagram.com/p/CMf-h2rrk7B/.

100. Kimberly Elchlepp, "ESPN Teams with Peloton for First Ever Pro-Athlete All-Star Ride," *ESPN Press Room,* May 26, 2020, https://espnpressroom. com/us/press-releases/2020/05/espn-teams-with-peloton-for-first-ever-pro-athlete-all-star-ride/.

101. "Meet the Champions," Peloton (blog), April 30, 2021, https://blog. onepeloton.com/champions-collection/.

102. Sarah Perez, "BAMTech Valued at $3.75 Billion Following Disney Deal," *Tech Crunch,* August 8, 2017, https:// techcrunch.com/2017/08/08/bamtech-valued-at-3-75-billion-following-disney-deal/?guccounter=1&guce_referrer=aHR0cHM6Ly93d3cuZ29vZ2xlLmNvbS8&guce_referrer_sig=AQAAABQkWrRRTzx-vek_

103. "The Walt Disney Company to Acquire Majority Ownership of BAMTech," The Walt Disney Company, August 8, 2017, https:// thewaltdisneycompany.com/walt-disney-company-acquire-majority-ownership-bamtech/.

INDEX

Holt, Kelly, 175–77
Holt, Lindsey, 175–77
Holt, Melissa, 175–77
Homecoming, 66, 156, 173, 175, 268
Home Rider Invasion (HRI), 117–18, 233
Houston Rockets, 217
Howick, Becky, 258
HRI. *See* Home Rider Invasion (HRI)

I
The Iliad, 227
iMac, in 1997, 9
in-class community energy, 28
indoor cycling (spinning/studio cycling),
    26, 48, 53, 105, 200, 244, 245
  addict, 64
  ballet training to, 54
  boutique fitness classes, 134
  and boutique fitness enthusiasts, 63
  brands, 55
  classes with Foley, 17
  community aspect of, 27
  creation of, 49–51
  endurance roots of, 186
  enthusiast, 16
  era of, 48
  Goldberg and, 53
  instructors on bike, 89
  in New York, 10, 30
  Nike SuperRep Cycle, 192
  Peloton and, 68, 81, 288
  Silicon Valley investors, 19
  SoulCycle, 31
Industrial Revolution, 42
initial core value of Peloton, 34
initial public offering (IPO)
  in 2019, 125
  in 2020, 189
  interviews with Foley and Cortese,
    19, 225
  J.P. Morgan in 2018, 109
  Peloton, 196, 208, 212, 215–16, 277
  We Company, 228
innovation. *See also* innovator
  and change, 87
  creativity and, 53, 99
  entrepreneur into economic theories,
    8
  entrepreneurship and, 1, 2, 7, 59, 258,
    276, 288
  era of, 204
  financial innovation, 208
  product innovation, 252
  and unexpected success, 145–47

value-producing innovations, 8
Innovation and Entrepreneurship in 1985
  (Drucker), 2, 145
innovator, 3, 240. *See also* innovation
  behaviors and, 145
  business model, 199
  disruptive innovators, 8
  and entrepreneurs, 193
  fitness innovator, 207
  and leaders, 211
  mass market innovators, 190
  media and technology, 272–75
The Innovator's Dilemma (Christensen),
  18
International Health, 56
Internet, 7–12, 261
  boom of the mid-1990s, 14
  Facebook and other social media
    platforms, 151
  Glassman's CrossFit, 52
  in Los Angeles, 15
  rise of, 253
  and software, 115
  and technology, 27
IPO. *See* initial public offering (IPO)

J
Jackman, Hugh, 71
Jacobs, Jennifer, iv, 93–96, 99, 209, 210,
  239, 255
Jäger, Erik, 253
James, LeBron, 72, 88
Jazzercise in 1969, 47
Jennifer Schreiber Sherman (JSS), 104,
  286
  Foley, John, 106
  JSS Tribe, 133, 134, 155, 182–84, 216
  quotes, 300
  ride, 133
  and Wilpers, Matt, 112, 113
Jeopardy, 73
Jewish Community Centers, 39
The Jimmy Kimmel Show, 163
Jobs, Steve, 9, 248
John, on digital leaderboards, 13
Johnson, Dwayne, 112
Jordan, Michael, 263
The Joy of Running in 1976, 47
JSS Tribe, 133, 134, 155, 182–84, 216

K
Kabbalah mysticism, 228
Kadakia, Payal, 56
Kennedy, John F., 45, 46

cool-down session and stretch,
287–89
enable life-changing outcomes,
291–92
Peloton experience, 284–85
platform for others, 283–84
positivity, hope, and happiness sell,
279–81
weakness to strength, 286–87
"Your ride is your ride," 289–90
zero-sum game, 285–86
Peloton-based producers, 190
Peloton bike, iv, vii, viii, 124, 183, 186,
187, 198, 199, 211, 279. *See
also* bike; Peloton riders
in 2015, 150
and business model, 116
classes on, 81, 168
and community, 123, 277
customers, 73
exercising on, 31
in gym, 138
and platform, iii, 48
studio, 117, 119
Technology Buyers, 68
and treads, 35, 66, 188, 232
Peloton Bike+, 5, 78, 231, 251–52. *See
also* Peloton bike; Peloton
riders
Peloton Blog, 266
Peloton business model, 18, 34, 57, 82, 85,
200. *See also* Peloton
digital economy, 18
initial, 20–21
innovation and entrepreneurship,
276
key elements in, 35, 79
Peloton community, 10, 61, 68, 131, 136,
214, 291. *See also* Peloton
accountability, 155
ambassadors and sales people/
members, 162–63
benefits of membership, 155–56
data, 160–61
Dedicated members in, 248
Drucker, Peter, 193
emergence of, 145–47
and media coverage, 280
membership to friendship, 150–52
members, value of, 147–50
Mills, John & Mills, Erica, 168–71
Pelo Celebrities, 164–65, 178
Peloton commercial ecosystem,
188–93

Peloton Monthly Challenge Team
(PMCT), 180–82
Peloton podcasts, 173
people and groups of, 164
Physician Moms Peloton Group
(#PMPG), 185–86
Power Zone Pack (PZP) group,
186–88
Prewitt, John, 175–77
rebooting with positive vibes, 153–54
Sherman, Jenn, 194
significant contributions, 193
social media pages and, 224
team, value of, 156–60
unexpected emergence of, 147
United Nations of Peloton, 179–80
Peloton Delivery Discussion Group, 231
Peloton Facebook page, 144, 165, 168–69,
179, 237
Peloton Health and Wellness Advisory
Council, 265
Peloton instructor, 282. *See also* Peloton
Alldis, Benjamin, 187, 298
Arzón, Robin. *See* Arzón, Robin
boutique fitness, 106
contact with customers, 89
Corbin, Hannah, 25, 107, 264, 299
creative economy, talent and, 108–10
D'Ercole, Christine. *See* D'Ercole,
Christine
digital consumer fitness relationship,
96
diversity of, 86–87, 114
Hainsby, Leanne, 299
indoor cycling, 89
King, Jess. *See* King, Jess
LinkedIn world, 110–13
Love, Ally, 112, 273, 299
Lovewell, Emma, 112, 247, 299
Maggiacomo, Matty, 299
markets driven by innovation and
creative output, 99
McGee, Kristin, 238, 245, 300
member engagement, 93
Morton, Denis, 84–85, 107, 110, 187,
189, 289, 300
Oyeneyin, Tunde, 221, 300
'Pedalton,' 90
Peloton challenge group, 84
quotes, 298–301
reality and lifestyle programming
with, 272
Rigsby, Cody, 107, 130, 175, 300
Samuela, Selena, 300

PSNY. *See* Peloton Studios New York (PSNY)
Putnam, Robert, 156
Pyeongchang, 273

Q
qualitative source of data, 161
Quigley, Colleen, 273

R
Racquet and Sportsclub Association, 56
Rahbar, Raymond, 211
Rayburn, Ross, 303
Related Companies' goal, 202
Reynolds, Ryan, 213–14
Riding High (Zukerman), 55
Rigsby, Cody, 107, 130, 175, 300
The Rise of the Creative Class (Florida), 107
Robbins, Tony, 10
Roberts, Chelsea Jackson, 221, 238, 246
Roberts, Robin, 86, 137
Roker, Al, 71, 86
Rolling Stone (Travolta), 47
RollingStone.com, 4, 10
Roosevelt, Theodore, 44
Ruiz, Monica, 213

S
Sabry, Hala, 185
Samuela, Selena, 250, 300
Sargent, Dudley, 44
Saturday Night Live, 6
Scholz, Irène, 253
Schumpeter, Joseph, 18
    changemakers, 8
    as entrepreneurship researcher, 9
    graduation, 7
    theory of "creative destruction," 8
sedentary lifestyles, 42
sensory-pleasing environment, 54
serial entrepreneur, 59
Shah, Aditi, 245, 303–6
Shark Tank, TV show, 1, 60
Sheehi, Stephen, 240–41
Sherman, Jennifer Schreiber. *See* Jennifer Schreiber Sherman (JSS)
Silicon Valley Sand Hill Road investor, 19
Sims, Jess, 124, 300
Smith, Adam, 285
social media
    challenges, 34
    community on, 250
    countless moments on, 66

documentation of Peloton, 212
leaderboards and, 77, 235
on-demand offerings and, 91
Peloton social media pages, 75, 90, 150, 218
postings and interviews, 74
posts, 36
quick positive comment on, 158
real world and, 61
riders and instructors through, 10
rise of, 11
role of, 164–65
Super Bowl ads and viral videos for, 162
vibrant community on, 173
web and, 285
"The Soft American" (Kennedy), 45
SoulCycle, 19, 27, 31, 55, 80, 134, 202–3
SPAC. *See* special purpose acquisition company (SPAC)
Spears, Britney, 113
Specialized brand mountain bike, 212
special purpose acquisition company (SPAC), 208
Speer, Andy, 301
Spinning and Boutique Enthusiasts, 62–64
Spintray, 188, 191
Stanton, Graham, 18, 282
Stern, Howard, 32, 72
Stewart, Martha, 113
Strahan, Michael, 137
"Sundays with Love" series, 224–25, 264
sweating community, 29, 61, 76, 81–82, 122–24, 143–44
"sweat with swagger," 101–4, 113

T
tabata style classes, vi, 102, 103, 148, 155, 159, 179
talent-supporting culture, 87
Technology Buyers, 68, 70
technology innovator, 272–75
Tectrix bike, iv
Telotalker, 163
Tennessee-based Echelon, 206
theory of "creative destruction" (Schumpeter), 8
"Think Different," Apple Computer, 8
Timberlake, Justin, 113
Today Show to *Inside Edition*, 213